Evolution of the

BOLIVIAN ECONOMY: A TIME-SERIES APPROACH

ANTONIO N. BOJANIC

Kendall Hunt
publishing company

Cover images © Shutterstock. Used under license Shutterstock, Inc.

Kendall Hunt
publishing company

www.kendallhunt.com
Send all inquiries to:
4050 Westmark Drive
Dubuque, IA 52004-1840

ISBN 978-1-4652-1141-5

Printed in the United States of America

10 9 8 7 6 5 4 3 2 1

CONTENTS

Appendices 53

PREFACE

It is often stated by those interested in doing research about Bolivia that finding data on the country is the most challenging aspect of the mission. It is argued that reliable sources of data are few; that historical data is non-existent; and that the few variables for which time-series data have been compiled are fairly recent, perhaps only starting in the 1980s, and hence of limited utility when the objective is to analyze long-term trends and relationships.

While some of these assertions have grains of truth, they hide the fact that much data has actually been compiled for quite a long time, at least since the first decades of the 1900s. It is my assertion that the main problem with finding data in Bolivia is not that it does not exist, but rather that it has to be dug out, often manually, from the historical archives of various institutions.

The more serious problem occurs after historical data say, before 1970—has been found. In order for it to be workable and comparable across time, it has to be adjusted, modified, and set in a way that will make economic sense. For instance, the definition of "non-traditional goods," commonly utilized when referring to certain export products, is a rather elastic concept, and as new goods appear and others phase out, the values that accompany this variable should be interpreted with caution, because they reflect constant and natural adjustments that occur through time. Likewise, particularly in a country like Bolivia, where the unit of account has changed twice during the 1900s, values for all time-series variables must be set in a common currency—either a specific Bolivian currency or some foreign currency, like the US dollar—so that proper comparisons through time may take place.

Here I address these problems by presenting and analyzing time-series data on five general topics: trade, prices, income, money and reserves, and government. The principal sources for the data are the historical archives of two government institutions: the Central Bank of Bolivia (CBB) and the National Institute of Statistics (NIS). Other complementary sources of data are the Ministry of Economy and Public Finance (MEPF), the National Tax Revenue Authority (NTRA), the Ministry of Hydrocarbons, Ministry of Mining, and the Customs Department—also public institutions—the World Bank (WB), and the International Monetary Fund (IMF). In all cases, I have gathered the raw information from these sources and constructed time-series data sets for multiple variables. When possible, I have crossed-referenced the values of the variables presented between different data sources. In those instances where this was not feasible, I have utilized the values of the primary institution—most often the CBB—providing the data.

I have also used a great deal of personal judgment in constructing several data sets. For instance, the aggregation of several variables—government expenditures on infrastructure, education, health, national defense, *M1*, and the various subcomponents of GDP, to mention a few—are my own and may not correspond to the current or official definition of these variables. Likewise, the monthly price indices presented reflect my personal beliefs about valid indicators of price volatility through time. Finally, and perhaps more importantly, the analysis of the data presented in each chapter is inevitably intertwined with my own views and opinions about what I perceive are the reasons behind the evolution of the Bolivian economy during the last several decades.

The process of obtaining the data has been arduous and time consuming. I am immensely thankful to all people working at the libraries of the CBB and of the NIS. In addition to their professionalism, dedication, and knowledge about national statistics, they were always patient with my constant requests, and even kind when confronted with my often impatient behavior. Contrary to what is sometimes stated about public servants in Bolivia, all the people I met in these libraries represent the best any researcher can hope for.

I am also grateful to the Kendall Hunt Publishing Company for believing in a project about Bolivia. I am particularly thankful to Linda Chapman and Jason McFaul for their willingness to accommodate all my requests, principally pertaining to data management.

Finally, I'll like to thank my family, and especially my parents. Without their constant support and encouragement, I could not have completed this work.

Antonio N. Bojanic
Universidad Mayor de San Andrés (UMSA)

Trade

CHAPTER 1

OVERVIEW

The pattern of trade in Bolivia since the early part of the twentieth century has remained remarkably consistent in some ways. In other respects changes have been fundamental. What has not changed is the country's reliance on a few mining and hydrocarbon commodities—referred throughout the book as traditional goods—as its most important source of export revenue, despite a tenuous reversal of this pattern in the 1990s and early 2000s with the still fragile consolidation of agricultural, textile, and other labor-intensive manufacturing products (non-traditional goods). Also unchanged is the little diversification in its export markets, depending heavily on a few countries, though the change in their relative importance has varied. Finally, the insignificant value-added that exports goods have shown for most of the country's recorded history has also been a constant. On the import side, the pattern of behavior is even more conspicuous as Bolivia's composition of imports has not changed in significant ways and its dependency on a few countries, notably for capital goods, has perdured.

Areas where changes have been substantial referred especially to the export side of trade. The composition of traditional goods has changed dramatically, as the relative importance of mining commodities has receded while that of hydrocarbon products—basically natural gas—has increased substantially, particularly since the 1980s. Important to point out, however, that while the share of mining commodities in traditional exports has diminished, they are still a fundamental source of export revenue and employment in the country, particularly in the western highlands.

The other significant development refers to a consolidation of sorts of non-traditional goods coming mainly from the eastern side of the country, particularly the lowland areas of Santa Cruz. A development that became noticeable in the 1970s, it reached a peak in 1994, when for the first time in Bolivia's history the share in total dollar exports of non-traditional products surpassed the one for traditional goods, cementing the relevance and importance of Santa Cruz as the new center of economic gravity of the country. Though the advent of this department[1] had been foretold for decades, 1994 set in place a milestone that despite some recent setbacks,[2] it is unlikely to unwind the growing significance of the eastern lowlands in the economic development of the country.

An introduction to Bolivia's trade is provided in Figure 1.1, where the dollar value of exports and imports, in log form, are presented for the 1900–2011 period. Table 1a in the appendix provides all the supporting data for this section.

An interesting fact illustrated in Figure 1.1 is the consistent surplus in the balance of trade of the country since 1900. With few exceptions, particularly during the 1960s, 1990s, and 2000s, the norm has been for the country to experience trade surpluses.

TRADE BY COUNTRIES

Throughout Bolivia's recorded history—certainly for the years analyzed here—the country's most important trading countries have been Great Britain, United States, Brazil, and Argentina. The relative importance of each has changed over time, but consistently these four nations have been Bolivia's most

[1] Bolivia is divided into nine states, or departments, as they are referred to in the country.

[2] During the first decade of the 2000s a worldwide boom in commodity markets positively affected Bolivia's exports of certain mining commodities. Concurrently, the export of natural gas to neighboring Brazil and Argentina also reached record levels, explaining the rise in the share of traditional products and the relative decrease in the importance of non-traditional products.

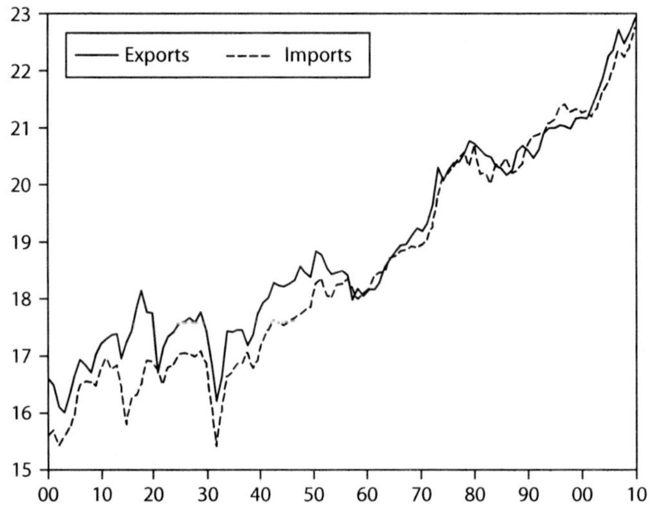

FIGURE 1.1 Total exports and imports (logs), 1900–2011

Source: Historical archives, Central Bank of Bolivia (CBB), National Institute of Statistics (NIS)

important trading partners.[3] Table 1.1 illustrates just how important these nations have been both as a destination of exports and as a source of imports. Table 2a in the appendix presents the actual data.

As can be observed, the reliance on these four nations for Bolivia's exports is quite overwhelming, with a concentration ratio easily exceeding the 85 percent mark from 1929 through the 1960s. During the 1940s and 1950s, almost all of the country's exports were destined to these four nations—with concentration ratios in the 97 to 99 percent range in many of the years—though the relative importance of Great Britain and the United States always exceeded Brazil and Argentina by a large margin. Though the preponderance of these four nations has diminished somewhat, it is still true that in the year 2005 over 62 percent of Bolivia's exports went to them. In 2011 the export concentration ratio diminished a bit, reaching 56 percent.

A more detailed analysis of the export concentration ratios reveals that until 1971, the US and Great Britain were by far the most important market destinations, consistently capturing over 50 percent of Bolivia's export supply. Beginning in 1972, the relative importance of Great Britain begins to dwindle and Argentina starts its ascent, changing the configuration and the relative composition of Bolivia's export market. Tellingly, in the 1980s, Argentina becomes the most important export market destination—with concentration ratios in the 30 and 40 percent range, and in 1985 with a record-level ratio of 55 percent—surpassing even the US, which by this time begins to diminish as a destination for Bolivia's goods just as it happened a decade earlier with Great Britain.[4] The importance of Brazil only becomes visible at the turn of the new century, when exports of natural gas to that country began in earnest, as the Gasbol pipeline linking Bolivia and Brazil finally became operational. By 2001 Brazil was the most important market destination, capturing 22 percent of the Bolivian export market. This position has only been accentuated throughout the first decade of the new century, reaching in 2008 a record-level 43 percent.

[3] China has become an important trade partner in the last few years, with exports in 2010 and 2011 reaching $208 and $330 million, respectively, easily placing it as one of the top ten export destinations for Bolivian goods. Imports from China during the same two years are even more significant: $536 million in 2010 and $937 million in 2011, which places the Asian giant as one of the top five import countries. However, for the period considered here, 1929–2011, the relative importance of China, in addition to being a fairly recent development, is not as compelling as the significance of Bolivia's more traditional partners. Given trade patterns at the time this chapter was written, however, it will not surprise anyone if at the end of the 2010s China becomes the biggest trade partner of Bolivia, and perhaps of several other countries in the Americas.

[4] Petroleum and natural gas are the main reasons behind Argentina's rise as the most important market destination of Bolivian goods. Exports of petroleum to that country became significant in the 1970s and exports of natural gas, which had began in 1972 with the Yabog pipeline, accelerated in the 1980s, hence the increase in Argentina's export concentration ratio for Bolivian commodities.

Table 1.1 Concentration of Export and Import Markets (%)		
Decade	Four-country export concentration ratio	Four-country import concentration ratio
1929–39	85.95	53.54
1940s	98.45	73.14
1950s	96.06	62.54
1960s	86.71	56.37
1970s	68.49	53.22
1980s	71.40	57.16
1990s	55.37	50.13
2000–11	53.09	49.65

Notes: Four-country refers to Argentina, Brazil, United States, and Great Britain.
Values in table reflect author's own estimations based on data from the historical archives of the Central Bank of Bolivia (CBB) and the National Institute of Statistics (NIS).

On the side of imports, the story is not that different. Consistently, four-country import concentration ratios have exceeded the 50 percent mark for each one of the decades between 1929 and 2011,[5] demonstrating the little diversification in Bolivia's sources of goods. Of the four countries, the US is the one with the most uniform evolution since 1929, as its share of sales to Bolivia has remained steadily in the two-digit range throughout the period analyzed, though 1971 is the last year in which it reached the 30 percent mark, a ratio that before that year was rather common. The year 1963 is when the US had its biggest participation in Bolivia's imports, with a 57 percent import concentration ratio. During the 1940s and late 1950s, its average was in the 40 percent range. The relative importance of Great Britain is uneven, with the 1930s representing the most important decade as its share of sales to Bolivia fluctuated around the low teens. After the end of that decade, its concentration ratio fluctuated around 4 percent until the mid 1980s, and then its descent became more pronounced, with yearly concentration ratios in the 2000s decade of less than 1 percent.

As of 2011, Brazil is the most important source of import goods for Bolivia, with Argentina and the US alternating as the second and third most important sources of goods. The relative importance of Brazil is rather recent since it only emerges in the 1970s: in 1974 its import concentration ratio reached an unprecedented 15 percent mark. Before that year, the Brazilian share of the Bolivian market never reached the two-digit percent mark. Consistently since then, Brazil has averaged a participation in the high teens. Argentina's share of the Bolivian market is more conventional, as its importance dates back to the very beginning of the time series analyzed here. Its concentration ratio has consistently been in the mid-teens and during the 1940s it easily averaged in the high 20 percent range. The peak share of Argentina in the Bolivian market happened in 1943, when its concentration ratio reached the 35 percent mark. This figure has not been repeated ever since.

THE EVOLUTION OF EXPORTS

Data for analyzing the evolution of exports since 1929 is not uniform, hence certain modifications and aggregations to the main categories of 'traditional' and 'non-traditional' goods have been made in order to make sense of year-to-year comparisons.[6] Official statistics for exports of mining commodities are the

[5] For the 12-year period between 2000 and 2011, the four-country import concentration was 49.65, a tad less than the marks of previous decades.

[6] Traditional goods can be any mining or hydrocarbon commodities that have been "traditionally" the main sources of income, employment, and economic growth of the country. Non-traditional goods include anything other than mining and hydrocarbon commodities. The composition of

best throughout the period analyzed, as the Central Bank of Bolivia (CBB) diligently kept track of its most important source of foreign exchange, especially during the 1930s, 40s, and 50s, when this sector was heavily regulated with foreign currency controls. For non-mining products, however, disaggregated data is patchy, and at times, simply non-existent. Between the years 1946 and 1965, reliable disaggregated data on non-traditional and petroleum exports is scattered and inconsistent, hence I chose not to report it.[7] For this period (1946–1965) the reported aggregated values for non-traditional exports are derived by subtracting total exports from mining exports, hence they represent rough estimates based on the best available information of the time. Due to these peculiarities of the data, I analyze first the evolution of exports between the years 1929 and 1945 (period 1929–1945), when reliable disaggregated export figures for traditional and non-traditional goods exist, and then focus on the years 1966–2011 (period 1966–2011), when the quality of disaggregated data improves once more. A more detailed analysis of the evolution of traditional (exports of traditional goods) and non-traditional goods (exports of non-traditional goods) is also presented. Table 3a in the appendix provides the data for the structure of exports between 1929 and 2011.

PERIOD 1929–1945

The period between the years 1929 and 1945 is characterized by low monetary—measured in unadjusted US dollars—exports receipts and high concentration in exports of mining commodities, with the overwhelming share of these commodities captured by tin. Figure 1.2 illustrates the composition of exports according to the general categories of traditional and non-traditional goods.

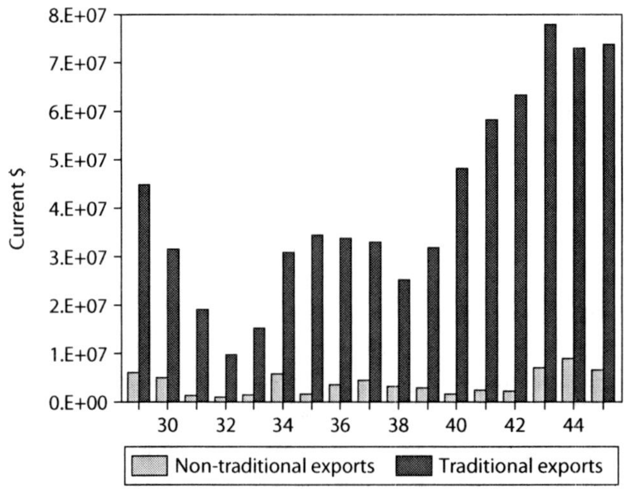

FIGURE 1.2 Composition of exports, 1929–1945

Source: Historical archives, CBB

As can be appreciated, traditional goods far outweigh non-traditional goods as the main export source of revenues in the country for the period under consideration. In percentage terms and for all years considered, traditional goods consistently comprise between 84 ($31 million in 1934) and 97 percent

products considered "non-traditional" has changed substantially over time, as the findings presented in this chapter will attest. Further, most of the export figures reported here refer to the export of raw products; that is, products with little, if any, value added.

[7] The main sources of official statistics are the "boletines estadísticos" published quarterly by the Central Bank of Bolivia (CBB) and the "anuario estadístico" published every year by the National Institute of Statistics (NIS). Particularly during the 1950s and 1960s, surely due to the political and economic turmoil of the times that will be discussed throughout the book, both institutions either did not publish or published summarized versions of these statistical official summaries, hence the difficulty in finding disaggregated export data—and other types of data—during those years.

($48 million in 1940) of total exports, demonstrating the high dependence of the country on these goods for its economic survival. Of the traditional goods, the most important commodity export is tin, which by itself captures between 59 percent ($22 million in 1937) and 80 percent ($16 million in 1931) of total exports during the period analyzed. Other, significantly less important traditional mining commodities, are wolfram—its relative importance ranges from less than 1 percent in the early 1930s to 12 percent of total exports in 1943 and 1944—silver, lead, copper, antimony, zinc, and bismuth. With the exception of wolfram and silver, the relative share on total exports of these commodities always remained in the low teens for the years considered. Recorded export figures for sulfur, gold and petroleum only begin in 1940, but their values are insignificant and their combined share of exports between 1940 and 1945 never reaches the 2 percent mark.

Non-traditional goods during this period include almonds and chestnut, rubber, quinoa, quinine coca leafs, leather, livestock, lumber, and other comparatively less important goods. As was the case with traditional goods, little, if any, value added accompanied the export of these goods. The year 1934 is when non-traditional goods reached their highest share of total exports, 16 percent ($6 million), and 1940 when their share was lowest, 3 percent ($1.5 million). Of these, the most important good is rubber; its share of total exports reached a high point of around 5 percent ($3.7 million) in 1945.

An alternative way to illustrate the high Bolivian export dependency on traditional goods—and, within this category of goods, the high dependency of its exports on tin—is illustrated in Table 1.2.

Table 1.2
Export Diversification, 1929-1945

Year	Herfindahl Index	Herfindahl Index without Tin
1929	0.55	0.16
1930	0.56	0.17
1931	0.64	0.16
1932	0.58	0.15
1933	0.55	0.18
1934	0.55	0.29
1935	0.62	0.23
1936	0.46	0.16
1937	0.37	0.13
1938	0.39	0.12
1939	0.44	0.13
1940	0.52	0.13
1941	0.51	0.15
1942	0.47	0.19
1943	0.44	0.17
1944	0.44	0.18
1945	0.57	0.12

Notes: Values reflect author's own calculations based on data from the CBB and the NIS.
Herfindahl Index $(H) = \Sigma(s_i)^2$, where s is share of a good in total exports
If $H \approx 0$, export structure well diversified;
If $H \approx 1$, export structure not well diversified

Table 1.2 reports the export diversification of Bolivia for the period 1929–1945 according to the Herfindahl Index.[8] This index is calculated by the following formula:

$$H = \sum_{i=1}^{N} (s_i)^2 \tag{1.1}$$

where s_i is the share of the exported product relative to total exports and N is the number of goods exported by Bolivia on a given period.

The index is a measure of how concentrated exports of Bolivia are on a range of products. As H approaches 1, the export diversification of the country worsens, and its dependency on a few products increases. Conversely, as H approaches 0, the export structure becomes better diversified, which means that the country ceases to be dependent on a small number of export products.

As the numbers in Table 1.2 illustrate, when all products are included in the analysis, the index is quite high, with a range of 0.37 (in 1937) to 0.64 (in 1931), reflecting the high concentration of Bolivian exports on a small number of traditional goods. However, when the most important traditional good, tin, is excluded altogether from the analysis, the Herfindahl index is significantly lower, consistently below 0.2, excepting years 1934 and 1935. These results reflect the high Bolivian dependency on tin over a sustained period of time—fifteen years—and how different the scenario becomes if the dominant commodity is taken out of the picture.

PERIOD 1966–2011

This period is characterized by a significant increase in the level of exports—both in volume and in monetary values—and by the consolidation of non-traditional goods[9] as an alternative source of economic activity and of exports receipts for the country. Figure 1.3 illustrates the evolution of mining, hydrocarbon, and non-traditional exports during the period between 1966 and 2011.

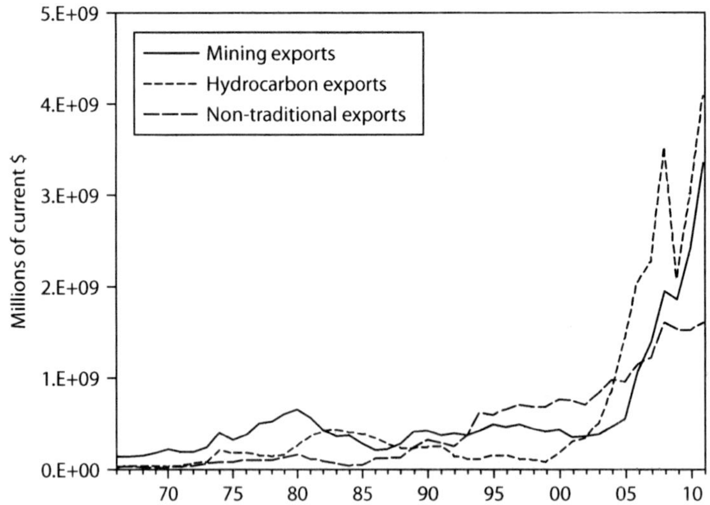

FIGURE 1.3 Evolution of traditional and non-traditional exports, 1966–2011

Source: NIS

[8] Albert O. Hirschman, *National Power and the Structure of Foreign Trade* (Berkeley and Los Angeles: University of California Press, 1945), pp. 157–162

[9] During the approximately four decades between 1966 and 2011, the non-traditional category grew to include a much wider variety of goods. The following is a non-exhaustive list: Brazilian nuts, unroasted coffee, cocoa grains and derivatives, soya beans and seeds, quinoa, unprocessed and processed cotton, different fruits, sesame seeds, sunflower seeds and derivatives, nuts, maize, sugar, beer, soft drinks, soya cake, oil and other derivatives, palm heart conserved food, different types of prepared food and oils, powder milk, tobacco products, textiles, unprocessed and processed leather, shoes, unprocessed and processed lumber (wood), paper and derivatives, chemical substances, software, furniture, and jewelry.

As Figure 1.3 shows, save the 69 percent drop in the export of mining commodities between 1980 and 1986, which was mostly the result of a reduction in tin exports due to the collapse of the tin cartel,[10] the behavior pattern of traditional goods—both mining and hydrocarbon commodities—did not suffer major fluctuations until around the turn of the new century. Conversely, during the same years, the evolution of non-traditional goods experienced some of its highest notes, as the level of exports of these goods increased from barely noticeable amounts ($12 million in 1966) to a formidable $754 million in 2000, recording an impressive 6,183 percent growth over these three decades. In 1994 and for the first time in the country's history, non-traditional goods surpassed traditional goods as the most important source of export revenues of the country, capturing more than 50 percent of total exports, and in the process, established itself as a real alternative to traditional exports.

Though during the first decade of the new century the behavior pattern of non-traditional goods has been overshadowed by the export boom of traditional goods, its evolution has been anything but disappointing, particularly in light of an economic and political environment within Bolivia that has become more complex, and despite economic policies implemented after 2006 that have plainly hindered the development of this group of export goods.[11] Between 2000 and 2011, exports of non-traditional goods have grown by a healthy 112 percent, from $754 million to over $1.5 billion, and the range of goods has expanded to include others—such are paper products, computer software, and some chemical by-products—that barely registered or even existed just few years earlier. Given the country's long-standing history with traditional goods, it seems that a continuous growth and expansion of the non-traditional sector is the best short- and medium-term bet for exporting products with greater value added, with greater utilization of economic capital, and hence with greater chances of domestic actors (i.e., entrepreneurs within Bolivia) affecting the final price of these goods. The (usual) alternative for products with little value added is for their prices to be determined in very competitive international markets, where the gains in efficiency are usually captured by the final consumer and not by the producers of these products.

The behavior and evolution of the traditional goods sector since 2000 is an illustration of why the exceptions to the rule—the rule being that the price of raw commodities is determined in very competitive international markets, usually favoring consuming countries—are sometimes proof of the difficulty in making sweeping generalizations in economics. As the world demand for raw mining commodities, driven mainly by China, continually increased throughout the 2000s, the price of these commodities reached record levels, and so did the coffers of countries, including Bolivia, highly dependent on these commodities. The mining export receipts of Bolivia increased by 709 percent between 2000 ($425 million) and 2011 ($3.4 billion). Additionally, and as exports of the other traditional good—natural gas—began to consolidate with ever increasing sales to Brazil, export receipts from these commodities soared, reaching an astonishing 2,369 percent growth rate between the year 2000 ($166 million) and the year 2011 ($4.1 billion). Figure 1.4 illustrates the evolution of Bolivian exports for the period 1966–2011, highlighting developments during the first decade of the new century.

As can be observed in Figure 1.4, the behavior pattern of traditional goods after the year 2000 is impressive. Though it is difficult to ascertain whether current conditions[12] will continue in the foreseeable future, what can be stated is that informed debate within Bolivia concerns the use and destination that

[10] On October 24, 1985, the International Tin Council (ITC)—the operative arm of an explicit production agreement among various tin producing countries, including Bolivia—announced that it was unable to repay debts and fulfill its contractual obligations. After this announcement was made, the ITC cartel effectively ceased to exist.

[11] Among the issues and economic policies negatively affecting the evolution of non-traditional exports, it is worth highlighting the following: the exclusion of Bolivia from the Andean Trade Preference Act and the Andean Trade Promotion and Drug Eradication Act—effective on December 15, 2008—which brought to a halt textile exports to the US and also brought to an abrupt end the growth of this manufacturing sector; the termination of a policy of gradual devaluation of the exchange rate—a system of exchange rate determination known as the 'crawling peg'—which basically ended almost 20 years worth of monetary subsidizing of the export sector; and the imposition of export controls to key agricultural commodities—sugar, rice, meat, soybeans and derivatives, to mention a few—which added to the uncertainty regarding the limits to individual liberties, respect for property rights, and the role the state should play in the economic affairs of the country.

[12] This chapter was written in March 2012.

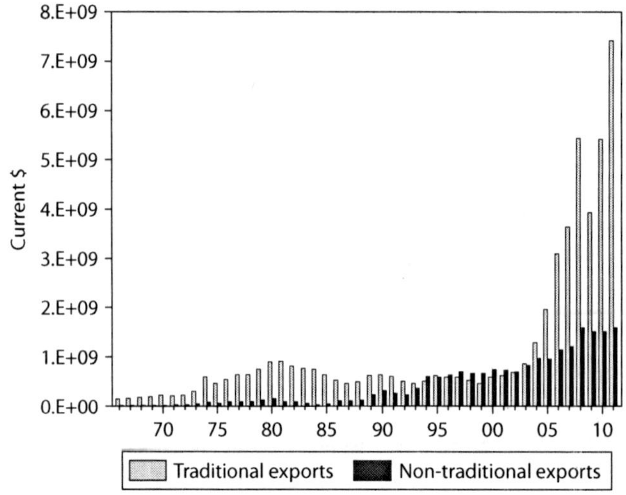

FIGURE 1.4 Composition of exports, 1966–2011

Source: CBB, NIS

government should place on the substantial windfall gains it is receiving, and on the need to plan for a future that may not be as plentiful as the one today.

Summarizing developments for the whole period between 1929 and 2011, while undeniable that Bolivia's supply of export goods has expanded, the reliance on certain key goods or commodities continues. Figure 1.5 illustrates how the Herfindahl index and exports of non-traditional goods have evolved during these years.

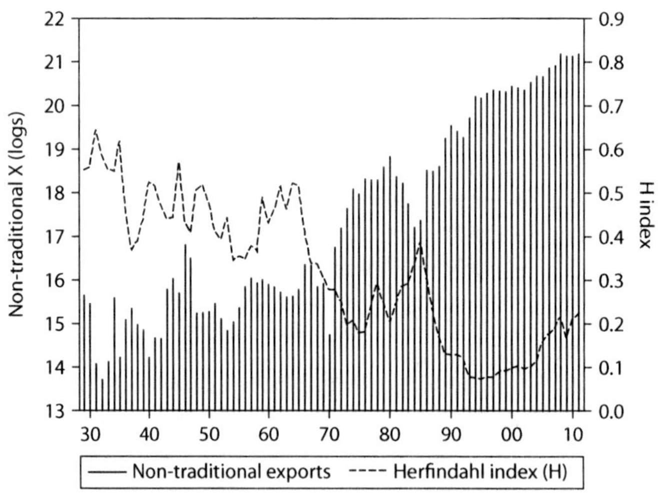

FIGURE 1.5 Export diversification, evolution of non-traditional exports, 1929–2011

Source: CBB, NIS

As can be appreciated, the Herfindahl index shows a marked tendency to decrease over time just as the importance of non-traditional exports increases, denoting the significance of this sector as an alternative to traditional goods. The pattern of behavior of the index illustrates progress, demonstrating that with the passing of time diversification has taken place, though perhaps not as rapidly as some may want. The challenge continues to be one of expanding the supply of export goods while at the same time adding greater value to them.

■ EXPORTS OF TRADITIONAL GOODS

As stated earlier, the best kept official statistics on exports occur with the mining industry. Table 1.3 reports average export values, by decades—in dollars and in metric tons—along with the most important export commodity for each decade. Table 4a in the appendix details yearly exports of mining products in current dollars.

Table 1.3
Mining Commodities: Average Export Values and Volume, by Decades, 1929-2011

Decade	Export Values (thousands current US dollars)	Export Volume (metric tons)[1]	Most Important Commodity (in dollar terms)
1929–39	28,172.41	65,824.24	Tin
1940s	74,571.90	91,383.36	Tin
1950s	99,036.70	90,610.33	Tin
1960s	108,086.00	97,886.88	Tin
1970s	344,216.70	154,215.20	Tin
1980s	367,211.50	105,801.36	Tin
1990s	416,844.10	218,995.56	Gold
2000–11	1,206,617.00	377,577.36	Tin

Notes: [1]For the 1929–39 decade, value refers only to the years 1937 through 1939;
For the 2000–11 decade, value refers only to the years 2000 through 2010.
Values in table reflect author's own estimations based on data from the CBB, NIS, and Customs Department.

Total exports of mining commodities increased from an average of around $28 million in the 1930s to over $1.2 billion (unadjusted dollar values) in the first decade of the new century. The volume increase, in metric tons, is also substantial, with an 840 percent growth rate between the years 1937 and 2010. Throughout the period analyzed, tin is the principal commodity, both in dollar terms and—along with zinc—volume wise, despite a significant monetary increase in gold exports during the 1990s. Other mining commodities with an important share in traditional exports include zinc, silver, wolfram, antimony, lead, copper, bismuth, and sulfur, though the latter two were not exported every year.

Important to point out is that mining commodities in Bolivia have traditionally been exported in their raw state, with very little added manufacturing, or as referred earlier in the text, with very little 'value-added.' For instance, metallic tin—whereby impure tin is heated in the presence of oxygen to oxidize any iron in the mixture—only began to be produced in Bolivia in 1971, and still is, 40 years later, the principal type of tin exported by the country. Despite significant advancements in the jewelry industry, particularly since the 1980s, most of the mining figures between 1929 and 2011 refer to export of commodities in their most basic, elemental state.

With regards to hydrocarbons exports, consistent, reliable data only appears during the latter part of the 1960s, though some official figures are also available for the 1940s. A summary of exports, by decade, is presented in Table 1.4. Table 5a in the appendix reports dollar export values of hydrocarbons since they became available in the 1940s.

As illustrated in Table 1.4, Bolivia has exported various types of hydrocarbon commodities, ranging from petroleum—including diesel oil and kerosene—to liquefied petroleum gas (gasoline), natural gas, propane gas, and butane gas. By far, natural gas is the most important of these hydrocarbons, and it has been ever since exports of it started in the 1970s. Average total exports of hydrocarbons have increased from around $90 thousand in the 1940s, $19 million in the 1960s, $107 million in the 1970s, $319 million in the 1980s, $131 million in the 1990s, to the astonishing figure of $1.7 billion during the years 2000 to 2011.

Table 1.4 Hydrocarbon Commodities: Average Export Values, by Decades, 1945-2011						
Decade	Export Values (thousands of current US dollars)					
	Petroleum	Gasoline	Natural Gas	Propane Gas	Butane Gas	Total Exports
1940–45	87.83	-	-	-	-	87.83
1966–69	19,166.20	-	-	-	-	19,166.20
1970–79	61,956.12	6,686.43	59,599.10	465.07	-	106,726.30
1980–89	10,464.73	5,146.68	307,157.82	2,536.29	2,500.36	319,501.37
1990–99	21,314.13	1,330.21	111,183.63	-	-	131,430.52
2000–11	183,072.14	21,323.54	1,509,733.45	-	-	1,714,129.13

Notes: Between 1945 and 1965, there is no reliable data on hydrocarbons exports, hence none is reported.
Petroleum column includes exports of diesel oil and kerosene.
During various years between 1966 and 2011, exports of some hydrocarbon commodities did not happen.
Values in table reflect author's own estimations based on data from the NIS and the Ministry of Hydrocarbons.

Though difficult to predict whether the export pattern of traditional commodities will extend beyond 2011, it is safe to assume that with mining products much will depend on China and its ability to sustain its demand for raw materials at the levels seen during the first decade of the new century. As for hydrocarbons, so long as Bolivia does not reduce the prices for natural gas agreed upon with Brazil and Argentina—a process that would involve a renegotiation of current contracts—and assuming neither of these countries begins production of its own natural gas reserves, it is not unreasonable to affirm that current levels of exports, both in volume and in monetary receipts, will continue at least into the mid 2010s.

EXPORTS OF NON-TRADITIONAL GOODS

Official, disaggregated statistics for exports of non-traditional goods began to be published regularly during the 1970s. Between 1929 and 1945 there is also reliable data on different types of exports, though the quantity and importance, in dollar terms, of these non-traditional exports is small relative to traditional exports. The interlude between 1946 and 1970 is one where reliable, consistent data on disaggregated exports is inexistent, though, as explained earlier, it is possible to derive aggregate values for non-traditional exports subtracting mining from total exports. Table 1.5 reports average export values, by decade, along with the most important non-traditional product for each decade. Table 6a in the appendix provides all supporting statistical data for yearly exports of non-traditional goods, in current dollars.

Table 1.5 Non-Traditional Products: Average Export Values, 1929-2011		
Decade	Export Values (current US dollars)	Most Important Good (in dollar terms)
1929–39	3,242,727.27	Rubber
1940–45	4,732,263.33	Rubber
1971–79	67,274,211.11	Lumber
1980s	99,751,130.00	Lumber
1990s	503,770,380.00	Soybeans
2000–11	1,125,413,008.33	Soybeans

Notes: Values in table reflect author's own estimations based on data from CBB, NIS, and Customs Department.

As can be observed, average export values increased from around $3 and $5 million in the 1930s and 1940s, to $67 million in the 1970s, $100 million in the 1980s, $504 million in the 1990s, and $1.1 billion between 2000 and 2011. Consistently, the most important good throughout the period analyzed has been an agricultural product from the Bolivian lowlands—rubber in the 1930s and 1940s, lumber in the 1970s and 1980s, and soybeans during the last two decades—confirming the significance of the agricultural sector and of the lowlands as the main source of key non-traditional goods.

While it is worthwhile to note that rubber is now being utilized in the production of other export goods such as textiles and shoes, unprocessed lumber has been finding its way to alternative economic activities—particularly in furniture manufacturing—and soybeans are now being converted into oil and different types of cakes, it still is true that these non-traditional commodities are mostly exported in raw form, and hence there is ample space for manufacturing processes to be added to these and other agricultural goods.

It is also worth noting the appearance of new products—textiles products with a variety of fabrics, computer software, pharmaceutical products, beverages, high-end jewelry artifacts, furniture, elaborated foodstuffs, tobacco products—that barely registered a few years back but that now seem to be showing significant export potential. These newer products come mainly from the three main departments—Cochabamba, Santa Cruz, and La Paz, or the 'main economic axis of the country,' as they have been referred to within Bolivia—but also from the other six departments, which speaks well of the gradual, though slow, diversification that is beginning to take place, both in terms of the variety of goods being produced and from the perspective of the geographical origin of these products.

THE EVOLUTION OF IMPORTS

According to the National Institute of Statistics (NIS), the government institution in charge of compiling official data on various areas, including trade, imports can be of three general types: consumer, intermediate, and capital imports. Consumer import goods are further subdivided into two general categories: perishable and non-perishable, and within these broad categories are any goods destined to the final consumer such are clothes, vehicles, computers, books (all examples of non-perishable goods) and different types of food and pharmaceutical products, which by definition have an expiration date and are hence considered 'perishable goods'. Intermediate import products are those which serve as inputs in the manufacturing processes of final goods and are subdivided into five subcategories: (1) fuels and oils lubricants (diesel oil is the most prominent of this kind), (2) inputs for agricultural purposes (e.g., seeds), (3) inputs for industry purposes (e.g., aluminum sheets), (4) inputs for construction purposes (e.g., cement), and (5) parts and accessories for transport equipment (e.g., wheels and batteries). Finally, capital import goods, much like intermediate goods, are also utilized in the manufacturing processes of final goods, but, unlike intermediate products, they tend to have greater value added, as they usually cannot be transformed to a different state. The NIS observes three different categories of capital goods: (1) those for agricultural purposes (e.g., specialized machinery to turn soybeans into oil), (2) those for industry purposes (e.g., satellite dishes for cable companies), and (3) transport equipment (e.g., tractors and heavy duty trucks). Here I refer to import data utilizing the definitions of NIS but without actually detailing the goods under any one of the categories.[13]

Import data disaggregated according to the general classification of consumer, intermediate, and capital goods has been available since 1962. An initial appraisal of import diversification is provided in Figure 1.6. Table 7a in the appendix provides the structure of imports since 1962.

Figure 1.6 illustrates that imports of all types have grown considerably since the beginning of the series. Total imports grew by 7,754 percent between 1962 ($97 million) and 2011 ($7.6 billion),

[13] Since 1991, Bolivia, along with all countries in the Andean Community, utilize the Nandina Nomenclature—a system based on the Customs Cooperation Council's Harmonized Description and Coding System—as a common language for classifying goods traded among countries. More detailed information on the goods and services traded by Bolivia can be found at http://apps.ine.gob.bo/comex/Main and more information on the Nandina system is found at www.comunidadandina.org/ingles/aduanas/nomenclatura.htm.

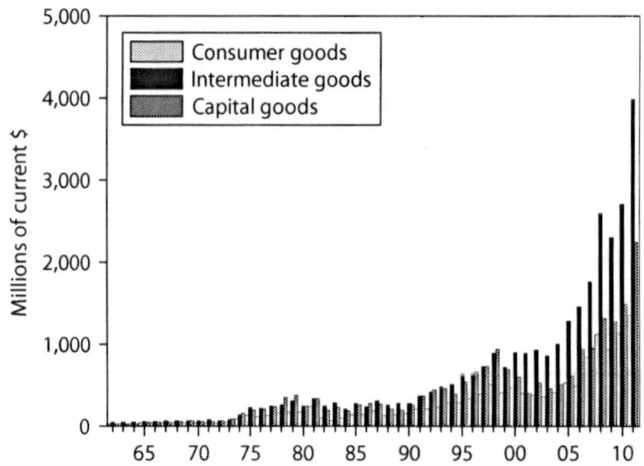

FIGURE 1.6 Import diversification, 1962–2011

Source: CBB, NIS

but growth rates differed among the different types of goods: consumer imports grew by 4,863 percent (from $27.3 million to $1.3 billion), intermediate goods by 8,820 percent (from $44.8 million to $4 billion), and capital imports by 9,048 percent ($24.6 million to $2.2 billion). Within consumer imports, non-perishable goods show a higher growth rate (9,170 percent) than perishable goods (2,552 percent), suggesting that Bolivia is, in relative terms, better at producing perishable goods than it is at producing non-perishable goods, but caution should accompany that statement as developments within the period analyzed and within the types of goods imported under each category may conceal or overemphasize important elements of the story. Additionally, and particularly when the initial monetary values are low, as is the case here, it is not surprising that growth rates will tend to overstate and amplify the state of certain economic activities. With those cautionary caveats in mind, it is noteworthy that with intermediate products the higher growth rates occur with agricultural inputs (91,420 percent) and construction inputs (29,199 percent), while with capital goods, agricultural equipment is easily the one with the highest growth rate, an astonishing 138,954 percent between 1962 ($450,000) and 2011 ($626 million).

An alternative way of analyzing how imports have evolved since 1962 is illustrated in Table 1.6, where average total import values by decade, along with the most rapidly growing import good, are presented.

Table 1.6 confirms that the growth of imports—measured in terms of the evolution of average imports by decade—since the 1960s has indeed been quite dramatic. From around $131 million in the

Table 1.6
Average Import Values and Highest Growth Product, by Decades, 1962–2011

Decade	Import Values (current US dollars)	Highest Growth Good[1]
1962–69	130,628,750.00	Capital goods—agricultural purposes (656%)
1970s	446,410,000.00	Intermediate goods—fuels and lubricants (991%)
1980s	653,450,000.00	Intermediate goods—fuels and lubricants (53%)
1990s	1,434,620,000.00	Intermediate goods—fuels and lubricants (1,594%)
2000–11	3,397,187,500.00	Capital goods—agricultural purposes (4,906%)

Notes: [1]Growth rate calculated between dollar import values of last year and first year of decade.
Values in table reflect author's own estimations based on data from NIS.

1960s, average imports increased to $446 million in the 1970s, $653 million in the 1980s, $1.4 billion in the 1990s, and $3.4 billion for the years between 2000 and 2011. As to the fastest growing import good for each decade, it is telling that in all cases the most important import product is not a consumer good but an intermediate product (fuels and lubricants, particularly diesel fuel, during the 1970s, 1980s, and 1990s), and capital goods destined to the increasingly more sophisticated agricultural sector of the Bolivian lowlands (during the 1960s, as this sector began to take its initial steps, and during the 2000s, when it established itself as a real economic alternative in the country). The growing importance of the agricultural sector is perhaps even more significant than the data in Table 1.6 indicates, as this sector has been the principal consumer of (subsidized) imported diesel fuel since extensive mechanization was incorporated in production processes, giving an added economic and political relevance to this industry.

Finally, Figure 1.7 illustrates how the shares of consumer, intermediate, and capital goods on total imports have varied during the years between 1962 and 2011.

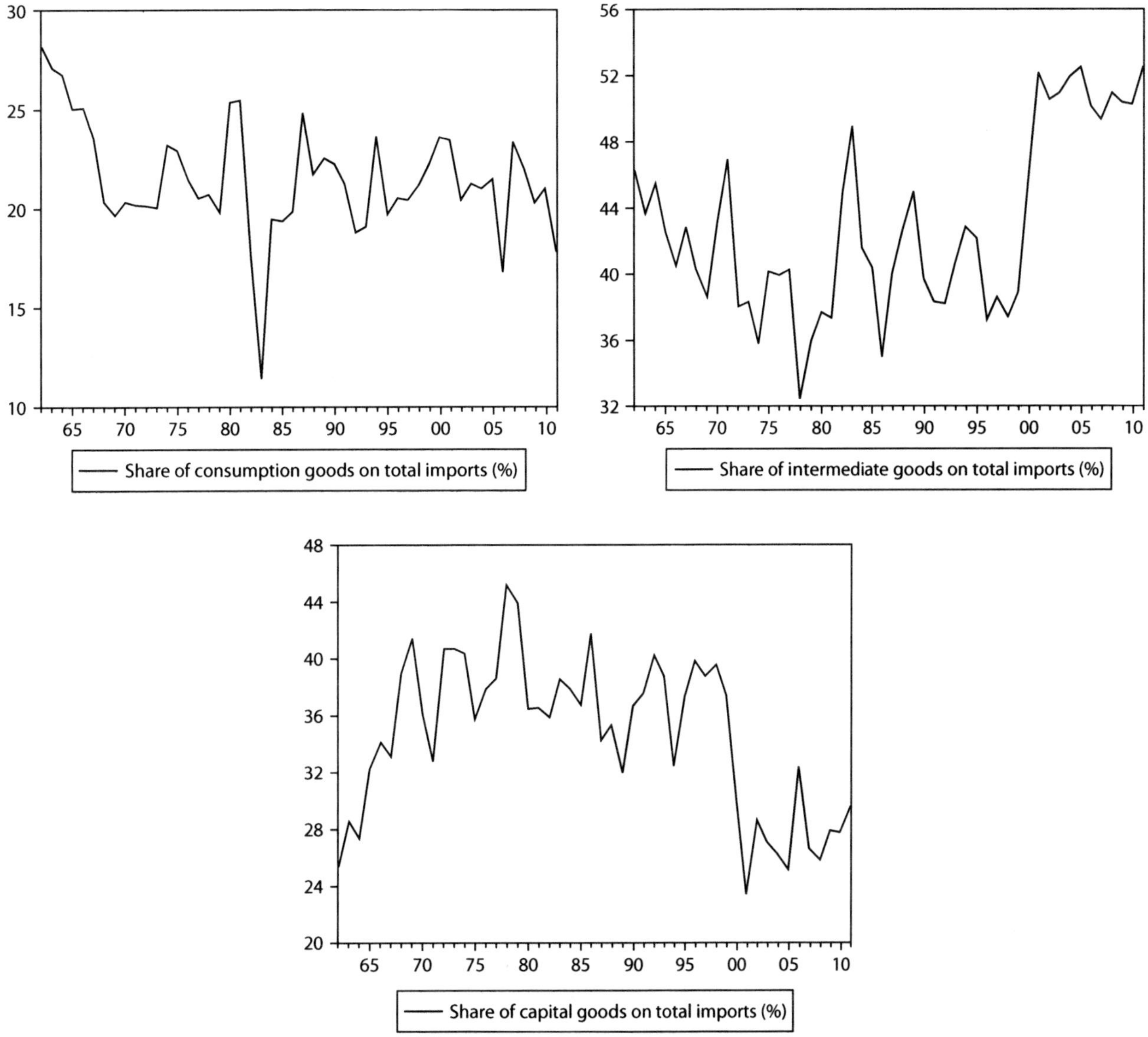

FIGURE 1.7 Share of consumer, intermediate, and capital goods on total imports, 1962–2011

Source: NIS, Customs Dept.

As illustrated in Figure 1.7, the share of consumption goods on total imports shows a clear downward trend, having decreased from a high of 28 percent in 1962 to 18 percent in 2011. During the 1980s it reached its lowest level (11 percent in 1983) but due to the particular economic circumstances of the time,[14] the share of consumption on total imports during that specific year (1983) is considered out of trend. With capital goods, the evolution of their share on total imports is more complicated, having risen consistently during the 1960s and 1970s (in 1978, it reached a maximum of 54.2 percent), then showing a clear downward trend throughout the 1980s and 1990s, and finally reversing to a more positive trend after 2001, when the share reached a low-point of 23.3 percent, to the 2011 mark of almost 30 percent. As for intermediate products, their share on total imports shows a negative trend through the 1960s and 1970s, reaching in 1978 a low point of 32.4 percent, but with a consistent positive trend thereafter, hitting the 50 percent mark repeatedly during the 2000s, and with a record high level of 52.5 percent in 2011.

As was the case with exports, and despite substantial increases in monetary value of imports, it is still true that Bolivia remains highly dependent on a few countries and is a net importer of intermediate and capital goods. In the future, greater sophistication and diversification of imports will only come with increasing levels of income spread across Bolivian society and with greater emphasis on finding alternative sources for these import goods.

[14] During the 1980s Bolivia experienced hyperinflation unprecedented at the time in a country at peace internally and with its neighbors. An analysis of the extreme price fluctuations during this period will be a central point of the chapter on prices.

Prices

CHAPTER 2

EVOLUTION OF PRICES

The evolution of prices in Bolivia since the 1930s is difficult to describe without the utilization of extreme adjectives: dramatic, chaotic, wild—these are all words that aptly describe what has happened to prices in the country during most of the twentieth century. Though the volatility has subsided, particularly after the last episode of hyperinflation in the 1980s, it is still remarkable to look back and contemplate how prices can change in the magnitudes seen in Bolivia, with such an apparent ease, and in a relatively short period of time.

Here, four different types of price series are analyzed: (1) a monthly consumer price index (CPI) beginning in January 1937 constructed out of several indices built by the Central Bank of Bolivia (CBB) over the approximately last 70 years; (2) a monthly industrial production index (IPI) also assembled by combining two wholesale indices constructed at various times by the CBB and by the National Institute of Statistics (NIS); (3) monthly and yearly exchange rates between the Bolivian currency, the US dollar, and the British pound; and (4) end-of-year interest rates for savings, time deposits, and short-term credits, in Bolivian currency (bolivianos) and in US dollars, since 1976.

CONSUMER PRICES[1]

The Central Bank of Bolivia (CBB) started compiling a consumer price index (CPI) for the city of La Paz[2] in the late 1930s (http://www.bcb.gob.bo/?q=indicadores/inflacion). With time, other price indices began to be constructed and urban centers different than La Paz began to be taken into account. In all, nine indices were developed over the course of approximately seventy years, though only six of these indices have been utilized to construct the single CPI utilized here.[3] The reason behind the utilization of six indices is that the CBB discontinued construction of older indices when a new index began to be collected, hence a single, unified index from the 1930s to the present is not available. Here, I fill that gap by presenting a single, unbroken monthly CPI between January 1937 and May 2012, built out of six indices that were constructed during this period of time.[4]

The methodology for putting together a single index out of the six indices that were utilized is fairly straightforward: the single index is built on the values that the initial index—the one that begins in 1937—would have if monthly rates of change of the other indices were applied to this initial index after it ceased to be compiled in 1956. The resulting values are then standardized by setting January 2000 as the base month. Table 1b in the appendix presents the price index, along with yearly inflation rates.

[1] The description on how the single consumer price index was built is also available in a paper I wrote ("Inflation and Inflation Uncertainty in Bolivia," *El Trimestre Económico*, forthcoming). Table 2.1 and Figure 2.1 in this chapter are partial reproductions from that paper.

[2] Bolivia is divided into 9 departments or provinces. The city of La Paz is the capital of the Department of La Paz and the seat of government of the country. The city of El Alto, also located in La Paz, is an important urban sprawling and, along with the other 9 capitals, is considered one of the most important economic centers of the country.

[3] The first index runs from January 1937 through 1956. Its base month is December 1936 and its coverage is the city of La Paz. The second index begins in 1956 and ends in 1965. Its base month is January 1956 and its coverage is the city of La Paz. The third index runs from 1957 through 1967. The base month is January 1957 and the coverage is the city of La Paz. The fourth index runs from 1967 through 1992. The base year is 1966 and the coverage includes the cities of La Paz and El Alto. The fifth index begins in 1992 and it is still being compiled. The base year is 1980 and it covers the cities of La Paz, Cochabamba, Santa Cruz, and El Alto. The sixth index runs from 2007 through the present. The base year is 2007 and it covers the 9 capital cities plus El Alto.

[4] The aggregation of different indices is problematic for a host of technical reasons, including the (incorrect) assumption that each index has the same degree of measurement error. Though aware of these difficulties, the single index presented in this work is an aggregation of various indices and the technical problems are addressed in my paper on the subject (footnote 1 above), where different statistical tests are carried out for different sub-periods between 1937 and 2011. The consistency of results found in these tests validates the worthiness of the single index presented here.

A continuous, unbroken price index series since 1937 provides a stark portrait of the volatility of prices in Bolivia. Table 2.1 reports summary statistics for the inflation rate in each of the decades covered by the index.

As Table 2.1 illustrates, the country experienced significant fluctuations in inflation rates throughout the years. The worst decade—unsurprising since only in 1985 the yearly inflation topped 4,800 percent—was the 1980s, when monthly rates consistently hit two and three figures, and the decade-long inflation rate was nearly 13 million percent. When inflation is calculated for the period January 1937 to March 2012, the rate is even more astonishing: nearly 370 billion percent![5] The 1950s were also a decade of significant price fluctuations but paled compared to the 1980s. During these years, the decade-long inflation rate was over 8 thousand percent. Since 1990, rates have consistently been in the lower one-digit figures, matching and often outperforming those of neighboring countries. Figure 2.1 plots the monthly inflation rate, together with the corresponding year-on-year growth rate, for the period 1938–2012.

Table 2.1
Summary Inflation Rates by Decade

Decade	Mean π	Median π	Monthly Maximum	Monthly Minimum	Q1 π	Q2 π	Q3 π	Q4π	Average π*
1930s	2.24	2.46	11.37	-8.19	1.87	2.61	1.52	2.93	111.73
1940s	1.18	0.66	12.14	-2.71	1.18	0.74	0.89	1.89	291.98
1950s	4.10	2.30	71.59	-30.83	2.24	4.47	2.21	7.49	8,182,67
1960s	0.48	0.50	8.21	-6.81	0.55	0.51	0.46	0.39	72.83
1970s	1.42	0.58	23.66	-2.11	1.18	0.79	1.12	2.61	407.87
1980s	12.00	2.49	182.77	-2.33	14.90	10.44	12.93	9.70	12,683,466.35
1990s	0.76	0.55	5.84	-1.05	0.87	0.55	0.68	0.94	144.72
2000s	0.43	0.37	2.68	-2.55	0.38	0.35	0.48	0.38	59.56
2010s	0.56	0.43	2.10	-0.12	0.54	0.10	0.61	0.95	15.63

Notes: All rates in %
*Estimated between December of last year and January of first year of decade
The 1930s values reflect the January 1937 through December 1939 period.
The 2010s values reflect the January 2010 through March 2012 period.
Values in table reflect author's own estimations based on data from the CBB and the NIS.

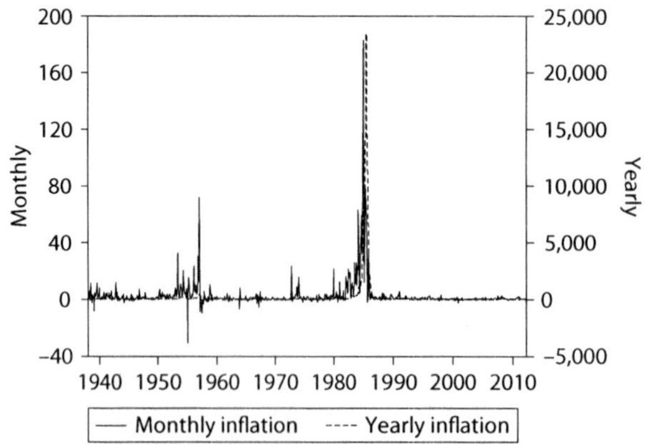

FIGURE 2.1 Monthly and yearly inflation rates, 1938–2012
Source: Central Bank of Bolivia (CBB), National Institute of Statistics (NIS)

[5] The unit of account of the country changed twice during the period 1937–2012, once in 1962 and then in 1987. In both instances, a new currency replaced a badly depreciated currency—the result of severe inflation during the 1950s and hyperinflation in the 1980s.

Visual inspection suggests significant variability in inflation rates up until the mid 1980s, when the hyperinflation period finally ended. The mid 1950s and 1980s are characterized by dramatic peaks in inflation, consistent with the two periods of greatest monetary disequilibrium. Since the latter part of the 1980s, inflation rates in single digits have been the norm, as successive governments placed price stability at the center of monetary policy and the country entered a self-enforcing cycle of low inflation and low uncertainty. Interestingly, even with the current administration of Evo Morales, the strict stance against inflation of his predecessors has apparently been maintained, which stands in stark contrast with economic and political events in the 1950s and in the 1980s, when other populist administrations—in many ways, very much like the current one—carried out significant structural reforms without regard to public finances, which generated severe episodes of hyperinflation[6] and abrupt ends to their regimes. It seems that the current populist reformers will embark on ambitious social and political projects, but aware of the fate of those who did not learn the economic lessons of their time, will not compromise on the monetary stability of the country.[7]

As to the reasons for the severe inflation of the 1950s and the hyperinflation of the 1980s, while low or moderate rates of inflation might be the result of a variety of factors in addition to excessive money growth (changes in the real demand for goods and services or scarcity of key commodities, to mention two of these additional factors) the Bolivian episodes of extreme inflation represent textbook representations of excessive growth of the money supply being the main reason for the wild price volatility seen during those decades. Figure 2.2 illustrates the close association between inflation and money supply growth between 1937 and 2011, where the correlation during the 1950s and 1980s is particularly evident.[8]

As is evident from Figure 2.2, the correlation between yearly inflation and money growth rates is almost perfect. During the 1950s, the correlation coefficient is 0.95; during the 1980s it rises to 0.99.

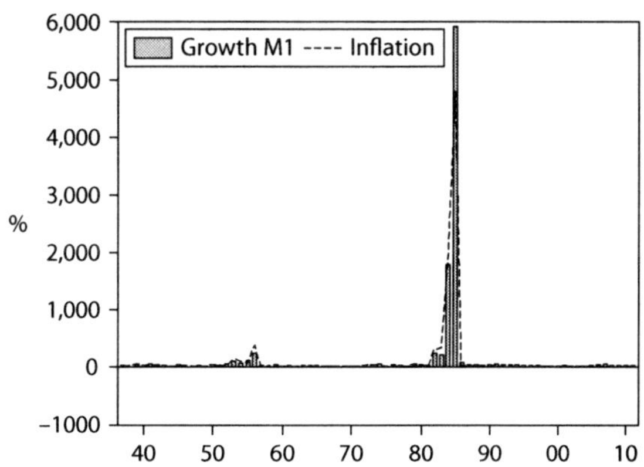

FIGURE 2.2 Inflation and growth of M1, 1937–2011

Source: CBB

[6] The inflation of the 1950s does not conform to the definition of hyperinflation—expressed by Phillip Cagan (1956)—which states that hyperinflation occurs when the monthly inflation rate exceeds 50%. The episode of severe price volatility during the 1980s, however, easily meets Cagan's rule.

[7] A qualification is in place, however, regarding the compromise of the Morales administration to price stability. In the new Constitution of the country approved and sanctioned by the Bolivian national Congress in October 2008, it is established (Article 236) that the Executive branch of government determines the objectives of monetary and exchange rate policies of the country, hence implicitly taking away the autonomy that the Central Bank had obtained as a result of previous political meddling into its policy activities. Law 1670 (Ley del Banco Central de Bolivia) enacted in October 1995, where this autonomy was explicitly declared as state policy, has been completely revamped by the new constitution and, as this chapter was written, was about to put into effect with a new central bank law where the activities of the bank would be explicitly directed, monitored, and controlled by the Ministry of Economy and Public Finances—part of the Executive branch. Time will tell whether this renewed effort to control monetary policy by the political establishment will bring the same economic meltdown observed in the 1950s and 1980s, when the CBB was also held hostage by the political class of the times.

[8] Money supply, or M1, was estimated by adding the amount of bills and coins with public and checking accounts in Bolivian currency, US dollars, and in Bolivian currency adjusted to changes in the value of the US dollar. Actual estimates for M1 are presented in the chapter on money.

For the whole period, 1937–2011, the coefficient is well above 0.90. Worth noting is that when inflation reached its highest level during the first episode of high inflation of the 1950s (the year was 1956 and inflation for that year was 366 percent) the growth in money supply also reached a record level rate of 239 percent. Likewise, during the hyperinflation period, 1984 and 1985 were the years when both inflation and money growth rates reached record levels concurrently. In 1984, the yearly inflation rate was 1,978 percent; its corresponding money growth rate was 1,782 percent. The following year, 1985, inflation toppled 4,800 percent and the corresponding money growth rate reached 5,929 percent. Severe inflation and hyperinflation in Bolivia, as orthodox economic theory predicts, have always been the result of monetary disequilibriums caused by excessive money growth rates.

As to the reasons why monetary disequilibriums of the magnitudes seen in the country occurred twice in the last century, it is worth mentioning that the 1950s and 1980s were decades characterized by momentous political transformations, when monetary and fiscal considerations took a distant second place to what policy makers of the time decided were more important objectives. During the 1950s the largest tin mines were nationalized, a sweeping agrarian reform transferred land to thousands, perhaps millions, of peasants, and literacy requirements for voting rights were abolished. Likewise, the hyperinflation of the 1980s occurred during the tenure of the first democratically elected government after more than two decades of military dictatorships. Monetary policy became a tool for grander political objectives (the social revolution of the 1950s, the consolidation of democracy during the 1980s) and it was unfortunately used capriciously and without regard to the consequences in the medium and long terms. The consequences were, of course, two of the biggest episodes of extreme price volatility ever seen by a country not engaged in a foreign or civil war. The evolution of prices throughout the period analyzed here is a clear representation of the political and social evolution Bolivia has taken since 1937.

INDUSTRIAL PRODUCTION PRICES

The production of reliable and consistent data for industrial prices is a recent development. During the late 1970s the NIS began compiling—at irregular intervals—a type of producer, or wholesale, price index. These initial efforts, however, were not sufficient to start a credible time series to measure fluctuations in these alternative prices. Starting in 1986, an index of industrial production prices—called "Indice de Precios de Producción Industrial" (IPPI), or Index of Prices for Industrial Production—began to be constructed with greater periodicity, and lasted until the end of 1989, when a new index was created measuring what might be construed as a more complete set of prices in key economic sectors. This latter index was called "Indice Global de Actividad Económica" (IGAE), or Global Index of Economic Activity. The combined index presented here, constructed with the same methodology used for the consumer price index of the previous section, is a combination of both of these indices—the IPPI starting in 1986, and the IGAE from 1990 to the present.[9] One of the drawbacks of the IGAE is that, as an index that measures the evolution of economic activity, it shows clear seasonal patterns through the year, with the index rising during high seasons—Christmas, particularly—and then dropping quite substantially during slower seasons, as usually happens during the first months of the year. Table 2b in the appendix presents the combined index (the IPI index) described here.

Figure 2.3 illustrates the evolution of both the combined IPI and CPI during the years 1986 through 2011.

[9] The IPPI and IGAE indices include data on prices collected across a variety of economic sectors, both public and private. The scope of the IGAE index is more extensive than the IPPI index as, in addition to prices in the industrial sector (agriculture, petroleum and natural gas, mining, manufactures, foodstuffs and beverages, and other smaller industries), it includes prices in the electricity, construction, and gas and water sectors, as well as prices in a variety of services in commerce, telecommunications, banking, and government-related activities. In the absence of a continuous and reliable industrial production index, the combination of the IPPI and the IGAE is the closest thing there is to a price index dedicated to measuring average changes over time in the selling prices received by Bolivian producers for their output.

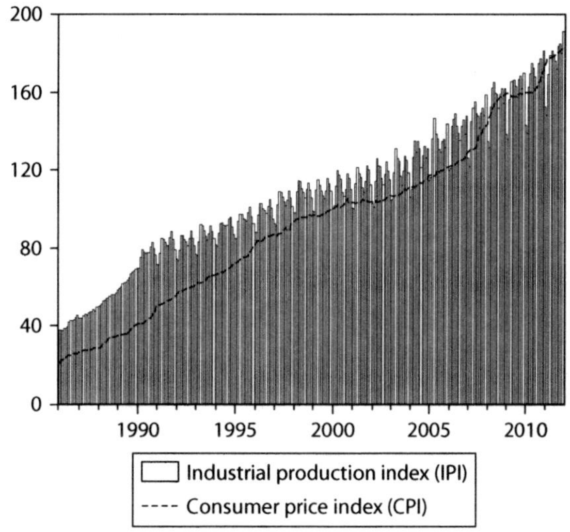

FIGURE 2.3 Evolution of IPI and CPI, 1986–2011

Source: CBB, NIS

Clearly, the tendency in both indices is to rise over time. The correlation between the series for the period 1986–2011 is 0.97, reflecting an almost identical perception of market prices by both indices. However, at the disaggregated level, the similarities between the two, as reflected in the different inflation rates calculated with each index, are less visible. Table 2.2 shows quarterly inflation rates calculated with both indices for the years 1986 through 2011, as well as average inflation for each decade.

Table 2.2
Inflation Rates with CPI and IPI

Decade	Q1 π		Q2 π		Q3 π		Q4 π		Average π*	
	CPI	IPI	CPI	IPI	CPI	IPI	CPI	IPI	CPI	IPI
1980s	1.51	0.48	1.61	1.47	1.63	1.86	1.06	1.43	95.63	84.69
1990s	0.87	1.68	0.55	1.34	0.68	0.42	0.94	−1.52	144.72	56.87
2000s	0.38	0.96	0.35	1.32	0.48	−0.58	0.38	0.73	59.56	69.97
2010s	0.62	−1.00	0.10	1.95	0.61	0.72	0.95	1.38	14.38	33.77

Notes: All rates in %
*Between December of last year and January of first year of decade
The 1980s values reflect the January 1986 through December 1989 period.
The 2010s values reflect the January 2010 through December 2011 period.
Values in table reflect author's own estimations based on data from the CBB and the NIS.

As can be observed, quarterly inflation rates estimated with the IPI index are more volatile than those estimated with the CPI index. The greater volatility in the IPI index is a reflection of the seasonal patterns embedded in the price series that was used to construct it. Seasonal patterns within a year are absent in the CPI index, which explains its smoother evolution over time. Notwithstanding the differences, both indices illustrate a clear long-term positive correlation throughout the period analyzed.

EXCHANGE RATES

Exchange rates presented here reflect the value of a foreign currency in terms of Bolivian currency; that is, they express the price of a foreign currency in Bolivian currency. An introduction to these prices is provided in Figure 2.4, where the exchange rates between Bolivian currency and the US dollar and the

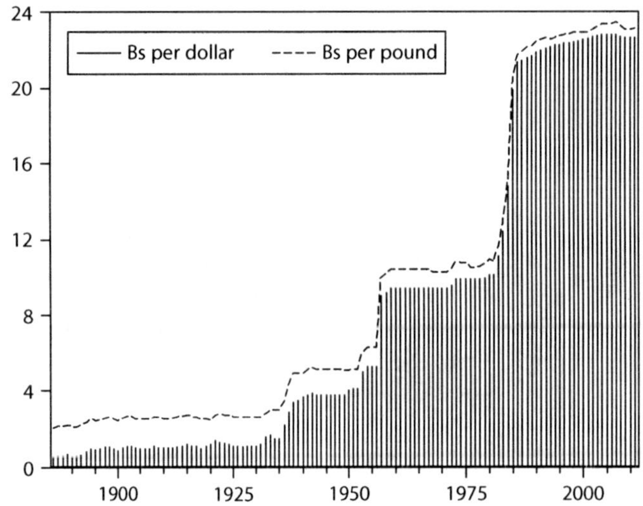

FIGURE 2.4 Exchange rates Bs per dollar and Bs per pound (logs), 1886–2011

Source: Historical archives, CBB, NIS

British pound are shown for the period 1886–2011. Table 3b in the appendix reports the exchange rates utilized in the construction of this figure.

The exchange rates Bs per dollar (Bs/dollar) and Bs per pound (Bs/pound) in Figure 2.4 are expressed in log form. Additionally, they represent the yearly average official selling exchange rate between Bolivian currency and both foreign currencies. Finally, and more importantly, they indicate what the dollar and pound currencies would have been worth in "old" bolivianos. That is, until 1962, the Bolivian currency was the boliviano. On July 13 of that year,[10] and due to the extreme depreciation of the boliviano during the severe inflation of the preceding 1950s, the government of the time decided to eliminate the boliviano and adopt a new currency, the peso boliviano, where the exchange rate between the new and old currencies was set at 1 peso boliviano = 1,000 bolivianos. Government effectively erased three zeros from the currency, gave it a new name, and printed new bills and coins. In 1986 the exact same thing happened again, as the government of that time, and due to the hyperinflation of the early 1980s, dropped the peso boliviano and adopted a new currency, the boliviano, utilizing the same name that had been used until 1962.[11] The exchange rate between the currencies was set at 1 boliviano = 1,000,000 pesos bolivianos. This time, six zeros were dropped from the old currency to come up with the new one. The exchange rates in Figure 2.4 are expressed in terms of how many old bolivianos are necessary to buy 1 dollar or 1 pound; that is, these rates have been adjusted to reflect the price of these foreign currencies in terms of the original boliviano.

There are a number of interesting facts illustrated in Figure 2.4. First, consistently throughout the period analyzed, the British pound has been valued higher than the US dollar. Although not that surprising given the behavior of both currencies in the last decades, it is remarkable to see how entrenched and sustained this trend has been for over 100 years. A second issue clearly evident from the figure is that since these rates represent official selling rates, they tend to remain on the same level for sustained periods of time; that is, starting in the 1940s through the early 1980s, Bolivia was on a fixed exchange rate regime—with the US dollar, and by default with other currencies—whereby government tried to keep the value of the Bolivian currency constant against other currencies. Adjustments to a given rate would occur periodically, whenever market rates would excessively diverge away from the current rate, making the fixed rate more difficult and expensive to maintain. In Figure 2.4, the plateaus, especially evident during the 1950s and 1970s, represent periods of time when the prices of the US dollar and the British

[10] Supreme Decree 6161 formalized the elimination of the boliviano and the adoption of the new currency, the peso boliviano.

[11] Law 901, from November 28, 1986, formalized the transition from the peso boliviano to the boliviano.

pound remained fixed for a time, only to be abruptly adjusted, usually upwards, when a given rate was no longer sustainable. Finally, it is remarkable to look at the rates themselves, to see how the prices of these foreign currencies in terms of Bolivian currency have changed over time. Table 2.3 reports average exchange rates between old bolivianos and the US and British currencies since 1886.

Table 2.3
Average Exchange Rates, 1886-2011

Period	Bs/$	Bs/£
1886–1929	2.57	12.17
1930s	11.20	49.83
1940s	42.63	167.93
1950s	3,057.28	8,547.44
1960s	11,885.00	32,369.87
1970s	17,858.04	38,700.12
1980s	946,621,490.00	1,548,899,231.50
1990s	4,603,000,000.00	7,514,000,000.00
2000–11	7,339,708,333.33	12,316,590,972.22

Notes: Exchange rates expressed in old bolivianos per foreign currency.
Values in table reflect author's own estimations based on data from CBB.
Rates estimated between values at the end and at the beginning of a period.

The average exchange rate between bolivianos and the dollar between 1886 and 1929 was 2.57 (12.17 with the pound). During the 1930s, this rate jumped to 11.20 (49.83 with the pound), and to 42.63 (167.93 with the pound) during the 1940s. Even though the devaluation of the boliviano with respect to the dollar exceeded, on average, 1,550 percent (1,279 percent with the pound) between 1886 and the 1940s, it was nothing compared to what would happen next: between the 1940s and 1950s, the price of the dollar jumped by over 7,000 percent (around 5,000 percent with the pound), reflecting the severe inflation the country experienced during the mid 1950s. The next two decades brought, comparatively speaking, mild average increases in the price of the dollar (and pound) with jumps of 289 percent between the 1950s and 1960s (279 percent with the pound) and 50 percent between the 1960s and 1970s (20 percent with the pound). By this time, the average exchange rate was at 17,858 bolivianos per dollar (38,700 bolivianos per pound) and the trend clearly pointed upwards. However, the magnitude of the increase in the average price of the dollar (and the pound) between the 1970s and 1980s was unexpected and unprecedented: 5.3 million percent (4 million percent for the pound), which this time around reflected the hyperinflation period of the early 1980s. During the 1990s and the twelve years between 2000 and 2011, the price of the dollar increased by 386 percent (385 percent with the pound) and 59 percent (64 percent with the pound), respectively. The actual, average rates between bolivianos and the dollar (pound) were 946.6 million per dollar in the 1980s (1.5 billion per pound), 4.6 billion per dollar (7.5 billion per pound) in the 1990s, and 7.3 billion per dollar (12.3 billion per pound) during the 2000s. In all, between the year 1886 and 2011, the price of the dollar, as measured in old Bolivianos, increased by 460 billion percent, while the price of the pound increased by 150 billion percent.

It is often argued that in countries like Bolivia, with serious monetary disequilibriums, market, or parallel exchange rates are commonly out of line with official rates. Proving that assertion for the years prior to 1982 is difficult because neither the CBB nor the NIS reported market rates with the periodicity necessary to construct a reliable time series dataset. Beginning in April 1982 this situation changes, as the CBB initiates reporting monthly rates in the parallel market between Bolivian currency and the US dollar, hence providing the opportunity to observe the divergence between official and market rates. In Figure 2.5, the official and market rates between bolivianos and dollars are pictured during the hyperinflation period of April 1982 through December 1986.[12] Tables 4b and 5b in the appendix report monthly official and market exchange rates since they began to be compiled in the 1980s.

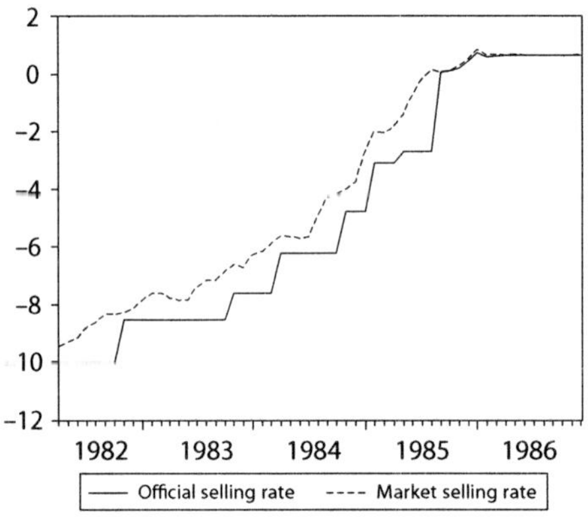

FIGURE 2.5 Official and market rates (bolivianos/$), in logs, 1982–1986

Source: CBB

Figure 2.5 clearly shows that market rates have consistently been above official rates during the hyperinflation period, though the divergence between the two becomes almost negligible beginning in September 1985. It seems that government, through the CBB, basically heeds to market forces in late 1985 once it realizes the folly in trying to fight it. When the same picture is done for the period 1982 through 2012, this pattern of aligning official to market rates becomes even more evident, as Figure 2.6 demonstrates.

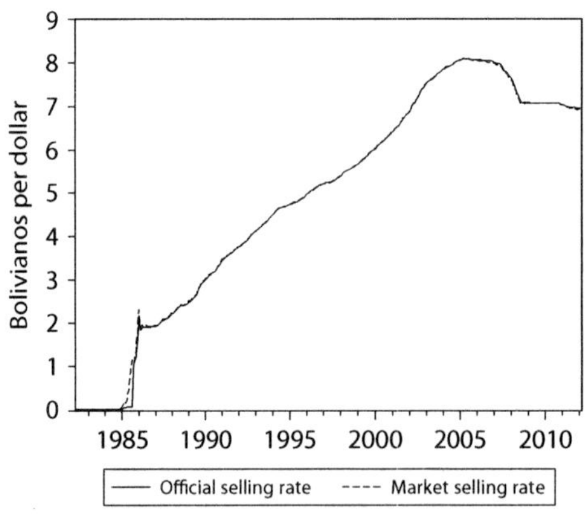

FIGURE 2.6 Official and market rates (bolivianos/$), 1982–2012

Source: CBB

Between April 1982 and February 2012, the divergence between official and market is negligible — the correlation between the series is 0.99—demonstrating that official and market rates have not swayed far apart from each other since the 1980s. In fact, during most months the difference between market

[12] The rates utilized in Figure 2.5, which run from April 1982 through December 1986, have been adjusted to reflect rates in bolivianos per dollar, where bolivianos refers to the currency adopted on November 1986 by Law 901. Additionally, these rates are selling rates and are expressed in log form.

and official rates, whether they be selling or buying rates,[13] has been at most two points, with market rates usually, but not always, quoted higher than official rates.

INTEREST RATES

Interest rates only begin to be compiled by the CBB at the end of the 1970s. Yearly data reported here starts in 1976, and includes end-of-period lending and savings rates of loans and time deposits in bolivianos and US dollars with maturities between 181 and 360 days, as well as rates offered by savings accounts also in bolivianos and dollars. The interest rates represent average rates reported by traditional banks only.[14] Table 6b in the appendix reports these interest rates for the period 1976–2011.

An introduction to the evolution of interest rates since 1976 is provided by Figure 2.7, where lending rates for short-term credits (maturity < 1 year) and savings rate for short-term deposits (maturity < 1 year) in bolivianos are reported.

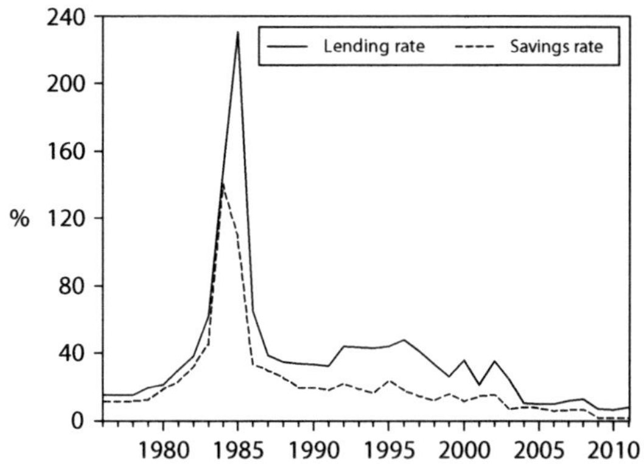

FIGURE 2.7 Lending, savings rates for credits and time deposits in Bs, 1976–2011

Source: CBB

As can be observed, the volatility of both lending and savings rates is significant, particularly during the hyperinflation years of 1982 to 1985, where lending rates easily surpassed the 230 percent mark (in 1985) and the savings rate reached 140 percent (in 1984). It is interesting to note that even after inflation receded and stabilized in the one-digit range during the 1990s and 2000s, interest rates remained in the upper double digits, averaging almost 39 percent (lending rate) and 17 percent (savings rate) during the 1990s, and 15.6 percent (lending rate) and 6.7 percent (savings rate) during the 2000–2011 period. Average spread rates between these periods were 21.4 percent (1990s) and 9 percent (2000s). It is likely that in addition to rooted mistrust in the capacity of the boliviano to sustain its value after the hyperinflation episode of the 1980s, other factors played a role as well, including the overt cartelization of the financial system due to a lack of antitrust legislation and blatant, endemic conflict of interests in government regulation of financial intermediaries.[15]

The evolution of lending rates for short-term credits (maturity < 1 year) and savings rate for short-term deposits (maturity < 1 year) in US dollars are illustrated in Figure 2.8 for the period 1985–2011.

[13] The official buying price was established by Supreme Resolution 042-051/89 and Decree 22139, dated February 21, 1989.

[14] Interest rates reported here do not include those offered by financial intermediaries such as savings and loans institutions, financial cooperatives, and other smaller financial institutions with the ability to make loans and offer savings accounts.

[15] Not uncommon in Bolivia for the government banking regulatory authority (during most of the period analyzed here, the *Superintendencia de Bancos y Entidades Financieras*, or as it is known now, *Autoridad de Supervisión del Sistema Financiero*) to be run by a banker, hence the perception of conflict of interests between regulators and regulated actors in the financial system.

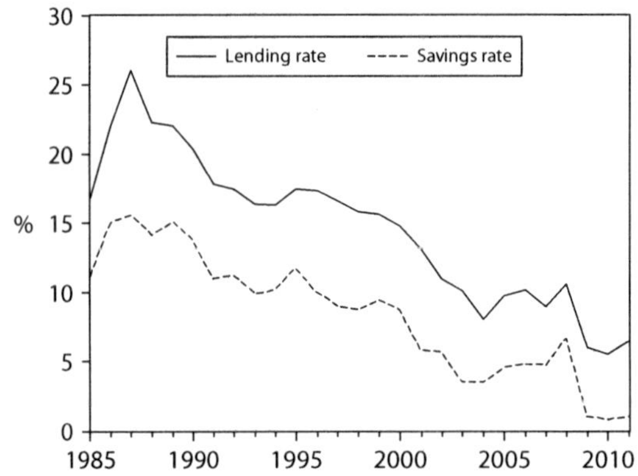

FIGURE 2.8 Lending, savings rates for credits and time deposits in $, 1985–2011

Source: CBB

Dollar denominated credits and time deposits are only available from 1985 onwards, hence the data begins as hyperinflation in the country was on its way out. The pattern of behavior of these rates is similar to those of credits and time deposits in bolivianos, though at considerably lower levels. The year 1987 is when the lending rate reached its highest level (26 percent), and since then the prevailing tendency has been downwards, averaging 17.1 percent in the 1990s and 9.52 during the 2000–2011 period. The savings rate also reached a peak in 1987 (15.56 percent) and consistently declined after that year, averaging 10.4 percent in the 1990s and 4.2 percent between 2000 and 2011. The high spread between the rates—averaging 6.6 percent in the 1990s and 5.32 during the 12 years of the new century—is difficult to explain by higher risk and higher administration costs alone (the industry's favorite two justifications), but must also be the result of the high degree of cooperation and lack of competition among financial intermediaries.

Finally, Figure 2.9 reports nominal interest rates offered by savings accounts in both bolivianos and dollars during the period 1988–2011.

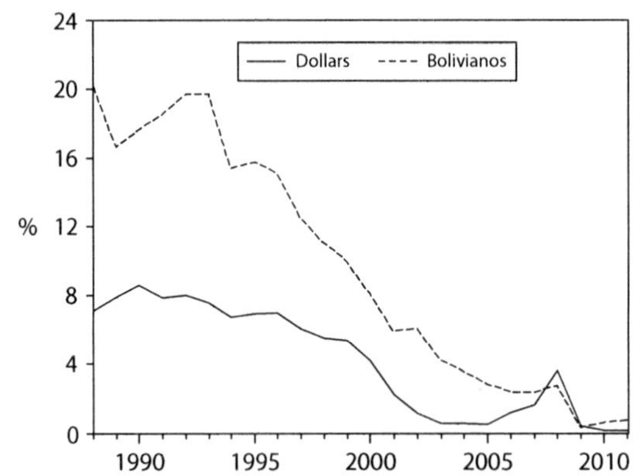

FIGURE 2.9 Savings accounts interest rates, in Bs and $, 1988–2011

Source: CBB

Data on savings rates in Bolivian currency is available since 1976 but since data for dollar savings accounts only begins in 1988, Figure 2.9 is limited to depicting this shorter time period. As can be clearly observed, savings rates in both currencies have consistently declined since 1988. Savings rate in bolivianos reached a peak in 1988 (20.15 percent)[16] and then continuously declined, averaging 15.53 percent during the 1990s and 3.29 percent during the 2000 to 2011 period. During the same periods, savings accounts in dollars averaged 6.95 percent (1990s) and 1.33 percent (2000–2011). In 1990, savings accounts in dollars offered 8.58 percent, the highest of the period analyzed. Particularly during the last few years, with negative real savings rates—real rates are estimated by subtracting average inflation rates from the nominal rates promised by financial instruments with a given maturity[17]—being offered by financial intermediaries, the lack of competition among them has become even more evident.

BEHAVIORAL PATTERN OF ALL PRICES

When all prices (CPI, IPI, exchange rate, interest rates) are analyzed at the same time, the pattern of behavior reflects expected relationships. Table 2.4 reports pairwise correlations among the price indices (CPI and IPI), exchange rates (Bs/$ and Bs/£), and two interest rates (lending and savings rate in Bs for short-term credits and time deposits).

Table 2.4
Pairwise Correlations

	Bs per dollar	Bs per pound	CPI	IPI	Lending rate time deposits, Bs	Savings rate time deposits, Bs
Bs per dollar	1					
Bs per pound	0.970	1				
CPI	0.890	0.834	1			
IPI	0.901	0.857	0.992	1		
Lending rate time deposits, Bs	-0.742	-0.755	-0.843	-0.857	1	
Savings rate time deposits, Bs	-0.885	-0.854	-0.925	-0.948	0.854	1

The correlation between the price indices and the exchange rates is positive and above 0.8, reflecting the upward trend in both the price level—whether measured in final markets or at the production level—and the price of foreign currencies. With interest rates, the correlation with price indices and exchange rates is negative due to the fact that as a special type of price, interest rates tend to decline as the financial system of a country becomes more developed, diversified, and generally more efficient. Disregarding the hyperinflation period, when interest rates did go up reflecting the general uncertainty of the times (illustrated in Figure 2.7) interest rates during the latter part of the 1980s, through the 1990s and the new century, have gone downwards, reflecting the greater development and stability of financial markets in the country. This behavior of interest rates is completely consistent with the low levels of inflation and stable exchange rates experienced during the same period.

Finally, Figure 2.10 illustrates the evolution of prices and exchange rates since 1937.

[16] Between 1976 and 1987, savings accounts in Bolivian currency averaged an interest rate of 34.89 percent, though this rate is greatly distorted by end-of-periods rates between 1982 and 1985—the hyperinflation years—when the average rate was 70.65 percent.

[17] According to the CBB (http://bcb.gob/bo/?q=indicadores/tasas) since 2005 every month through June of 2011, savings accounts in bolivianos and in dollars have resulted in negative real rates. In 2010, the average real saving rate in bolivianos was -0.78 percent and for dollars it was -1.45 percent. During the first 6 months of 2011, the average real rate in bolivianos was -4.45 percent and -5.08 percent for dollars.

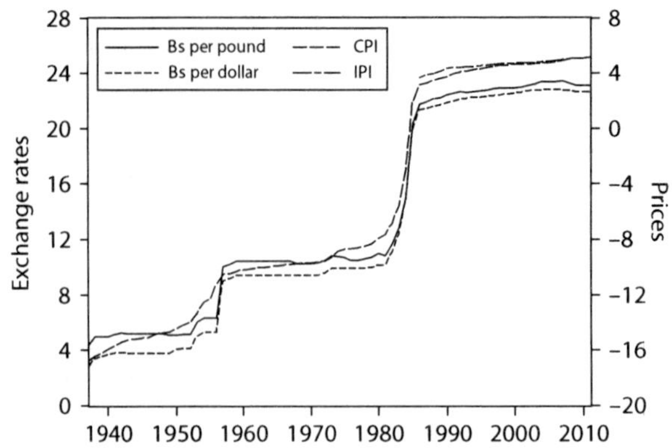

FIGURE 2.10 Exchange rates, CPI and IPI (logs), 1937–2011

Source: CBB, NIS

As is clearly observed, prices and exchange rates move in lockstep with each other since 1937. The close correlation simply confirms that price fluctuations in Bolivia during the last several decades were not confined to any one particular sector, but were a reflection of what was happening throughout the economy. Figure 2.10 also makes evident the extent and severity of price fluctuations that have occurred in the country, particularly during the severe inflation and hyperinflation years of the mid-1950s and early 1980s.

Income

CHAPTER 3

EVOLUTION OF INCOME

A widely utilized indicator of national income is gross domestic product (GDP). Formal estimation of this variable by the Central Bank of Bolivia (CBB) only began in the 1940s, when yearly estimates were first reported. During the 1950s disaggregated yearly estimates of GDP—by economic activity—surfaced, and estimations by type of expenditure emerged the following decade, making the calculation and analysis of this key variable a central part of the CBB's functions. During the 1980s, estimation of GDP by department was added to the mix of habitual, systematic technical expertise of the CBB, and during the 1990s quarterly figures for GDP emerged, based on a more detailed set of categories for economic activities.

Here, the evolution of different types of GDP indicators are reported since they first became available.[1] Specifically, the following time series are analyzed: GDP and GDP per capita in current dollars (since 1940), GDP by economic activity (since 1958), by type of expenditure (since 1964), by Department (since 1988), and quarterly estimations by economic activity (since 1990).

GROSS DOMESTIC PRODUCT SINCE 1940

The evolution of gross domestic product since 1940 is irregular. Figure 3.1 shows yearly GDP and GDP per capita from 1940 through 2013.[2] Table 1c in the appendix reports the actual data.

As illustrated in Figure 3.1, despite an erratic evolution throughout the period analyzed, GDP and GDP per capita show an ascending, upward trend. Not surprisingly, during times of economic upheaval (1950s and 1980s), income shrank considerably, but rebounded during the ensuing years. The data shows that the bounce back after the severe inflation of the 1950s took longer than after the hyperinflation of the 1980s. Positive, sustained growth only began in 1960 after the economic collapse of the mid-1950s, while after the crisis of the mid-1980s growth resumed almost immediately—in 1987, the year after the largest shrinkage in GDP. One possible reason for the slower recovery after the 1950s crisis is that the country did not confront the root causes of inflation head on (pronounced increase in government budget deficits, complaisant monetary policy, and decrease in productivity of newly nationalized tin mines, to mention a few of the factors that contributed to generating conditions for the inflation during this decade) but more or less continued with the social revolution even after Victor Paz Estenssoro, the main culprit of the economic mismanagement, was voted out of office in 1956. His successor, Hernán Siles Zuazo (1956–1960), himself a revolutionary, tried to deepen the reforms started in 1952 and may inadvertently have contributed in prolonging the economic recession of the country. By contrast, during the 1980s economic debacle, the country—once again led by Victor Paz Estenssoro (1985–1989)—did

[1] During the 1940s, GDP figures were reported in Bolivian currency. During the 1950s, some years' GDP figures were reported in dollars and other years (since 1958) in Bolivian currency. Here, I've converted all figures in Bolivian currency into dollars at the official (average) yearly selling exchange rate.

[2] Values utilized for Figure 3.1 are current, unadjusted GDP yearly estimates. Values for 2010 and 2011 are preliminary estimates. Values for 2012 and 2013 are forecasts.

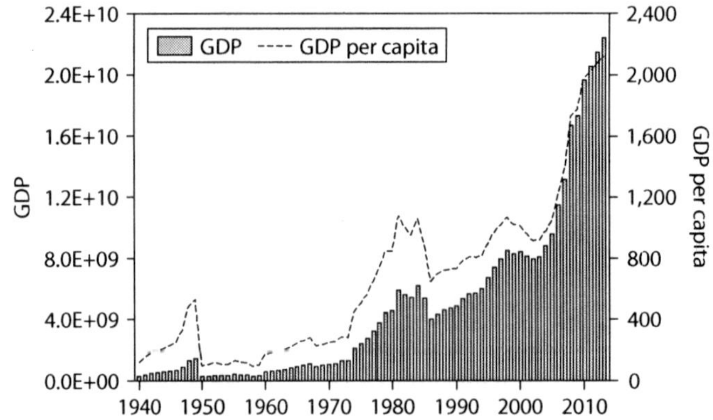

FIGURE 3.1 GDP and GDP per capita (current $), 1940–2013

Source: Central Bank of Bolivia (CBB), World Bank Figures 2012, 2013 are forecasts

go after the root causes of the hyperinflation and through the now infamous Supreme Decree #21060 (DS 21060),[3] tried to address the structural issues that had put the country into such dire straits.[4]

Back to the evolution of income reflected in Figure 3.1, GDP and GDP per capita are, as expected, positively correlated, signifying that not only the economic performance of the country has improved since 1940—albeit with considerable contractions over the course of several years—but also that living standards, as measured by GDP per capita, have been raised since 1940.[5] Table 3.1 reports in more detail how GDP and GDP per capita, at current prices, have fluctuated during the decades between 1940 and 2013.

As Table 3.1 shows, fluctuation of income among the different decades is substantial. The very high average and year-specific fluctuations, particularly during the 1940s through the 1980s, can be attributed to a variety of factors. First, it is not surprising that in a small economy like Bolivia, small changes in income are likely to be reflected with very high percentage fluctuations. For instance, between 1940 and 1941, GDP increased from $287 million to $375 million, which might not seem that much in dollar terms but represents a 31 percent growth. The high percentage figures, particularly during the 1940s, are perhaps a reflection of this small-numbers feature. Second, the 1950s saw a severe contraction of the Bolivian economy due to the social revolution and the accompanying severe case of inflation of the times. This, along with the small-numbers feature, may partly explain the high volatility of the 1950s and 1960s. During the 1970s, Bolivia and many other developing nations were benefitted—or perhaps cursed—with easy money (i.e., petrodollars) at very affordable rates. The greater amount of external financing coupled with an authoritarian government with a zeal for large infrastructure projects, particularly in the low lands of the country, may in turn explain, at least partially, the high growth rates of income observed in the 1970s. Lastly, the hyperinflation of the 1980s would certainly be the main cause of the high fluctuations observed during that decade. The 1990s and the years of the new century have brought mostly one-digit growth rates, which, on the surface, would appear to represent a more natural evolution of income over time.

[3] DS 21060 served as the foundation and principal pillar of what was then called "New Political Economy." Among the many things it did, the following are worth mentioning: It dismantled price controls, freed up trade, eliminated many, but not all, subsidies, opened the way for private participation in key public utilities and in the energy and mining sectors, set up the foundations for a more flexible labor market, liberalized the exchange rate of the newly created currency with the dollar, and established the foundations for a more decentralized government structure.

[4] In a famous speech to the nation, Paz Estenssoro—an older, much more pragmatic, and perhaps wiser statesman with little resemblance to the man of the 1950s and 1960s—justifying the painful reforms to be implemented with DS 21060, stated that "our Bolivia is dying...," unless the underlying root causes of the hyperinflation problem were tackled in a decisive way.

[5] GDP per capita is the most widely utilized indicator of standard of living. As several authors and organizations have noted, however (notably Sudhir Anand and Amartya Sen in several theoretical articles on the subject, and the United Nations Development Program with its on-the-ground work), other variables should also be considered in conjunction with income per capita as a measure of quality of life. These include proxies for determining access and quality of health care, education, and income, and indicators of gender inequality.

Table 3.1 GDP and GDP per Capita, 1940-2013						
Decade	Average GDP (current US dollars)	Average Growth GDP (%)	Average GDP per Capita (current US dollars)	Average Growth GDP per Capita (%)	Highest Growth GDP per Capita (year)	Lowest Growth GDP per Capita (year)
1940s	692,814,990	20.19	265.67	19.13	49.45 ('48)	3.55 ('43)
1950s	314,480,000	-4.86	105.38	-6.86	12.69 ('51)	-82.62 ('50)
1960s	823,950,668	13.35	219.72	10.82	71.04 ('60)	-18.09 ('68)
1970s	2,327,729,266	17.50	480.03	14.71	62.28 ('74)	-1.99 ('73)
1980s	5,058,818,482	1.70	862.81	-0.49	27.03 ('81)	-27.97 ('86)
1990s	6,639,104,038	5.88	891.36	3.54	9.77 ('95)	-4.51 ('99)
2000s	10,943,672,398	8.06	1,194.79	6.11	25.04 ('08)	-4.81 ('02)
2010s	21,016,319,408	6.71	2,046.84	4.57	11.54 ('10)	2.25 ('13)

Notes: Values for the 2010s are forecasts.
Growth rates based on GDP measured at current US dollars
Values in table reflect author's own estimations based on data from the CBB and the World Bank.

It is worth emphasizing that over the course of more than 70 years, and despite the dramatic economic setbacks of the 1950s and 1980s, Bolivia's GDP has grown substantially, by over 7,050 percent between 1940 and 2011 in unadjusted prices. Growth in GDP per capita over the same period has also been significant, 1,644 percent, demonstrating that at snail's pace, or perhaps more accurately at Bolivian's pace, the country is moving forward notwithstanding the occasional economic debacle.

GDP BY ECONOMIC ACTIVITY

Beginning in 1958, the CBB started reporting yearly GDP disaggregated by economic activity. Three main categories of activities have consistently been utilized over the years: (1) goods, (2) basic utilities, and (3) other services. The goods category includes activities in the mining, energy, agricultural, manufacturing, and construction sectors. Basic utilities refer to expenditures in the electricity, gas, water, telecommunications, and transport and storage sectors. Other services include the commerce, financial intermediation and real estate, and public administration sectors. Tables 2c, 3c, and 4c in the appendix report the actual data for GDP by economic activity in dollars (Table 2c), yearly growth (Table 3c), and as a share of each activity on GDP (Table 4c). Figures 3.2, 3.3, and 3.4 illustrate growth rates for all components of the three categories along with growth rates for GDP.

A common characteristic of all these figures is the very high volatility in growth rates of all types of economic activity. It is worth noting that in the Goods category, both the energy (crude oil and natural gas) and the mining (metallic and non-metallic minerals) sectors show the most erratic behavior—economic sectors that have been termed "traditional" sectors of economic activity in the country. In the Basic Utilities category, greater volatility is observed with electricity, gas, and water services, while in the Other Services category considerable fluctuations are seen in the commerce and financial intermediation and real estate sectors. In all cases, however, the correlation between growth rates of all economic activities and GDP is positive. Furthermore, the greatest volatility in all variables is observed, unsurprisingly, during the hyperinflation years of the mid 1980s.

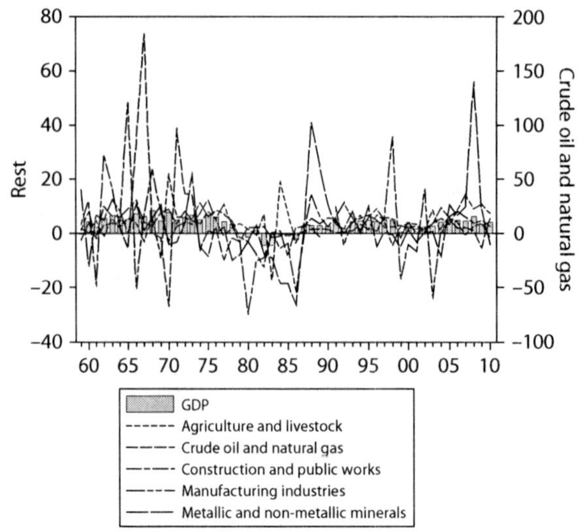

FIGURE 3.2 Growth rates GDP and goods (%), 1959–2010

Source: CBB, NIS

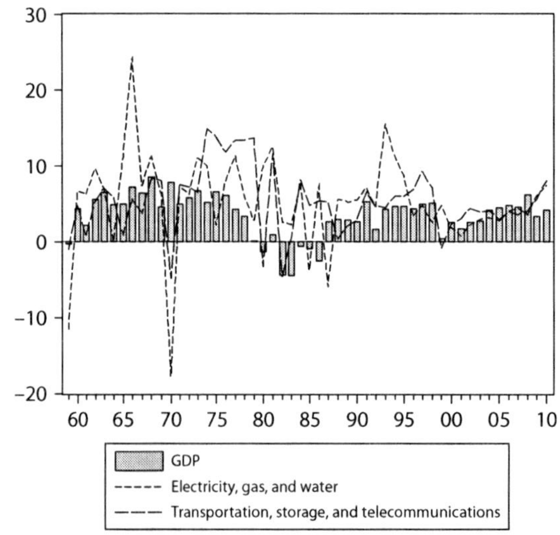

FIGURE 3.3 Growth rates GDP and basic utilities (%), 1959–2010

Source: CBB, NIS

An alternative way of analyzing the evolution of GDP is by estimating the share of each type of economic activity on GDP. Figures 3.5 (goods), 3.6 (utilities), and 3.7 (other services) show the share of each economic activity on GDP for the period 1958–2010.

Goods have consistently comprised the biggest share of GDP over the period analyzed, ranging from a high of 61 percent of GDP (in 1959) to the mid-40s during the new century. Of those, agriculture and livestock commodities have historically been the most important ones, but since 1990 they have been overtaken by manufacturing goods, which represent the most important economic activity in this category, averaging in the high teens since the 1990s.

The share of basic utilities—electricity, gas, and water; and transportation, storage, and telecommunications—on GDP has ranged from the high one-digit percentages in the 1950s and 1960s to the low teens during the 1990s and the years of the new century. Between 1978 and the mid-1980s there is a big drop in the share of these utilities, which may partially be attributed to the economic and political uncertainty of the times. Of these utilities, transportation, storage, and telecommunications are the

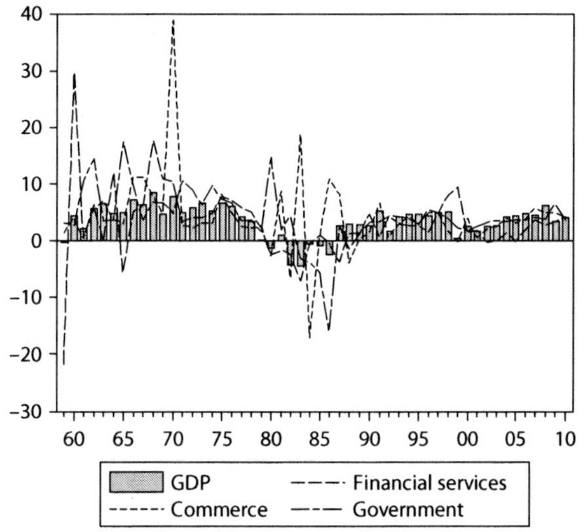

FIGURE 3.4 Growth rates GDP and other services (%), 1959–2010

Source: CBB, NIS

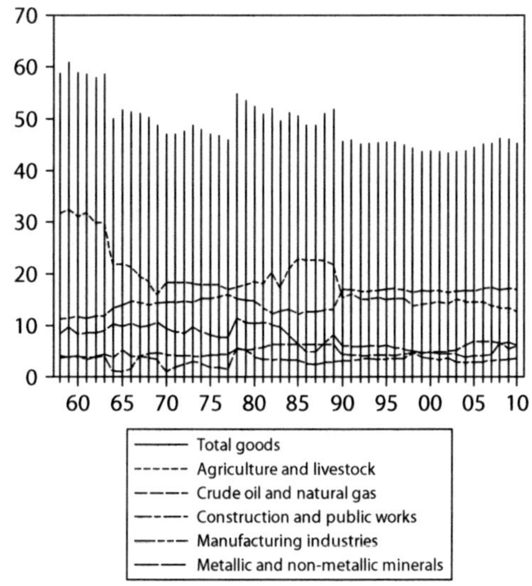

FIGURE 3.5 Share of goods on GDP (%), 1958–2010

Source: CBB, NIS

most important ones, closely mirroring the evolution of basic utilities throughout the period analyzed. The share on GDP of electricity, gas, and water, by contrast, has consistently remained in the low teens, denoting little, if any, tangible progress since 1958.

Lastly, the share of other services—commerce, financial, and real estate sectors, and government—on GDP has fluctuated between the low 30 percent range during the 1950s and 1960s, to mid-40s during the 1970s, high 30s during the 1980s and 1990s, and low 30s during the years of the new century. Of these, the financial and real estate sector is the most important economic activity, consistently averaging in the mid to upper teens—in percentage terms—since the mid-1960s. Interestingly, the share of government on GDP has persistently remained in the high one-digit percentage range, excepting the period 1980–1985, when the share climbed to the low teens. Even during the presidency of Evo Morales (2006–2010),[6] the share of government on GDP remains on the levels of previous years, despite grandiloquent claims and announcements to the contrary.

[6] Evo Morales' current term as president is due to conclude in 2014.

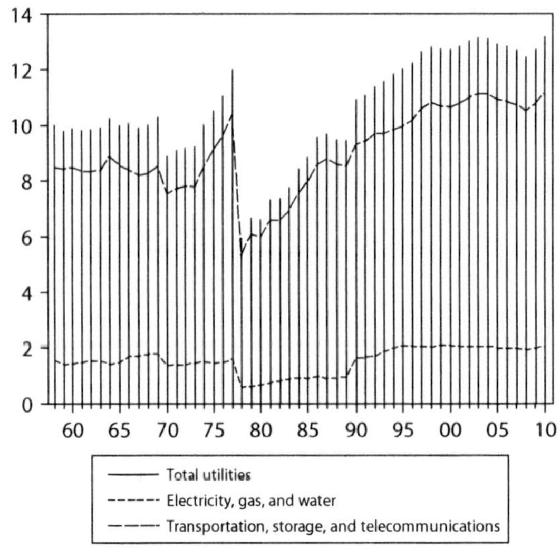

FIGURE 3.6 Share of utilities on GDP (%), 1958–2010

Source: CBB, NIS

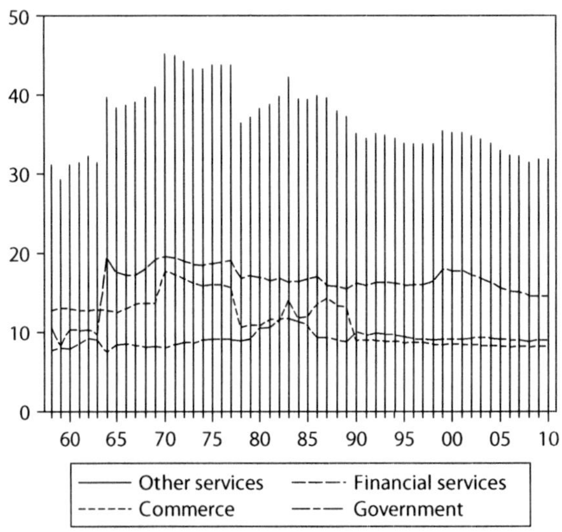

FIGURE 3.7 Share of other services on GDP (%), 1958–2010

Source: CBB, NIS

GDP BY TYPE OF EXPENDITURE[7]

In 1964 the CBB started estimating GDP by type of expenditure. The three types of expenditure are consumption, investment, and trade. Within the first category a distinction is made between two types of consumption: (1) government; and (2) households and not-for-profit firms' consumption. The investment category includes two components: (1) gross fixed capital formation and (2) inventory provisions. Finally, the trade category includes exports and imports of goods and services. Tables 5c, 6c, and 7c in the appendix report the actual data for GDP by type of expenditure in dollars (Table 5c), yearly growth (Table 6c), and as a share of each expenditure on GDP (Table 7c). Likewise, Figure 3.8 (consumption), Figure 3.9

[7] Regarding the consistency of GDP estimates with the two approaches—by economic activity and by type of expenditure—some small discrepancies are found during the years 1969 and 1970. The expenditure approach tends to slightly underestimate GDP during these two years. For the rest of the years, both approaches produce the same results. I've chosen not to smooth out or correct the data in any way, so as to let the data tell its own story.

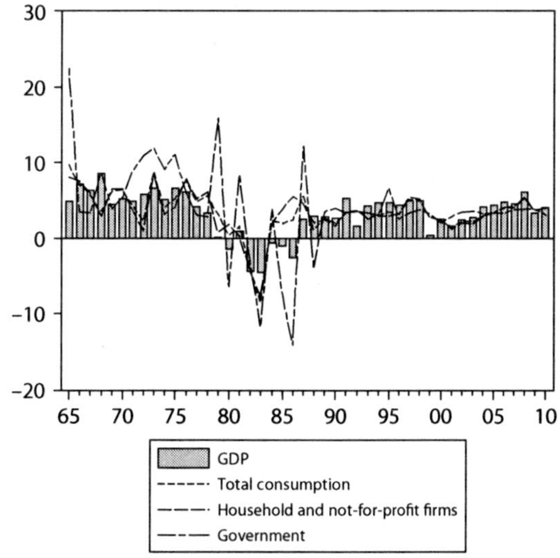

FIGURE 3.8 Growth rates GDP and consumption (%), 1965–2010

Source: CBB, NIS

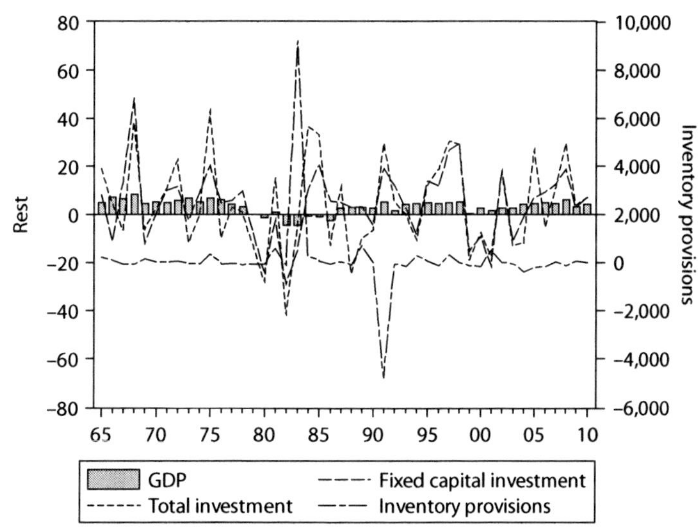

FIGURE 3.9 Growth rates GDP and investment (%), 1965–2010

Source: CBB, NIS

(investment), and Figure 3.10 (trade) illustrate yearly growth rates of GDP and of these types of expenditures during the 1965–2010 period.

As Figure 3.8 shows, there is a close correlation between GDP and consumption expenditures' growth. Of the two components of consumption, government consumption is more volatile, and this volatility is accentuated during types of economic crisis, as evident from the sharp fluctuations during the hyperinflation years of the 1980s. The volatility in investment (Figure 3.9) and trade (Figure 3.10) expenditures is even more pronounced and tends to stretch out over the entire period. A positive correlation between GDP and investment and trade expenditures is still present, but it is not as prominent as it was with consumption expenditures. Some factors that may partly explain the high volatility in investment and trade growth figures is the economic uncertainty generated by the economic crises of the 1950s—reflected in the sharp fluctuations observed in the following decade—and 1980s, as well as the very significant readjustments in the trade pattern of Bolivia during these decades (the evolution in the pattern of trade is the main subject of the chapter on trade) and the uncertainty throughout these decades on the rules and regulations regarding private investment in the country.

The evolution of the share of different types of expenditures on GDP is illustrated in Figure 3.11 (consumption), Figure 3.12 (investment), and Figure 3.13 (trade).

Figure 3.11 illustrates that consumption is by far the most important expenditure component of GDP throughout the period analyzed. Within this component, household and not-for-profit firms' expenditures are significantly more important than government expenditures, consistently averaging in the high 60- and 70-percent ranges. By contrast, government expenditures reach a peak of 14.10 percent of GDP in 1982, but remain below that mark the rest of the period, even during the current Morales presidency, notwithstanding persistent announcements that the government's role in the economy would increase considerably during his presidency.

As it refers to investment (Figure 3.12), the share of total investment on GDP has averaged in the mid teens since the beginning of the period. Of the two components, gross fixed capital formation is

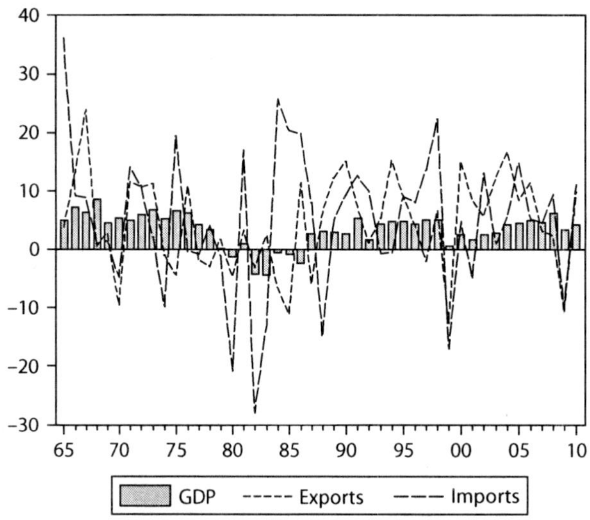

FIGURE 3.10 Growth rates GDP and trade (%), 1965–2010

Source: CBB, NIS

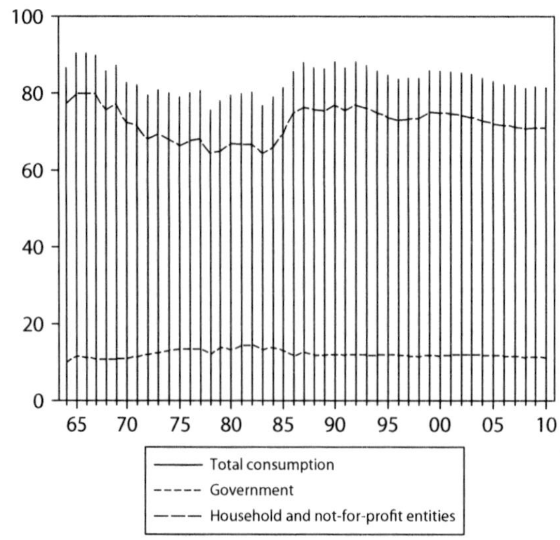

FIGURE 3.11 Share of consumption on GDP (%), 1964–2010

Source: CBB, NIS

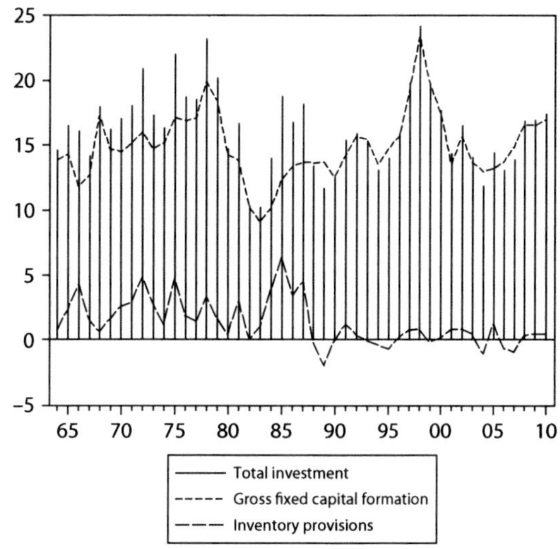

FIGURE 3.12 Share of investment on GDP (%), 1964–2010

Source: CBB, NIS

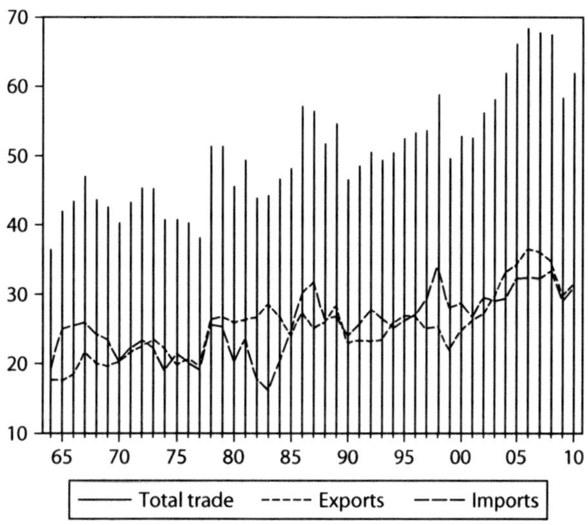

FIGURE 3.13 Share of trade on GDP (%), 1964–2010

Source: CBB, NIS

by some ways the most important one, averaging also in the teens and reaching a peak in 1998, with 23.43 percent. As an indicator of the value of acquisitions of new or existing fixed assets by the business sector, government, and households, less disposals of fixed assets, it is an indicator of the new value added in the economy that is invested rather than consumed. That it reached a maximum level in the 1990s, as Bolivia was in the midst of a process whereby many enterprises, particularly public utilities, had been transferred to the private sector through the privatizations of previous years, says something about the importance of the private sector in generating necessary levels of investment. Unsurprisingly, in times of economic or political uncertainty (e.g., the hyperinflation years of the 1980s; the populist wave during the new century) total investment, particularly gross fixed capital formation, has tended downwards, though after a low point of around 12 percent in 2004, investment has picked up again, surely as a result of increases in government investment in a number of areas.

Lastly, the share of trade (exports and imports) on GDP (Figure 3.13) has consistently increased since 1964 and it highlights the very high dependence of the Bolivian economy on economic relations with other nations. The combined share of exports and imports on GDP has averaged 51 percent over the entire period, but since 2000, the share has averaged 61 percent, denoting how essential it is for any government to promote the country's export sector as a source of foreign currency and employment in Bolivia, and also to keep the country open to imports of all types to meet domestic demand for an ever increasing array of goods and services.

GDP BY DEPARTMENT

Estimations of department GDP are only available since the 1980s. Here, I report them starting in 1988. Even though the data is rather recent, it offers an interesting appreciation of how wealth, economic growth, and regional inequalities have fared over the last decades. In the appendix, Tables 8c (department GDP in current dollars), 9c (GDP growth), 10c (GDP per capita), 11c (GDP per capita growth), and 12c (share of department's GDP on national income) present the actual data. A brief summary is offered in Table 3.2.

There are some intriguing patterns that emerge from the data. First, the department of Pando[8] is the one with the lowest GDP, ranging from \$33.5 million in 1988 to \$89.2 million in 2006, and the lowest share of national income, consistently below 1 percent of GDP throughout the period analyzed.[9] However, it is not the poorest, as Potosí—department located in the southern highlands—has regularly shown the lowest GDP per capita throughout the 22-year period. Between 1988 and 1995, the department of La Paz[10] had the highest GDP, but since 1996 that distinction has gone to Santa Cruz, in the eastern lowlands. Not surprisingly, these two departments have also had the highest contribution to national income, representing anywhere between (approximately) 28 to 30 percent of GDP during the 1980s and early 1990s (La Paz), to between (approximately) 29 to 31 percent during the late 1990s and new century (Santa Cruz). Interestingly,

Table 3.2
Summary Statistics, Income by Department, 1988-2010

Period	Department GDP		GDP per Capita		GDP per Capita Growth		Share on National GDP	
	Highest	Lowest	Highest	Lowest	Highest	Lowest	Highest	Lowest
1988–90	La Paz (\$1.32 billion, 1990)	Pando (\$33.5 million, 1988)	Santa Cruz (\$1,052, 1990)	Potosí (\$456, 1988)	Oruro (6.03%, 1989)	Oruro (-8.21%, 1990)	La Paz (28%, 1988)	Pando (0.72%, 1989)
1991–95	La Paz (\$1.98 billion, 1995)	Pando (\$38.0 million, 1991)	Santa Cruz (\$1,187, 1995)	Potosí (\$426, 1993)	Oruro (14.75%, 1995)	Potosí (-11.49%, 1993)	La Paz (30%, 1995)	Pando (0.68%, 1992)
1996–2000	Santa Cruz (\$2.63 billion, 1998)	Pando (\$55.2 million, 1996)	Pando (\$1,481, 1998)	Potosí (\$543, 1996)	Tarija (17.93%, 1997)	Santa Cruz (-11.44%, 1999)	Santa Cruz (31%, 1998)	Pando (0.75%, 1996)
2001–2005	Santa Cruz (\$2.83 billion, 2005)	Pando (\$70.0 million, 2003)	Pando (\$1,470, 2001)	Potosí (\$499, 2002)	Tarija (33.76%, 2005)	Pando (-11.36%, 2002)	Santa Cruz (31%, 2001)	Pando (0.86%, 2004)
2006–2010	Santa Cruz (\$5.35 billion, 2010)	Pando (\$89.2 million, 2006)	Tarija (\$4,257, 2010)	Potosí (\$809, 2006)	Potosí (50.01%, 2008)	Beni (-4.08%, 2007)	Santa Cruz (29%, 2006)	Pando (0.78%, 2006)

Notes: Numbers represent current US dollars.
Values in table reflect author's own estimations based on data from the CBB, NIS, and World Bank.

[8] Pando is the youngest of the 9 departments that constitute Bolivia. It was created on September 24, 1938, during the presidency of Germán Busch. Located on the tropical lowlands in the Northeast of the country—part of the Amazon—it is also the least populated department.

[9] Dollar figures represent current, or unadjusted, values.

[10] The capital of the department of La Paz is Nuestra Señora de La Paz, or simply known as La Paz. This city is also the seat of government of Bolivia. As the administrative capital of the country, its most important industries are government-related services.

the combined preponderance of the three biggest departments—La Paz, Santa Cruz, and Cochabamba, or the "main axis," as they are commonly referred to—ranges from 67.3 percent of national income (in 2010) to 75.47 percent (in 1996), denoting the overwhelming economic importance of these departments.

The highest GDP per capita during the 1980s and early 1990s was observed in Santa Cruz (ranging from $1,052 in 1990 to $1,187 in 1995). However, since 1996 the highest income per capita has migrated to Pando (latter 1990s, reaching $1,481 in 1998; early 2000s, with $1,470 in 2001) and Tarija (latter 2000s, reaching a record-level $4,257 in 2010), signifying a positive diversification in the economic prosperity of the nation. To complement this tendency, the highest GDP per capita growth throughout the period has not occurred in the usual suspect departments (La Paz and Santa Cruz), but rather in Oruro (1980s, early 1990s), Tarija (late 1990s, early 2000s), and Potosi (late 2000s). The reasons for this shift in the pattern of growth have to do with natural resources: Oruro and Potosí, with a long tradition for mining activities, have been positively affected by an increased world demand for mining commodities during the last several years. Likewise, Tarija is the department with the largest reservoirs of natural gas, the new star commodity and one whose importance as a source of export revenues has grown exponentially, particularly during the late 1990s and the new century. As has been suggested in the chapter on trade, as long as world demand for mining commodities and natural gas remain at current levels—perhaps due to contractual obligations with natural gas and (expected) sustained Chinese demand for mining commodities—the regional balance of economic activity in Bolivia is likely to continue shifting towards those departments rich in natural resources, which in itself is welcome news in a country that has tended to be geared towards only a handful of places (the main axis departments) instead of spreading income-generating activities to the rest of the nation.

QUARTERLY GDP BY ECONOMIC ACTIVITY[11]

Quarterly GDP calculations by economic activity are available since 1990. The list of economic activities in these latest quarterly calculations is similar to those activities recorded for yearly estimations, however the scope of activities under each category is more refined and better describes the type of economic undertaking being scrutinized. Specifically, as opposed to the 10 types of activities analyzed with yearly estimations of GDP, there are 11 types of activities examined with quarterly estimations:

1. agriculture, forestry, livestock, and fisheries;
2. crude oil and natural gas;
3. metallic and non-metallic minerals;
4. manufacturing industry;
5. electricity, gas, and water;
6. construction industry;
7. commerce industry;
8. transport and communications;
9. finance, insurance, real estate, and other business services;
10. public administration services; and
11. other services.

Table 13c in the appendix presents the actual data, Table 14c reports quarterly growth rates, and Table 15c shares of each activity on GDP.

An appraisal of the evolution of quarterly GDP by economic activity is offered in Figure 3.14 (GDP; agriculture, forestry, livestock, and fisheries; construction; and manufacturing), Figure 3.15 (GDP; commerce; finance, insurance, real estate, and other business services; and other services), Figure 3.16 (GDP;

[11] GDP figures reported here may differ a bit from yearly GDP estimations of previous sections. The difference is the result of the exchange rate (average quarterly exchange rates in the parallel markets) utilized in converting values from bolivianos to dollars.

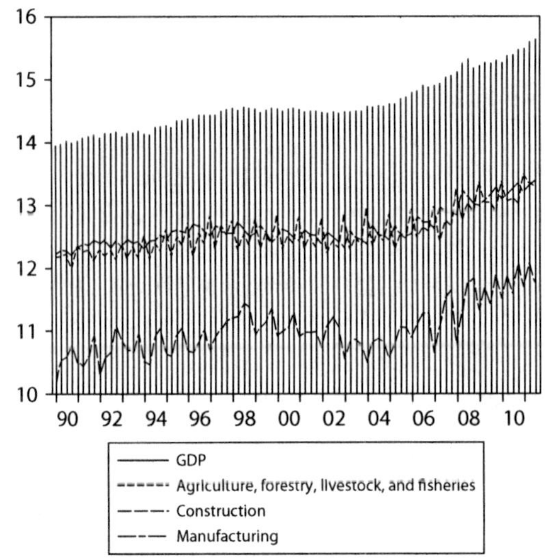

FIGURE 3.14 GDP, agriculture, construction, and manufacturing (logs), 1990–2011

Source: CBB, NIS

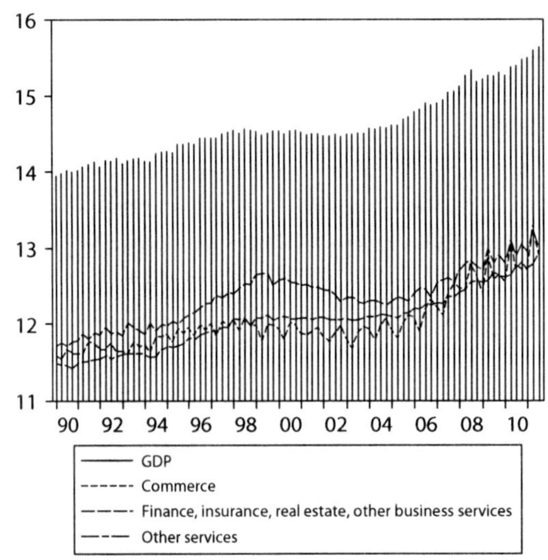

FIGURE 3.15 GDP, commerce, finance, and other services (logs), 1990–2011

Source: CBB, NIS

government; and transport and telecommunications), and Figure 3.17 (GDP; electricity, gas, and water; metallic and non-metallic minerals; and crude oil and natural gas).

As can be observed, in all cases there is a positive correlation between GDP and economic activities. Greater volatility is observed in those sectors with expected seasonal fluctuations (e.g., agriculture, forestry, livestock, and fisheries; construction; and commerce) and those experiencing a substantial increase in demand and in production capacity, particularly during the late 1990s and the years of the new century. The natural gas and mining sectors fall under the latter category of commodities. The figures also demonstrate that the long-term tendency of GDP and its various components is positive; that is, GDP and all economic activities show an upward, ascending trend. This observation is consistent with previous analysis, which highlighted that, despite economic setbacks, the Bolivian economy maintains a positive long-run growth trend. One can only wonder what could happen with the economic outlook of the

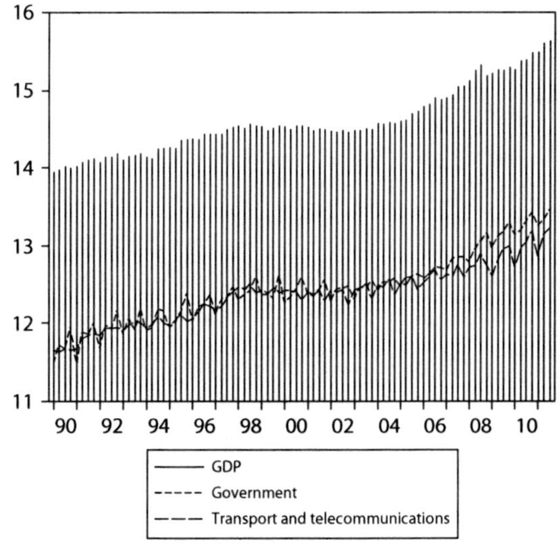

FIGURE 3.16 GDP, government, and transport and telecommunications (logs), 1990–2011

Source: CBB, NIS

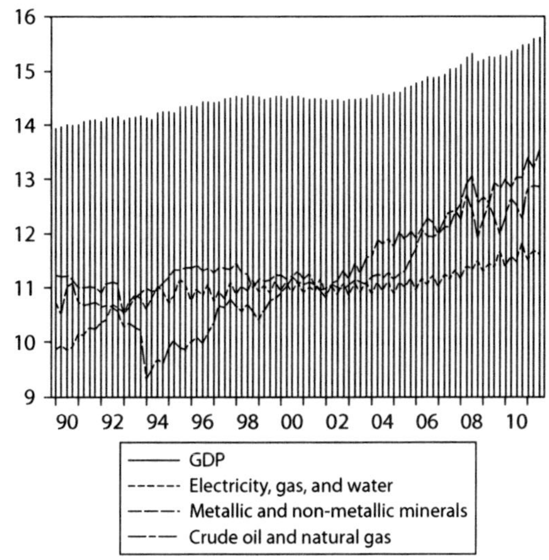

FIGURE 3.17 GDP, oil and gas, mining, and electricity, gas, and water (logs), 1990–2011

Source: CBB, NIS

country if more consistency and greater continuity in economic policies were sustained over time, without falling into the populist traps that seem to engulf the country every so often, which, at current pace seem to occur every 30 years or so. Under that interpretation and for the years that have been analyzed in this chapter, the mid-1950s, early 1980s, and the years of the Morales administration (2006–present), represent the populist intervals that one's wishes would fade away.

Money and Reserves

CHAPTER 4

OVERVIEW

The expansion of money in the Bolivian economy very much reflects the economic cycles of the country. Likewise, the evolution of international reserves held by the Central Bank of Bolivia (CBB) is an appropriate indicator of the progression of the country. How both money and international reserves have changed over time highlights the many obstacles and difficulties the country has experienced over the years. Here I concentrate on reporting how money has changed since 1911 and then account for the evolution of international reserves held by the CBB since 1929. The starting dates reflect the years when official statistics on both variables began to be compiled.

MONEY

The evolution of money since 1911 has been breathtaking. Before analyzing the actual data, it is important to point out that during the period of interest, 1911–2011, the country changed its unit of account twice: on July 13, 1962, the "boliviano" became the "peso boliviano." This new currency was created by eliminating three zeros from the old currency; that is, 1 peso boliviano = 1,000 bolivianos. On January 1, 1987, this exercise was repeated as a new currency—once again, the boliviano—came into existence with an exchange rate between the new and old currencies set at 1 boliviano = 1,000,000 pesos bolivianos. Figures reported here refer to the amount of money in "old" bolivianos; that is, the amount of different types of money—bills and coins and checking deposits—in its original unit of measurement.

An introduction to how much the amount of money has changed in the country is observed in Table 4.1, where the evolution of different monetary aggregates by decade is illustrated. Table 1d in the appendix presents the complete dataset.

Table 4.1 illustrates how three different types of monetary aggregates have changed since 1911. Values represent decade averages. An indicator of the money supply is *M1*, found by adding bills and coins with checking deposits. In all cases, the expansion is substantial, confirming previous assertions (see chapter on prices) that price fluctuations in the country—periods of severe inflation and hyperinflation—are best explained by monetary considerations; that is, by the amount of money in circulation. The 1950s and 1980s are, unsurprisingly, the periods when average growth of *M1* was highest—67.6 and 837.2 decade-average percent growth, respectively—lending credence to the hypothesis that the severe inflation and hyperinflation of those decades were indeed a monetary phenomenon. It is also interesting to observe the mere size of each of these variables. During the 1910s, the average quantity of *M1* was approximately 28 million bolivianos. By the 1950s, the average quantity of money had increased to 137 billion bolivianos; to almost 5 trillion during the 1970s; 246 quadrillion in the 1980s; and 40 quintillion during the 2010s.

Complementing the summary statistics, by decade, of Table 4.1, Figure 4.1 illustrates how checking deposits, bills and coins, and the sum of both of these categories, *M1*, have evolved since 1911.

The figure is a clear illustration of the constant—rapid, during particular years—progression of each one of these variables for the last 100 years. The gradual upward movement in the quantity of all variables is interrupted twice, during the 1950s and during the 1980s, when there is a clear spike in the growth of these monetary aggregates. The two years during the 1950s of fastest growth in the money supply was 1954–55, when *M1* grew by 109 percent, and 1955–56, when growth reached 239 percent. The steep ascent in Figure 4.1 during those years bears witness to the significant growth of *M1* and its

Table 4.1 Evolution of Monetary Aggregates (in old bolivianos), by Decade, 1911-2011				
Decade	Bills and Coins	Checking Deposits	*M1*	Average Growth *M1* (%)
1910s	14,055,556	13,866,667	27,922,222	40.72
1920s	34,232,600	21,148,700	55,381,300	2.56
1930s	149,895,700	153,199,500	303,095,200	34.73
1940s	1,369,454,600	966,561,400	2,336,016,000	20.31
1950s	99,872,610,900	37,099,531,400	136,972,142,300	67.58
1960s	699,592,800,000	175,235,500,000	874,828,300,000	13.50
1970s	3,368,700,000,000	1,628,530,000,000	4,997,230,000,000	22.89
1980s	189,449,840,750,000,000	56,411,356,660,000,000	245,861,197,410,000,000	837.21
1990s	1,460,004,200,000,000,000	2,214,426,800,000,000,000	3,674,431,000,000,000,000	24.52
2000s	7,391,857,000,000,000,000	7,035,398,300,000,000,000	14,427,255,300,000,000,000	18.31
2010s	24,149,206,500,000,000,000	15,883,628,000,000,000,000	40,032,834,500,000,000,000	18.96

Notes: Average values estimated by adding end-of-the-year balances and dividing the sum by years in each decade.
M1 = bills and coins + checking deposits; Official *M1* calculated by the Central Bank of Bolivia (CBB) differs from the one reported here.
Checking deposits include those in bolivianos, in US dollars (beginning in mid-1980s) and in bolivianos, adjusted to changes in the exchange rate with the US dollar.
Values in table reflect author's own estimations based on data from the CBB and the National Institute of Statistics (NIS).

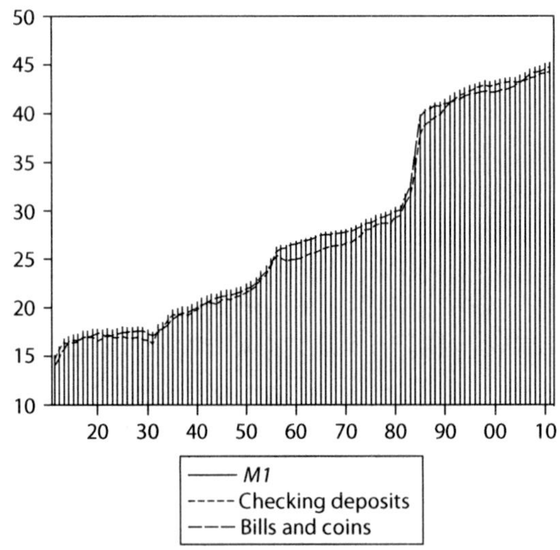

FIGURE 4.1 Evolution of monetary aggregates (logs), 1911–2011

Source: Central Bank of Bolivia (CBB)

components. Before these years, growth in *M1* had been substantial between 1911–12 (142 percent), 1912–13 (121 percent), 1931–32 (111 percent), and 1933–34 (107 percent), but never, until that moment, in consecutive years and at the rates observed between 1954 and 1956. During the 1980s the percentage growth rates of *M1* would reach triple digits once again, although this time they exceeded anything that had been experienced before. The growth rates between 1981–82 and 1982–83 were a robust 230 and 210 percent, respectively. High as they were, they paled to what happened next: between 1983 and 1984, the growth rate in *M1* reached 1,782 percent. The following year (1984–85), growth in *M1* toppled 5,930 percent. In Figure 4.1, the almost vertical ascent of *M1* during the 1980s is proof of the extraordinary growth rates in the money supply—mirrored in equally extraordinary inflation rates—the country experienced during these years, a result that prompted many Bolivian historians to call the hyperinflation-plagued 1980s as the 'lost decade,' due to the devastating effects of this phenomenon on the economic and social rubric of the country.

■ INTERNATIONAL RESERVES

The term "international reserves" refers to assets held by the CBB. Among them, gold and foreign exchange reserves are the most important types. Other, less important assets are silver coins, special drawing rights (SDRs),[1] International Monetary Fund reserve positions, and different types of securities, particularly foreign bonds. Table 4.2 presents decade-average international reserves, in current dollars, since 1929. Table 2d in the appendix introduces the actual data.

Net reserves are estimated by subtracting total liabilities from total reserves. Since liabilities only started to be officially recorded in 1963, the 1960s represents the decade when estimation of net reserves was initiated. As Table 4.2 shows, the level of international reserves has continually increased throughout the decades. During the 1930s, the average level of reserves was around $7 million and by the 2000s it had increased to $3,163 billion, a decade-average growth of 45,000 percent. It is important to point out, however, that the bulk of growth only occurred after the hyperinflation episode of the 1980s was placed safely behind. Until the 1980s, the decade-average level of international reserves never surpassed the

Table 4.2
International Reserves Held by the Central Bank of Bolivia, Decade Averages
(millions of current US dollars)

Decade	Total Reserves				Total Liabilities	Net Reserves
	Gold	Foreign Exchange	Silver Coins	Other		
1929	3.33	16.68	0.01	0.48	-	20.50
1930s	2.71	4.34	0.02	0.14	-	7.22
1940s	15.98	8.88	0.03	0.01	-	24.89
1950s	11.88	8.18	0.04	28.48	-	48.58
1960s	8.12	15.85	0.00	11.14	8.20	26.91
1970s	19.24	98.74	-	26.25	44.48	99.75
1980s	36.59	176.96	-	88.50	292.31	9.74
1990s	83.19	636.59	-	66.91	155.86	630.83
2000s	519.73	2,622.03	-	75.79	54.89	3,162.66
2010, 2011	1,852.65	8,755.05	-	266.95	0.50	10,874.15

Notes: Average values estimated by adding end-of-the-year balances and dividing the sum by years in each decade.
Before 1962 no information on liabilities is available.
Figures in Bolivian currency were converted to dollars at current, official selling (spot) rate between Bolivian currency and dollars.
Values in table reflect author's own estimations based on data from the CBB and the NIS.

[1] SDRs were created by the International Monetary Fund in 1969. Originally intended to be an asset like any other currency, its most important current role is to act as the IMF's official unit of account.

$100 million mark, which demonstrates that the quite significant increase in the CBB's reserves is a fairly recent development. It is also interesting to note that during the 1980s the level of international reserves decreased to a decade-average low of $9.74 million, the lowest since the 1930s. This record low is directly attributed to the hyperinflation of that decade and reflects the frail state of the CBB and of the economy as a whole, as the ability of the country's monetary authority to affect the value of the Bolivian currency was basically non-existent.

The yearly evolution of net international reserves and its two most important components, foreign exchange reserves and gold, is illustrated in Figure 4.2. Values utilized in the construction of the figure represent current dollars.

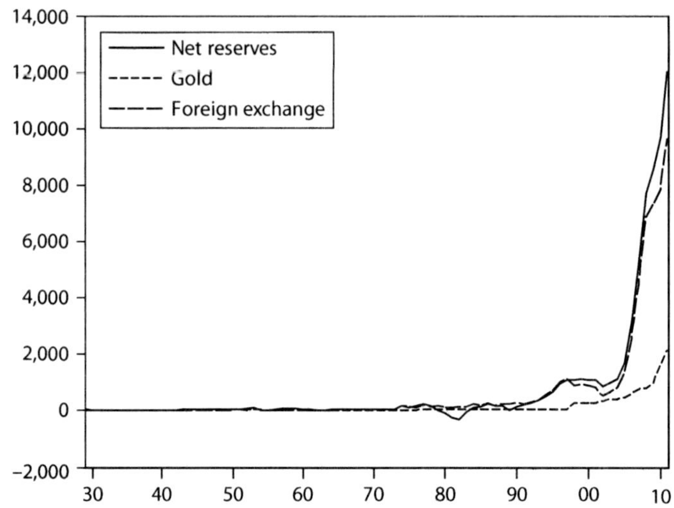

FIGURE 4.2 Net reserves (current million of dollars), 1929–2011

Source: CBB

Figure 4.2 demonstrates that 1990 is when the growth of reserves in the country really takes off. Before then, the level of international reserves had been quite modest: during the 1930s, 1936 is when reserves reached a peak, $12.2 million; during the 1940s, it was 1945, with $35.2 million; the next decade saw its highest level in 1953, with $96 million; during the 1960s it was 1960, with $41.5 million; in the 1970s, the year with the highest level of reserves was 1977, with $216.4 million, a record figure until then; and finally during the 1980s, the year 1986, with $246.6 million, was when reserves reached a highest point. It is also important to point out that during the 1950s the level of reserves decreased to a decade low of $7 million in 1955, a result of the monetary crisis of the times. Likewise, during the hyperinflationary 1980s, the level of net international reserves was negative several years in a row—in 1980, 1981, 1982, and 1983—evidencing the seriousness of the looming monetary crisis.

With the ending of the hyperinflation years in the 1980s, international reserves gradually began to recuperate. In 1989 the level of reserves was $18.6 million but by 1990 it jumped to $132.3 million, a one-year growth of more than 600 percent. From that point onwards, the growth in the level of reserves has been significant and the long-term trend positive. In 1997, a milestone of sorts was accomplished when, for the first time in the country's history, the level of international reserves held by the CBB surpassed the $1 billion mark. The first decade of the new century witnessed a level of reserves that only a few years back would have been unthinkable: in 2006 international reserves surpassed the $3 billion mark; in 2008 the level of reserves was at $8.6 billion; at last count, in 2011, the level of international reserves had jumped to $12 billion.

Several factors account for why the level of international reserves has increased so dramatically in the last two decades. The first is that with the stabilization of the economy at the end of the 1980s and first part of the 1990s, Bolivia entered a sustained cycle of responsible fiscal and monetary policies that allowed the private sector to emerge as the most important pillar of the economic recovery, especially throughout the 1990s. Private exports, particularly of non-traditional goods, reached record levels; the level of foreign private investment—basically foreign direct investment—increased dramatically with a wave of privatizations of government-owned utilities; and a general increase in other types of private investment, particularly in agribusiness, construction, financial services, and commerce also ensued.[2]

Second, during the new millennium, other ingredients came into play that explain the dramatic rise in international reserves: An impressive and, so far, lasting demand for mining commodities, particularly from China, generated an awakening of an industry that had been dormant in previous years; mining exports (analyzed in the chapter on trade) reached record levels during the 2000s; and exports of natural gas (in volume and in dollars) to Argentina and especially Brazil reached record highs, providing yet again a source of windfall gains.

Finally, and notwithstanding the sharp drop in foreign private investment during the 2000s, the level of remittances has increased dramatically and, more controversially, with a lax policy on coca cultivations[3] by the administration of Evo Morales (2006–2014),[4] the level of foreign exchange generated by the illegal portion of the coca market has increased as well.

Whether current levels of international reserves will be maintained in the future depends to a large extent on what happens with exports of both mining and hydrocarbon commodities. As stated elsewhere in the text, if export levels of mining commodities, particularly to China, and of natural gas, particularly to Brazil, remain on current levels, international reserves held by the CBB are likely to continue with their ascending trend.

[2] Other factors may have also played an important role in attracting foreign reserves into the country during the 1990s, but they are presumed to have played a less important role. Some of those other factors include the illegal coca trade—which, during that decade was in decline due to aggressive government eradication efforts—improvements in the tourism industry, and remittances from abroad.

[3] Coca leafs are utilized in the production of cocaine, an illegal drug. Coca leaf production in Bolivia, which within certain limits is not illegal, dates back centuries, and is consumed in its raw state—as coca leaf—by a significant number of Bolivians, particularly in rural areas.

[4] In addition to being president of Bolivia, Evo Morales holds another post as president of the Bolivian Coca Growers Association (Federación de Productores de Coca de Bolivia). On several occasions he has maintained that he sees no conflict of interest between his two posts.

Government

CHAPTER 5

OVERVIEW

The concept of government is wide and the range of government activities is far-reaching: from its basic fiscal functions of revenue generation and spending, to its power to affect the behavior of economic agents through a variety of economic and social regulations. Here, I limit the analysis of what the government of Bolivia does to its core functions as revenue collector and as a generator of public expenditures. Specifically, yearly aggregate government operations—total revenues and total expenditures—since 1940 to 2011 are presented. Additionally, yearly tax collection data, by department, are introduced for the period 1987–2010. Finally, yearly data on central government expenditures, by sector, are introduced for the period 1940–2010.

GOVERNMENT OPERATIONS

Tax collection and government expenditures data is only available since 1940. Sporadic information on government activities—expenditures and revenue-related activities—is found before that year, but nothing that would allow the construction of continuous, reliable data sets. An introduction to revenues and expenditures of the central government for the period 1940–2011 is presented in Figure 5.1. The actual data set is introduced in Table 1e in the appendix.[1]

As is evident from Figure 5.1, the level of revenues and expenditures has changed dramatically since 1940. Only during the 1970s (in 1973 revenues reached the $123 million mark; in 1970 expenditures totaled $105 million) revenues and expenditures surpassed the two-digit barrier; before then, total level of government operations were modest, with recurrent fiscal deficits in most years, with notable exceptions during the period 1948–50, 1953, 1957, and 1961, when either revenues were greater than expenditures or they were of equal magnitude. The 1970s was the decade when both revenue generation and government expenditures began a dramatic ascent, but, like in previous decades, throughout this latter period and until the present, government has, for most fiscal years, experienced a deficit. The years 2006 and 2007 represent the exceptions, as during both years considerable surpluses—of $395 million and $295 million, respectively—were recorded. In 2008, however, expenditures began to outpace revenues again, and the fiscal position of the country has returned to its normal course of continuous deficits. It is interesting to note that the highest deficits for the whole period occurred in 1984 and 1985, during the hyperinflation years, as the deficit level in both years exceeded one billion dollars. In no time after 1985 and certainly before 1984 has the country experienced a deficit so large, confirming the notion that the 1980s was a period of great economic anomalies and one that is only likely to be repeated under the most extreme social and political conditions.

A summary of the evolution of revenues and expenditures during the years 1940–2011 is presented in table 5.1.

Table 5.1 reflects the significant growth in both revenues and expenditures throughout the decades. While during the 1970s both revenues and expenditures reached the three-digit mark, it was only during the 1980s (1984, with $1.3 billion) that expenditures surpassed the billion dollar milestone, and the 1990s

[1] The values for revenues and expenditures represent aggregate values in current US dollars. Furthermore, they refer to actual revenues collected and actual expenditures carried out by the central government of Bolivia. The exchange rate utilized for converting values from Bolivian currency to dollars was the yearly average, official selling exchange rate between both currencies.

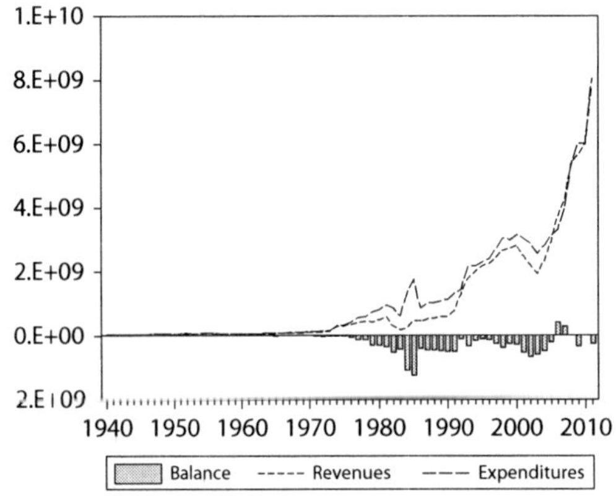

FIGURE 5.1 Central government operations (current dollars), 1940–2011

Source: Central Bank of Bolivia(CBB), Ministry of Economy and Public Finance (MEPF)

Table 5.1
Average Revenues and Expenditures (current US dollars), 1940–2011

Period	Revenues	Growth Revenues (%)	Expenditures	Growth Expenditures (%)	Balance
1940s	24,066,301.32	11.69	25,177,760.72	6.46	−1,111,459.41
1950s	41,732,043.54	3.96	43,462,794.31	10.09	−1,730,750.78
1960s	51,025,752.44	9.29	60,522,146.45	10.61	−9,496,394.01
1970s	249,192,389.34	21.38	336,897,390.02	26.51	−87,705,000.68
1980s	420,436,339.00	12.19	1,019,269,668.58	11.15	−598,833,329.58
1990s	1,861,948,046.29	18.13	2,156,339,324.50	11.49	−294,391,278.21
2000–11	3,956,775,738.43	10.37	4,194,307,342.99	9.49	−237,531,604.55

Notes: Average values estimated by adding end-of-the-year values each year and dividing the sum by years in each period.
Growth figures refer to average growth for each period.
Balance refers to average difference between revenues and expenditures for each period.
Values in table reflect author's own estimations based on data from the Central Bank of Bolivia (CBB) and Ministry of Economy and Public Finance (MEPF).

for revenues (the exact year was 1992) when revenues totaled $1.3 billion. Table 5.1 also shows the recurring deficits experienced by government, highlighting the 1980s as the worst decade for out-of-control public expenditures, with an average deficit almost equal to $600 million. It is also worth noting that the fastest average decade-growth in both revenues and expenditures occurred in the 1970s, with 21.4 percent and 26.5 percent, respectively, setting the stage for the monetary and fiscal imbalances of the next decade. Since then, growth in both fiscal aggregates has been more moderate, though still averaging in the two-digit percentage level. During the 1990s and the years of the new century, both average revenues and expenditures have comfortably surpassed the one billion dollar mark, and in 2011—the last year analyzed here—revenues neared 8 billion dollars while expenditures were a tad above that level. Finally, and to underline the considerable evolution of government operations between 1940 and 2011, it is compelling to simply look at the growth rates in both revenues and expenditures between these years: 58,751 percent and 55,723 percent, respectively, signifying the extensive growth of government during the last seven decades.

■ TAX COLLECTION BY DEPARTMENTS

Tax collection data by departments only begins during the 1980s. Here I present data disaggregated by taxes collected in the nine departments for the period 1987–2010. Department tax values represent aggregate indicators of all national taxes collected by the National Tax Revenue Authority (NTRA).[2] Table 2e in the appendix introduces the actual data and Table 5.2 below presents relevant summary statistics.

Table 5.2
Average Tax Collection by Departments, 1987-2010 (current US dollars)

Years	Highest Contributor	Lowest Contributor	Fastest Growing Contributor	Slowest Growing Contributor	Share of Main Axis
1987-89	La Paz ($154 million)	Pando ($144 thousand)	Pando (44%)	Potosí (1.5%)	0.93
1990-94	La Paz ($234 million)	Pando ($265 thousand)	Oruro (25%)	La Paz (9.8%)	0.92
1995-99	La Paz ($388 million)	Pando ($484 thousand)	Tarija (24%)	La Paz (7.3%)	0.91
2000-04	La Paz ($342 million)	Pando ($280 thousand)	Tarija (27%)	Potosí (-7.2%)	0.91
2005-10	La Paz ($604 million)	Pando ($1 million)	Potosí (88%)	Oruro (11.1%)	0.88

Notes: Average values estimated by adding end-of-the-year balances and dividing the sum by years in each period.
Main axis refers to the combined contributions of the departments of La Paz, Santa Cruz, and Cochabamba.
Share of main axis (in decimals) estimated as share on total tax collections in nine departments.
Values in table reflect author's own estimations based on data from the National Tax Revenue Authority (NTRA) and the National Institute of Statistics (NIS).

As Table 5.2 shows, average tax collection has increased substantially for all departments since 1987. Throughout this period, the department of La Paz has consistently been the highest contributor, with average tax collection revenues increasing from $154 million during the late 1980s, to $234 during the 1990–94 period, $388 million during the 1995–99 years, $342 million during the 2000–04 period, and $604 million during the 2005–10 period. The department of Santa Cruz has been a close second throughout, and in 2005, it even surpassed La Paz as the biggest contributor to the national coffers. In other years—1999, 2001, and 2010—the difference between the two has been minimal. The lowest contributor has consistently been Pando, the youngest and least-populated department of the nation. As to which department is the fastest-growing or lowest-growing contributor during the period analyzed, there is no clear-cut tendency, but, unsurprisingly, mining departments (Oruro, Potosí) will tend to grow faster when demand for their products increases, and hydrocarbon departments (mainly Tarija) will also see a surge in their revenues when their principal export commodity begins to be traded at ever-growing volumes with other nations. The late 1990s and the years of the new millennium have been particularly positive for certain mining commodities and for natural gas, hence it is not surprising to see that during these years the departments of Oruro, Tarija, and Potosí have shown the fastest rates of revenue growth. The slowest growing contributors have been those departments highly dependent on few economic sectors (Potosí and Oruro) that tend to be heavily affected with downturns on their poorly diversified economies, and the department of La Paz, with a more mature economy that tends to show little variation between the years. Finally, and as the last column in Table 5.2 demonstrates, the share of La Paz, Cochabamba,

[2] National taxes include a value-added tax, income tax, and other minor taxes; until 2004 figures for department taxes also included hydrocarbon taxes, but from 2005 to the present hydrocarbon taxes are accounted as a separate entry and, hence, are not included as part of department taxes.

and Santa Cruz on total department taxes is substantial, consistently surpassing the 90 percent mark (0.90 in decimals), and denoting the significant dependence of the country on the well being of these three key departments. During the 2005–10 period the share of these departments on total department taxes decreased to 88 percent, a welcome development, but still a sign of the considerable impact these regional economies have on the welfare of the nation as a whole.

PUBLIC EXPENDITURES BY SECTOR

Government expenditures by sector are estimated for the 1940–2010 period. The four sectors considered are infrastructure, education, health, and national defense.[3] In all cases, expenditures refer to those carried out by the central government and do not necessarily include expenditures on the same sectors by the nine departments or by decentralized public institutions. Finally, and due to the lack of consistency on official data since 1940, the data does not differentiate between current (administrative) and capital expenditures. An introduction to the data is presented in Table 5.3, where average shares of central government expenditures, by sector, are introduced. Table 3e in the appendix presents the actual data in current dollars.

Table 5.3
Average Shares of Central Government Expenditures, by Sector (%)

Decade	Infrastructure	Education	Health	National Defense	Other
1940s	9.72	17.58	5.48	24.50	42.73
1950s	3.21	12.18	2.64	11.19	70.78
1960s	5.94	17.30	3.19	13.05	60.51
1970s	10.56	24.98	8.41	15.90	40.16
1980s	10.49	9.60	3.34	15.21	61.36
1990s	10.18	1.35	1.21	13.94	73.31
2000–10	10.11	2.30	1.49	4.63	81.46

Notes: Average values estimated by adding shares in each year and dividing the sum by years in each period.
Shares estimated by dividing expenditures in each sector by total central government expenditures.
Expenditures refer to those made by the central government.
Expenditures may not reflect those carried out by departments or by decentralized government agencies.
Values in table reflect author's own estimations based on data from the NIS.

As Table 5.3 shows, of the four sectors considered, infrastructure and national defense have been the ones where government expenditures have shown greater consistency and greater outlay of financial resources. Since the 1970s, infrastructure spending has consistently hovered around 10 percent of total government expenditures, while expenditures on national defense denote a downward trend, with the share of average expenditures in the new millennium reaching an all-time low of approximately 5 percent.

With respect to education, the data shows that from the 1940s to the 1970s, government expenditures on this sector were quite significant, consistently surpassing the two-digit percentage mark on total expenditures and even reaching a record average level of 25 percent during the 1970s. Beginning in the 1980s, the share of education expenditures has declined considerably, though during the years of the

[3] The infrastructure sector includes central government expenditures on roads, telecommunications, and urban housing. The education sector includes central government expenditures on education at the primary, secondary, and tertiary levels, as well as expenditures on culture, tourism, and information-related activities. The health sector comprises central government expenditures in public health programs, including prevention and educational programs. Finally, expenditures on national defense comprise all expenditures on defense, including administrative activities in institutions related to national defense.

new millennium there has been a spike in government spending on education as its share rose from its previous 1990s average of 1.4 percent to an average of around 2.3 percent of total expenditures.[4]

The average share of government expenditures on health is the lowest in every one of the decades analyzed here and, beginning in the 1970s, there is a notable downward trend in central government outlays on health-related programs. As was the case with education, health expenditures have spiked a bit after 2000 (from an average share of 1.2 percent in the 1990s to approximately 1.5 percent in the next decade), but it seems that central government expenditures on these two key sectors—education and health—should stand at much higher levels if the country hopes to attain higher levels of economic development.

Finally, it is interesting to note that the "other" category has grown considerably through the decades, demonstrating that central government expenditures are increasingly dedicated to maintaining an expanding bureaucracy, often at the expense of other sectors (such as the four that have been emphasized here) that would seem to be crucial to the economic well-being of the country.

[4] It should be noted that education and health expenditures are not only carried out by the central government but also by departments, municipalities, and decentralized public institutions, usually funded by external institutions (World Bank, United Nations Development Program, Inter-American Development Bank, non-governmental organizations). Data presented here only refers to expenditures carried out by the central government.

Appendices

Table 1a: Total Exports and Imports, 1900–2011 (CIF values, current US dollars)			
Year	Total Exports	Total Imports	Balance of Trade
1900	15,797,665.37	5,909,533.07	9,888,132.30
1901	14,230,019.49	6,418,128.65	7,811,890.84
1902	9,707,744.76	4,895,275.21	4,812,469.56
1903	8,798,638.13	5,680,933.85	3,117,704.28
1904	12,283,349.56	6,601,752.68	5,681,596.88
1905	16,799,610.89	8,161,478.60	8,638,132.30
1906	22,426,006.79	14,138,767.59	8,287,239.20
1907	20,111,758.99	15,145,772.59	4,965,986.39
1908	17,610,705.60	14,686,131.39	2,924,574.21
1909	24,278,752.44	14,069,200.78	10,209,551.66
1910	29,829,766.54	19,250,972.76	10,578,793.77
1911	32,318,911.04	22,829,363.15	9,489,547.89
1912	34,262,773.72	18,822,384.43	15,440,389.29
1913	34,698,149.95	20,272,638.75	14,425,511.20
1914	22,642,998.03	13,683,431.95	8,959,566.07
1915	29,957,183.63	7,102,759.28	22,854,424.36
1916	36,534,795.04	11,196,377.50	25,338,417.54
1917	56,765,126.25	12,048,594.57	44,716,531.68
1918	75,192,949.02	14,411,624.58	60,781,324.44
1919	51,372,288.62	22,080,566.62	29,291,722.00
1920	50,637,596.19	21,205,569.81	29,432,026.38
1921	17,644,341.80	18,683,602.77	-1,039,260.97
1922	27,537,643.93	14,521,700.62	13,015,943.31
1923	33,490,393.41	19,569,990.85	13,920,402.56
1924	36,289,752.65	19,805,653.71	16,484,098.94
1925	42,225,977.79	24,094,640.27	18,131,337.52
1926	43,479,105.93	25,102,040.82	18,377,065.11
1927	46,349,052.02	24,107,924.16	22,241,127.86
1928	42,374,695.86	23,508,515.82	18,866,180.05
1929	50,998,193.30	26,014,065.08	24,984,128.22
1930	36,545,935.83	20,919,202.72	15,626,733.11
1931	20,347,278.91	10,010,562.36	10,336,716.55
1932	10,650,378.68	4,867,791.02	5,782,587.66

Table 1a: Total Exports and Imports, 1900-2011 (CIF values, current US dollars) continued			
Year	Total Exports	Total Imports	Balance of Trade
1933	16,444,012.71	8,938,385.59	7,505,627.12
1934	36,753,808.56	16,583,733.00	20,170,075.57
1935	35,920,666.67	17,969,465.69	17,951,200.98
1936	37,279,279.32	20,675,039.76	16,604,239.56
1937	37,438,790.90	21,023,979.24	16,414,811.67
1938	28,490,066.01	24,931,902.20	3,558,163.81
1939	34,669,523.28	19,214,004.43	15,455,518.85
1940	49,738,926.46	21,833,577.17	27,905,349.29
1941	60,669,778.23	31,299,568.55	29,370,209.68
1942	65,735,362.39	37,519,927.36	28,215,435.03
1943	85,195,900.82	44,228,434.22	40,967,466.60
1944	82,056,510.12	42,280,096.85	39,776,413.27
1945	80,430,782.00	40,369,844.00	40,060,938.00
1946	85,082,094.12	43,464,596.24	41,617,497.88
1947	89,733,532.21	46,559,275.49	43,174,256.72
1948	115,160,000.00	49,654,070.53	65,505,929.47
1949	103,140,000.00	52,748,512.21	50,391,487.79
1950	94,219,000.00	55,843,000.00	38,376,000.00
1951	150,590,000.00	85,837,000.00	64,753,000.00
1952	141,303,000.00	92,620,000.00	48,683,000.00
1953	112,664,000.00	68,006,000.00	44,658,000.00
1954	99,453,000.00	65,483,000.00	33,970,000.00
1955	102,374,000.00	82,394,000.00	19,980,000.00
1956	107,437,273.91	84,057,757.09	23,379,516.82
1957	97,667,409.42	92,245,934.27	5,421,475.15
1958	63,907,605.19	79,592,482.09	-15,684,876.90
1959	77,635,000.00	64,986,000.00	12,649,000.00
1960	67,828,000.00	71,477,000.00	-3,649,000.00
1961	76,136,000.00	77,192,000.00	-1,056,000.00
1962	76,735,000.00	96,930,000.00	-20,195,000.00
1963	86,404,000.00	103,270,000.00	-16,866,000.00
1964	113,866,000.00	102,710,000.00	11,156,000.00
1965	131,836,000.00	133,850,000.00	-2,014,000.00
1966	150,436,000.00	138,430,000.00	12,006,000.00
1967	166,325,000.00	150,960,000.00	15,365,000.00
1968	170,648,000.00	153,840,000.00	16,808,000.00
1969	198,191,000.00	165,040,000.00	33,151,000.00
1970	225,591,000.00	159,200,000.00	66,391,000.00
1971	215,920,000.00	169,700,000.00	46,220,000.00
1972	244,420,000.00	185,400,000.00	59,020,000.00

Table 1a: Total Exports and Imports, 1900–2011 (CIF values, current US dollars) continued			
Year	Total Exports	Total Imports	Balance of Trade
1973	338,315,000.00	229,400,000.00	108,915,000.00
1974	650,832,000.00	390,000,000.00	260,832,000.00
1975	521,430,000.00	557,900,000.00	-36,470,000.00
1976	623,080,000.00	587,600,000.00	35,480,000.00
1977	715,150,000.00	665,900,000.00	49,250,000.00
1978	725,500,000.00	777,200,000.00	-51,700,000.00
1979	857,200,000.00	860,900,000.00	-3,700,000.00
1980	1,036,060,000.00	678,400,000.00	357,660,000.00
1981	995,320,000.00	975,400,000.00	19,920,000.00
1982	898,200,000.00	577,500,000.00	320,700,000.00
1983	817,500,000.00	589,100,000.00	228,400,000.00
1984	782,100,000.00	491,600,000.00	290,500,000.00
1985	672,500,000.00	690,900,000.00	-18,400,000.00
1986	637,750,000.00	674,000,000.00	-36,250,000.00
1987	569,600,000.00	766,300,000.00	-196,700,000.00
1988	622,150,000.00	590,500,000.00	31,650,000.00
1989	866,660,000.00	620,000,000.00	246,660,000.00
1990	955,920,000.00	702,700,000.00	253,220,000.00
1991	882,440,000.00	993,700,000.00	-111,260,000.00
1992	767,580,000.00	1,130,500,000.00	-362,920,000.00
1993	890,620,000.00	1,177,000,000.00	-286,380,000.00
1994	1,185,930,000.00	1,196,200,000.00	-10,270,000.00
1995	1,304,070,000.00	1,433,500,000.00	-129,430,000.00
1996	1,321,380,000.00	1,537,400,000.00	-216,020,000.00
1997	1,376,770,000.00	1,850,900,000.00	-474,130,000.00
1998	1,362,500,000.00	1,983,100,000.00	-620,600,000.00
1999	1,290,240,000.00	1,755,000,000.00	-464,760,000.00
2000	1,551,950,000.00	1,829,900,000.00	-277,950,000.00
2001	1,587,330,000.00	1,707,700,000.00	-120,370,000.00
2002	1,553,320,000.00	1,774,700,000.00	-221,380,000.00
2003	1,888,920,000.00	1,615,800,000.00	273,120,000.00
2004	2,438,670,000.00	1,876,900,000.00	561,770,000.00
2005	3,161,790,000.00	2,431,000,000.00	730,790,000.00
2006	4,617,620,000.00	2,915,800,000.00	1,701,820,000.00
2007	5,145,080,000.00	3,585,700,000.00	1,559,380,000.00
2008	7,463,200,000.00	5,081,400,000.00	2,381,800,000.00
2009	5,768,600,000.00	4,544,900,000.00	1,223,700,000.00
2010	7,038,160,000.00	5,383,700,000.00	1,654,460,000.00
2011	9,109,290,000.00	7,612,550,000.00	1,496,740,000.00

Note: Values in table reflect author's own estimations based on data from the Central Bank of Bolivia (CBB), National Institute of Statistics (NIS), and Customs Department.

Table 2a: Trade by Countries as a Share of Total Exports and Total Imports, 1929-2010 (values expressed in %)															
Year	Exp to UK	Exp to US	Exp to Germany	Exp to Argentina	Exp to Brazil	Exp to Chile	Exp to Peru	Exp to Rest of World	Imp from UK	Imp from US	Imp from Germany	Imp from Argentina	Imp from Chile	Imp from Peru	Imp from Brazil	Imp from Rest of World
1929	77.22	13.92	1.36	2.03	0.84	0.27	0.03	4.33	16.58	33.72	13.63	9.65	6.49	4.48	0.52	14.93
1930	76.46	12.97	2.69	3.11	1.25	0.16	0.05	3.31	16.68	27.81	13.57	11.28	7.05	5.48	0.53	17.60
1931	82.08	0.05	1.03	3.14	0.61	0.20	0.04	12.84	16.45	25.20	17.02	10.81	5.71	8.16	0.70	15.95
1932	82.72	3.58	0.70	4.03	0.58	0.68	0.03	7.69	18.29	24.07	12.26	13.08	6.16	10.16	1.25	14.73
1933	83.53	4.60	0.64	4.35	0.49	0.21	0.01	6.17	22.16	30.24	5.93	8.57	4.34	9.39	0.92	18.45
1934	90.09	2.40	0.97	0.79	0.19	0.14	0.04	5.37	12.70	36.89	13.58	5.57	5.13	8.01	1.22	16.90
1935	86.02	4.05	1.01	1.58	0.22	0.10	0.04	6.98	9.18	23.78	21.21	7.75	3.18	6.28	1.34	27.28
1936	74.83	7.82	1.48	2.70	0.55	0.31	0.08	12.23	10.85	29.20	12.66	13.86	4.66	8.64	1.44	18.69
1937	59.91	7.28	1.10	1.94	0.57	0.27	0.13	28.80	8.22	28.90	13.87	13.44	4.03	12.12	1.36	18.06
1938	62.48	4.61	1.20	1.94	1.46	0.24	0.23	27.84	7.24	26.39	18.59	13.41	4.48	9.56	0.79	19.54
1939	64.78	9.15	0.53	1.68	0.79	0.48	0.23	22.37	6.47	25.40	13.89	13.92	4.66	12.47	1.06	22.13
1940	70.84	24.32	0.03	1.13	0.17	0.12	0.10	3.29	7.19	41.21	1.71	18.78	6.35	6.99	1.71	16.06
1941	35.34	60.04	0.00	1.74	0.77	0.11	0.00	2.00	5.62	41.64	0.31	20.38	6.65	9.61	4.41	11.38
1942	31.94	65.67	0.00	1.98	0.23	0.05	0.12	0.01	5.89	39.92	0.02	26.04	5.86	14.94	2.94	4.39
1943	34.25	63.30	-	1.99	0.25	0.14	0.04	0.04	5.50	32.36	-	35.09	5.92	12.55	6.70	1.88
1944	33.79	63.13	-	1.53	0.41	0.13	0.08	0.93	3.59	33.65	-	26.50	9.47	15.76	8.90	2.13
1945	34.07	61.87	-	2.73	0.25	0.15	0.16	0.77	3.40	31.80	-	25.30	8.35	19.00	9.05	3.10
1946	35.34	59.55	-	3.51	0.46	0.10	0.33	0.71	3.57	37.05	-	23.23	9.54	13.87	4.51	8.23
1947	35.38	60.56	-	2.20	0.37	0.19	0.37	0.94	3.83	49.42	-	20.31	6.21	10.55	2.49	7.19
1948	35.21	62.62	-	1.36	0.11	0.27	0.07	0.37	6.07	49.14	-	16.22	5.49	10.25	2.95	9.88
1949	30.44	64.07	0.06	1.51	0.13	0.22	0.03	3.53	5.46	52.27	0.28	15.86	4.57	8.11	1.43	12.03
1950	29.64	66.68	0.07	2.29	0.31	0.17	0.01	0.82	7.05	42.25	0.77	17.66	5.28	10.82	2.07	14.10
1951	32.02	65.69	0.04	0.86	0.54	0.16	0.14	0.54	8.15	42.22	2.48	13.44	4.76	10.21	2.53	16.22
1952	31.10	65.19	0.16	0.78	1.13	0.47	0.14	1.02	8.35	40.96	5.51	13.75	3.27	7.02	2.73	18.42
1953	35.98	61.14	0.03	1.10	0.55	0.86	0.17	0.17	6.83	31.77	4.82	14.30	3.38	14.04	1.79	23.08
1954	33.18	63.04	0.12	1.75	0.90	0.88	0.02	0.11	6.62	38.09	6.14	11.71	2.05	11.28	0.94	23.18
1955	32.86	60.62	1.10	0.85	0.91	0.94	0.02	2.70	7.37	37.91	9.60	10.20	0.98	6.66	2.33	24.95
1956	37.54	53.31	1.35	2.52	2.58	1.29	0.06	1.35	5.80	45.94	9.26	14.61	1.77	6.33	1.64	14.65
1957	53.46	33.91	3.29	4.74	1.99	0.68	0.53	1.39	8.51	46.97	11.51	6.48	2.22	7.50	1.88	14.93

Table 2a: Trade by Countries as a Share of Total Exports and Total Imports, 1929–2010 (values expressed in %) continued

Year	Exp to UK	Exp to US	Exp to Germany	Exp to Argentina	Exp to Brazil	Exp to Chile	Exp to Peru	Exp to Rest of World	Imp from UK	Imp from US	Imp from Germany	Imp from Argentina	Imp from Chile	Imp from Peru	Imp from Brazil	Imp from Rest of World
1958	51.22	31.84	2.82	9.33	0.85	0.94	0.72	2.29	5.90	46.41	12.30	8.13	2.65	4.61	0.23	19.77
1959	45.52	34.79	4.46	5.94	1.95	0.19	0.71	6.43	4.70	44.24	11.68	12.43	3.80	6.52	0.54	16.09
1960	52.32	34.97	4.91	3.80	2.84	0.44	0.12	0.60	5.00	43.10	12.69	5.94	3.64	3.72	0.92	24.99
1961	51.60	27.32	5.99	3.43	3.08	0.59	0.16	7.83	4.87	42.16	12.22	8.50	4.00	1.50	0.61	26.14
1962	53.76	30.23	6.04	2.47	0.99	0.34	0.18	5.99	6.04	40.05	12.07	8.15	4.42	1.63	0.59	27.05
1963	46.90	32.34	5.40	2.38	0.77	0.16	0.12	11.93	5.54	57.35	13.27	3.93	1.55	1.64	1.53	15.19
1964	48.27	35.65	4.67	0.87	0.72	0.14	0.19	9.50	4.80	51.45	11.18	3.15	1.73	1.46	1.64	24.59
1965	44.60	42.66	5.06	0.68	1.01	0.50	0.43	5.05	5.22	43.75	11.00	5.45	1.33	1.60	1.56	30.09
1966	45.46	39.24	5.26	2.18	0.87	0.69	1.37	4.93	4.64	41.17	12.36	6.27	1.54	1.09	1.20	31.73
1967	40.56	43.44	4.95	3.18	0.73	0.49	1.22	5.43	4.60	41.15	11.63	5.94	1.36	1.15	1.98	32.19
1968	44.90	35.35	3.32	4.82	0.46	0.82	1.33	8.99	4.69	43.38	11.85	7.47	1.30	1.38	1.56	28.37
1969	45.80	30.67	2.63	5.35	0.47	0.00	1.66	13.42	5.05	31.12	12.41	10.26	1.21	1.33	1.89	36.73
1970	38.11	34.80	2.39	5.11	0.54	0.45	2.19	16.41	4.95	33.93	10.70	10.61	1.41	1.18	2.27	34.95
1971	27.94	32.04	2.90	7.35	1.76	2.61	6.74	18.65	5.48	30.48	12.99	10.43	1.40	1.43	3.95	33.84
1972	25.54	27.12	4.11	13.72	4.44	3.85	3.61	17.62	3.91	25.32	10.49	15.84	1.09	1.59	7.52	34.24
1973	18.38	27.30	3.95	16.41	5.54	5.09	2.09	21.25	3.89	24.30	10.01	16.89	1.15	1.56	8.04	34.16
1974	11.63	30.77	5.02	17.55	4.36	4.16	2.50	24.01	2.56	26.44	7.98	14.95	0.97	1.07	15.52	30.51
1975	10.44	30.82	3.38	25.88	3.54	1.11	1.43	23.40	2.44	25.02	7.75	14.40	1.89	1.56	14.32	32.62
1976	9.02	34.36	3.12	22.76	3.31	1.45	2.81	23.16	2.70	23.22	8.90	13.21	3.92	2.79	11.00	34.26
1977	11.45	35.30	3.90	17.90	2.86	1.98	0.90	25.70	3.33	29.50	8.43	12.67	3.58	2.62	10.96	28.91
1978	11.79	31.19	4.59	17.32	3.98	2.86	1.55	26.72	2.87	27.63	9.43	11.26	3.24	2.25	9.47	33.85
1979	8.86	33.01	5.25	15.57	5.08	4.12	2.87	25.24	3.01	27.93	8.40	10.93	3.13	2.16	9.01	35.43
1980	6.88	25.73	5.29	23.66	3.51	4.52	3.11	27.30	2.96	28.47	9.60	11.01	3.80	5.45	6.58	32.13
1981	3.85	26.75	3.65	36.14	1.28	0.85	3.13	24.35	4.81	22.93	8.07	9.90	3.97	3.14	14.11	33.07
1982	3.45	26.14	3.71	44.53	2.17	1.20	2.56	16.24	4.01	29.38	8.09	13.27	2.82	2.61	9.52	30.30
1983	2.34	20.78	2.93	47.56	1.56	1.02	1.78	22.03	3.79	28.08	5.48	14.19	3.05	2.53	13.87	29.01
1984	5.21	18.42	3.20	48.79	1.03	0.89	1.20	21.26	2.82	21.81	7.21	14.49	3.30	5.12	20.17	25.08
1985	8.87	13.51	4.99	55.87	0.67	1.58	1.89	12.62	4.36	20.29	7.52	16.94	3.43	3.67	19.41	24.38
1986	7.89	14.76	5.61	53.44	3.54	3.38	2.49	8.89	4.60	22.26	6.81	11.22	5.09	2.21	18.46	29.35

Table 2a: Trade by Countries as a Share of Total Exports and Total Imports, 1929–2010 (values expressed in %) continued

Year	Exp to UK	Exp to US	Exp to Germany	Exp to Argentina	Exp to Brazil	Exp to Chile	Exp to Peru	Exp to Rest of World	Imp from UK	Imp from US	Imp from Germany	Imp from Argentina	Imp from Chile	Imp from Peru	Imp from Brazil	Imp from Rest of World
1987	10.93	16.25	5.45	45.62	3.31	2.08	4.30	12.06	3.03	24.02	6.56	13.56	3.51	1.93	19.40	27.99
1988	11.83	17.03	5.73	37.91	1.88	4.92	3.77	16.93	1.52	21.19	5.35	15.21	6.21	2.29	19.14	29.09
1989	14.06	13.24	4.52	27.88	5.77	7.62	5.48	21.43	1.76	26.13	6.58	12.43	6.52	2.75	20.49	23.34
1990	12.30	19.94	4.30	25.52	8.42	3.64	5.73	20.15	1.55	23.17	5.83	13.12	5.63	5.52	24.40	20.78
1991	12.13	14.64	3.16	30.61	4.84	4.74	5.63	24.25	1.33	21.98	7.94	10.49	12.49	3.16	16.78	25.83
1992	18.15	16.00	4.57	21.79	1.75	2.19	8.13	27.42	0.90	25.93	8.41	11.16	6.37	2.15	14.31	30.77
1993	21.11	22.65	4.28	16.60	2.83	2.08	9.94	20.51	5.43	23.54	4.87	12.05	7.38	4.30	10.46	31.97
1994	14.62	29.22	5.40	13.92	3.11	1.80	11.64	20.29	1.29	18.17	4.66	10.43	7.50	5.03	14.54	38.38
1995	13.99	24.09	5.18	12.00	1.74	2.28	13.68	27.04	1.84	22.08	4.97	8.86	7.46	5.34	12.22	37.23
1996	12.72	20.09	4.95	12.46	3.51	3.56	12.71	30.00	0.75	26.29	3.90	8.82	6.89	5.31	10.75	37.29
1997	13.00	16.12	4.76	15.95	2.50	4.69	13.11	29.87	1.20	23.34	3.07	13.81	6.40	5.07	11.39	35.72
1998	18.72	14.53	1.99	11.54	2.34	3.15	13.08	34.65	0.70	26.25	2.34	9.60	5.72	3.70	10.27	41.42
1999	17.01	21.57	1.46	6.02	3.65	2.33	6.73	41.23	0.84	23.62	2.64	13.14	7.00	4.71	14.51	33.54
2000	11.62	24.23	0.92	3.36	11.38	2.02	4.16	42.31	0.53	21.78	2.00	15.31	8.25	5.00	14.10	33.03
2001	5.33	13.48	0.57	4.80	22.05	2.45	4.94	46.38	0.75	16.50	2.04	16.89	8.34	5.26	16.29	32.93
2002	2.30	13.01	0.51	1.96	22.42	2.05	4.89	52.86	0.64	16.24	1.69	16.90	6.99	5.22	21.70	30.62
2003	2.03	14.24	0.41	3.39	30.03	2.63	5.40	41.87	0.78	15.98	2.28	16.98	7.37	6.26	20.83	29.52
2004	2.40	16.08	0.46	6.22	31.21	2.29	6.16	35.18	0.60	13.89	1.98	15.35	5.82	6.77	25.90	29.69
2005	2.11	14.52	0.55	9.45	36.40	1.43	4.51	31.03	0.81	14.11	1.84	16.71	6.81	6.43	22.25	31.04
2006	1.89	9.69	0.42	9.22	37.47	1.60	5.88	33.83	0.62	11.86	2.31	15.54	8.09	6.51	20.14	34.93
2007	2.18	8.85	0.33	8.92	36.02	1.25	4.81	37.64	0.53	11.39	2.38	16.45	6.35	6.33	20.06	36.50
2008	1.30	7.13	0.37	7.36	43.18	1.23	4.15	35.29	0.45	10.87	1.81	14.36	6.90	6.98	18.21	40.42
2009	1.36	9.02	0.37	8.36	30.64	1.53	5.39	43.31	0.63	13.81	2.16	13.83	5.43	7.08	17.35	39.71
2010	1.46	10.11	0.46	8.31	34.69	1.41	5.77	37.80	0.60	13.25	2.07	12.99	5.64	7.22	18.59	39.64
2011	1.72	9.77	0.56	11.16	33.30	1.73	5.11	36.65	0.58	11.18	1.84	12.51	4.04	6.14	18.13	45.59

Notes: Between 1943–48 there is no recorded trade with Germany.
Values in table reflect author's own estimations based on data from CBB, NIS.

Table 3a: Structure of Exports (millions of current US dollars)

Products	1929	%	1930	%	1931	%	1932	%	1933	%	1934	%	1935	%	1936	%	1937	%	1938	%	1939	%
Minerals	**44.92**	**88.09**	**31.57**	**86.37**	**19.09**	**93.82**	**9.77**	**91.67**	**15.10**	**91.90**	**30.98**	**84.29**	**34.45**	**95.92**	**33.77**	**90.56**	**32.95**	**88.01**	**25.37**	**89.02**	**31.91**	**92.04**
Tin	37.37	73.29	26.94	73.71	16.24	79.83	8.08	75.85	12.08	73.52	26.66	72.54	28.00	77.96	24.65	66.10	21.95	58.62	17.34	60.83	22.44	64.72
Zinc	0.17	0.33	0.45	1.23	0.78	3.83	0.50	4.69	0.84	5.11	0.66	1.80	0.59	1.64	1.00	2.68	1.26	3.37	0.71	2.50	0.54	1.57
Silver	2.58	5.06	2.07	5.66	1.25	6.14	0.72	6.76	1.43	8.70	2.03	5.52	3.52	9.80	4.26	11.42	3.74	9.99	2.45	8.60	2.91	8.39
Antimony	0.53	1.04	0.14	0.38	0.13	0.64	0.10	0.94	0.17	1.03	0.23	0.63	0.64	1.78	1.06	2.84	1.26	3.37	1.13	3.96	1.63	4.70
Wolfram	0.57	1.12	0.25	0.68	0.06	0.28	0.06	0.53	0.05	0.30	0.49	1.33	0.68	1.89	0.80	2.15	1.55	4.14	1.84	6.46	2.19	6.32
Gold	-	-	-	-	-	-	-	-	-	-	-	-	-	-	-	-	0.14	0.38	0.35	1.23	0.31	0.89
Others[6]	3.70	7.26	1.72	4.71	0.63	3.10	0.31	2.91	0.53	3.23	0.91	2.48	1.02	2.84	2.00	5.36	3.05	8.15	1.55	5.44	1.89	5.45
Hydrocarbons	-	-	-	-	-	-	-	-	-	-	-	-	-	-	-	-	-	-	-	-	-	-
Petroleum[1]		-		-		-		-		-		-		-		-		-		-		-
Natural gas		-		-		-		-		-		-		-		-		-		-		-
Propane gas		-		-		-		-		-		-		-		-		-		-		-
Butane gas		-		-		-		-		-		-		-		-		-		-		-
Others[2]		-		-		-		-		-		-		-		-		-		-		-
Non-Traditional Products	**6.07**	**11.91**	**4.98**	**13.63**	**1.26**	**6.18**	**0.89**	**8.33**	**1.33**	**8.10**	**5.77**	**15.71**	**1.47**	**4.08**	**3.52**	**9.44**	**4.49**	**11.99**	**3.13**	**10.98**	**2.76**	**7.96**
Fruits and almonds		-		-		-		-		-		-		-		-		-		-		-
Almonds and chestnut	0.08	0.15	0.18	0.49	0.08	0.40	0.12	1.13	0.13	0.79	0.21	0.57	0.18	0.50	0.57	1.53	0.63	1.68	0.64	2.25	0.42	1.21
Quinoa	0.07	0.14	0.14	0.38	0.09	0.45	0.08	0.77	0.08	0.49	0.18	0.49	0.24	0.67	0.34	0.91	0.41	1.10	0.38	1.33	0.33	0.95
Quinine	-	-	-	-	-	-	-	-	-	-	-	-	-	-	-	-	-	-	-	-	-	-
Coffee		-		-		-		-		-		-		-		-		-		-		-
Coca leafs	0.39	0.76	0.40	1.09	0.34	1.67	0.18	1.69	0.12	0.73	0.14	0.38	0.30	0.84	0.53	1.42	0.38	1.01	0.37	1.30	0.27	0.78
Lumber (maderas)	-	-	-	-	-	-	-	-	-	-	-	-	-	-	-	-	-	-	-	-	-	-
Sugar		-		-	-	-	-	-	-	-	-	-	-	-	-	-	-	-	-	-		-
Rubber	1.05	2.06	0.62	1.70	0.24	1.18	0.07	0.69	0.25	1.52	0.14	0.38	0.13	0.36	0.87	2.33	0.55	1.47	0.29	1.02	0.37	1.07
Leather products	0.31	0.61	0.22	0.60	0.16	0.79	0.09	0.82	0.11	0.67	0.18	0.49	0.33	0.92	0.66	1.77	0.54	1.44	0.25	0.88	0.24	0.69
Soja (grains, flour, cake)		-		-		-		-		-		-		-		-		-		-		-

Table 3a: Structure of Exports (millions of current US dollars) continued

Products	1929	%	1930	%	1931	%	1932	%	1933	%	1934	%	1935	%	1936	%	1937	%	1938	%	1939	%
Metal-mechanic goods		-		-		-		-		-		-		-		-		-		-		-
Handicrafts		-		-		-		-		-		-		-		-		-		-		-
Chestnut (castana)		-		-		-		-		-		-		-		-		-		-		-
Livestock	0.24	0.47	0.34	0.93	0.09	0.42	0.03	0.23	0.03	0.18	0.05	0.14	0.08	0.21	0.16	0.43	0.18	0.48	0.45	1.58	0.23	0.66
Meat		-		-		-		-		-		-		-		-		-		-		-
Cotton		-		-		-		-		-		-		-		-		-		-		-
Textiles		-		-		-		-		-		-		-		-		-		-		-
Soja oil		-		-		-		-		-		-		-		-		-		-		-
Jewelry products		-		-		-		-		-		-		-		-		-		-		-
Others[3]	3.93	7.71	3.08	8.43	0.26	1.28	0.32	3.00	0.61	3.71	4.87	13.25	0.21	0.58	0.39	1.05	1.80	4.81	0.75	2.63	0.90	2.60
Total (A)	**50.99**	**100.00**	**36.55**	**100.00**	**20.34**	**100.00**	**10.65**	**100.00**	**16.43**	**100.00**	**36.75**	**100.00**	**35.92**	**100.00**	**37.29**	**100.00**	**37.44**	**100.00**	**28.50**	**100.00**	**34.67**	**100.00**
Others[4] (B)		-		-		-		-		-		-		-		-		-		-		-
Total CIF (A)+(B)	**50.99**	**100.00**	**36.55**	**100.00**	**20.34**	**100.00**	**10.65**	**100.00**	**16.43**	**100.00**	**36.75**	**100.00**	**35.92**	**100.00**	**37.29**	**100.00**	**37.44**	**100.00**	**28.50**	**100.00**	**34.67**	**100.00**
Adjustments ©	-		-		-		-		-		-		-		-		-		-		-	
Realization expenses																						
Others[5]																						
Total FOB (A)+(B)+©	**50.99**		**36.55**		**20.34**		**10.65**		**16.43**		**36.75**		**35.92**		**37.29**		**37.44**		**28.50**		**34.67**	

Table 3a: Structure of Exports (millions of current US dollars) continued

	1940	%	1941	%	1942	%	1943	%	1944	%	1945	%	1946	%	1947	%	1948	%	1949	%
Minerals	**48.27**	**97.05**	**58.33**	**96.15**	**63.41**	**96.46**	**78.07**	**91.62**	**72.97**	**88.95**	**73.88**	**91.83**	**65.39**	**76.86**	**75.24**	**83.84**	**111.15**	**96.53**	**99.04**	**96.02**
Tin	35.51	71.40	42.82	70.58	43.93	66.83	54.99	64.53	53.11	64.74	60.28	74.92	52.00	61.12	54.65	60.90	80.18	69.63	72.87	70.65
Zinc	1.67	3.36	0.83	1.37	1.46	2.22	2.81	3.30	2.18	2.66	2.80	3.48	2.56	3.01	1.95	2.17	2.81	2.44	2.36	2.29
Silver	2.09	4.20	2.58	4.25	3.04	4.62	3.12	3.66	2.95	3.60	3.36	4.18	4.35	5.11	4.34	4.84	5.48	4.76	4.65	4.51
Antimony	2.31	4.64	2.52	4.15	3.70	5.63	3.84	4.51	1.58	1.93	1.18	1.47	2.08	2.44	4.71	5.25	6.23	5.41	4.19	4.06
Wolfram	3.26	6.55	5.37	8.85	7.77	11.82	10.08	11.83	10.06	12.26	3.30	4.10	1.53	1.80	2.83	3.15	2.90	2.52	2.25	2.18
Gold	0.41	0.83	0.31	0.51	0.21	0.31	0.15	0.18	0.16	0.20	0.11	0.14	0.10	0.11	0.28	0.31	0.14	0.12	1.81	1.75
Others[6]	3.01	6.06	3.90	6.43	3.30	5.02	3.08	3.61	2.93	3.57	2.85	3.54	2.77	3.26	6.48	7.22	13.41	11.65	10.91	10.58
Hydrocarbons	**0.01**	**0.02**	**0.05**	**0.09**	**0.09**	**0.13**	**0.10**	**0.12**	**0.14**	**0.17**	**0.14**	**0.18**	-	-	-	-	-	-	-	-
Petroleum[1]	0.01	0.02	0.05	0.09	0.09	0.13	0.10	0.12	0.14	0.17	0.14	0.18		-		-		-		-
Natural gas		-		-		-		-		-		-		-		-		-		-
Propane gas		-		-		-		-		-		-		-		-		-		-
Butane gas		-		-		-		-		-		-		-		-		-		-
Others[2]		-		-		-		-		-		-		-		-		-		-
Non-Traditional Products	**1.46**	**2.94**	**2.29**	**3.77**	**2.24**	**3.41**	**7.04**	**8.26**	**8.93**	**10.88**	**6.44**	**8.00**	**19.69**	**23.14**	**14.50**	**16.16**	**4.00**	**3.47**	**4.10**	**3.98**
Fruits and almonds		-		-		-		-		-		-		-		-		-		-
Almonds and chestnut	0.32	0.64	0.44	0.73	0.19	0.29	0.00	0.00	-	-	-	-		-		-		-		-
Quinoa	0.32	0.64	0.22	0.36	0.12	0.18	0.41	0.48	0.36	0.44	0.34	0.42		-		-		-		-
Quinine	-	-	0.00	0.00	0.05	0.07	0.12	0.14	0.28	0.34	0.29	0.36		-		-		-		-
Coffee		-		-		-		-		-		-		-		-		-		-
Coca leafs	0.23	0.46	0.21	0.35	0.23	0.35	0.19	0.22	0.25	0.30	0.32	0.39		-		-		-		-
Lumber (maderas)	0.01	0.01	0.06	0.10	0.01	0.02	0.02	0.02	0.04	0.05	0.03	0.04		-		-		-		-
Sugar	-	-	-	-	-	-	-	-	-	-	-	-		-		-		-		-
Rubber	0.39	0.78	0.66	1.09	1.30	1.98	2.02	2.37	2.91	3.55	3.69	4.59		-		-		-		-
Leather products	0.17	0.34	0.21	0.35	0.25	0.38	0.18	0.21	0.18	0.22	0.27	0.34		-		-		-		-
Soja (grains, flour, cake)		-		-		-		-		-		-		-		-		-		-

Table 3a: Structure of Exports (millions of current US dollars) continued

	1940	%	1941	%	1942	%	1943	%	1944	%	1945	%	1946	%	1947	%	1948	%	1949	%
Metal-mechanic goods		-		-		-		-		-		-		-		-		-		-
Handicrafts		-		-		-		-		-		-		-		-		-		-
Chestnut (castana)		-		-		-		-		-		-		-		-		-		-
Livestock	0.02	0.04	0.45	0.74	0.09	0.14	0.10	0.11	0.20	0.24	0.11	0.14		-		-		-		-
Meat		-		-		-		-		-		-		-		-		-		-
Cotton		-		-		-		-		-		-		-		-		-		-
Textiles		-		-		-		-		-		-		-		-		-		-
Soja oil		-		-		-		-		-		-		-		-		-		-
Jewelry products		-		-		-		-		-		-		-		-		-		-
Others[3]	0.00	0.01	0.03	0.05	0.00	0.00	4.00	4.69	4.71	5.74	1.39	1.73		-		-		-		-
Total (A)	**49.74**	**100.00**	**60.67**	**100.00**	**65.73**	**100.00**	**85.21**	**100.00**	**82.04**	**100.00**	**80.46**	**100.00**	**85.08**	**100.00**	**89.74**	**100.00**	**115.15**	**100.00**	**103.14**	**100.00**
Others[4] (B)		-		-		-		-		-		-		-		-		-		-
Total CIF (A)+(B)	**49.74**	**100.00**	**60.67**	**100.00**	**65.73**	**100.00**	**85.21**	**100.00**	**82.04**	**100.00**	**80.46**	**100.00**	**85.08**	**100.00**	**89.74**	**100.00**	**115.15**	**100.00**	**103.14**	**100.00**
Adjustments ©	-		-		-		-		-		-		-		-		-		-	
Realization expenses																				
Others[5]																				
Total FOB (A)+(B)+©	**49.74**		**60.67**		**65.73**		**85.21**		**82.04**		**80.46**		**85.08**		**89.74**		**115.15**		**103.14**	

Table 3a: Structure of Exports (millions of current US dollars) continued

	1950	%	1951	%	1952	%	1953	%	1954	%	1955	%	1956	%	1957	%	1958	%	1959	%
Minerals	**90.02**	**95.54**	**145.59**	**96.68**	**137.75**	**97.49**	**109.97**	**97.61**	**96.18**	**96.69**	**97.76**	**95.51**	**100.02**	**93.09**	**88.47**	**90.57**	**55.74**	**87.20**	**68.89**	**88.74**
Tin	63.59	67.49	93.36	61.99	84.78	60.00	72.33	64.20	54.91	55.20	57.29	55.97	59.21	55.10	57.39	58.75	36.29	56.77	52.88	68.12
Zinc	5.29	5.61	12.18	8.09	13.15	9.31	5.56	4.94	4.74	4.77	5.73	5.60	5.02	4.67	5.41	5.54	3.23	5.05	0.86	1.11
Silver	4.77	5.06	6.32	4.20	5.96	4.22	5.26	4.67	4.37	4.39	4.98	4.87	6.72	6.25	4.79	4.90	5.31	8.31	4.08	5.26
Antimony	2.09	2.22	7.48	4.97	4.23	2.99	1.79	1.59	1.71	1.72	1.89	1.85	1.53	1.42	1.67	1.71	1.25	1.96	1.48	1.91
Wolfram	2.68	2.84	11.29	7.50	14.22	10.06	13.75	12.21	14.16	14.24	15.67	15.31	14.43	13.43	6.39	6.54	1.20	1.88	1.32	1.70
Gold	0.06	0.06	0.04	0.03	0.29	0.21	0.04	0.03	7.53	7.57	2.58	2.52	0.84	0.78	1.64	1.68	0.66	1.03	1.22	1.57
Others[6]	11.54	12.25	14.92	9.91	15.12	10.70	11.24	9.98	8.76	8.81	9.62	9.40	12.27	11.42	11.18	11.45	7.80	12.20	7.05	9.08
Hydrocarbons	-	-	-	-	-	-	-	-	-	-	-	-	-	-	-	-	-	-	-	-
Petroleum[1]		-		-		-		-		-		-		-		-		-		-
Natural gas		-		-		-		-		-		-		-		-		-		-
Propane gas		-		-		-		-		-		-		-		-		-		-
Butane gas		-		-		-		-		-		-		-		-		-		-
Others[2]		-		-		-		-		-		-		-		-		-		-
Non-Traditional Products	**4.20**	**4.46**	**5.00**	**3.32**	**3.55**	**2.51**	**2.69**	**2.39**	**3.29**	**3.31**	**4.60**	**4.49**	**7.43**	**6.91**	**9.21**	**9.43**	**8.18**	**12.80**	**8.74**	**11.26**
Fruits and almonds		-		-		-		-		-		-		-		-		-		-
Almonds and chestnut		-		-		-		-		-		-		-		-		-		-
Quinoa		-		-		-		-		-		-		-		-		-		-
Quinine		-		-		-		-		-		-		-		-		-		-
Coffee		-		-		-		-		-		-		-		-		-		-
Coca leafs		-		-		-		-		-		-		-		-		-		-
Lumber (maderas)		-		-		-		-		-		-		-		-		-		-
Sugar		-		-		-		-		-		-		-		-		-		-
Rubber		-		-		-		-		-		-		-		-		-		-
Leather products		-		-		-		-		-		-		-		-		-		-
Soja (grains, flour, cake)		-		-		-		-		-		-		-		-		-		-

Table 3a: Structure of Exports (millions of current US dollars) continued

	1950	%	1951	%	1952	%	1953	%	1954	%	1955	%	1956	%	1957	%	1958	%	1959	%
Metal-mechanic goods		-		-		-		-		-		-		-		-		-		-
Handicrafts		-		-		-		-		-		-		-		-		-		-
Chestnut (castana)		-		-		-		-		-		-		-		-		-		-
Livestock		-		-		-		-		-		-		-		-		-		-
Meat		-		-		-		-		-		-		-		-		-		-
Cotton		-		-		-		-		-		-		-		-		-		-
Textiles		-		-		-		-		-		-		-		-		-		-
Soja oil		-		-		-		-		-		-		-		-		-		-
Jewelry products		-		-		-		-		-		-		-		-		-		-
Others[3]		-		-		-		-		-		-		-		-		-		-
Total (A)	94.22	100.00	150.59	100.00	141.30	100.00	112.66	100.00	99.47	100.00	102.36	100.00	107.45	100.00	97.68	100.00	63.92	100.00	77.63	100.00
Others[4] (B)		-		-		-		-		-		-		-		-		-		-
Total CIF (A)+(B)	94.22	100.00	150.59	100.00	141.30	100.00	112.66	100.00	99.47	100.00	102.36	100.00	107.45	100.00	97.68	100.00	63.92	100.00	77.63	100.00
Adjustments ©	-		-		-		-		-		-		-		-		-		-	
Realization expenses																				
Others[5]																				
Total FOB (A)+(B)+©	94.22		150.59		141.30		112.66		99.47		102.36		107.45		97.68		63.92		77.63	

Table 3a: Structure of Exports (millions of current US dollars) continued

	1960	%	1961	%	1962	%	1963	%	1964	%	1965	%	1966	%	1967	%	1968	%	1969	%
Minerals	**59.88**	**88.27**	**68.71**	**90.24**	**70.20**	**91.47**	**80.54**	**93.20**	**107.88**	**94.74**	**124.73**	**94.61**	**131.50**	**87.39**	**131.35**	**78.97**	**138.90**	**81.43**	**167.18**	**84.35**
Tin	42.86	63.18	50.33	66.10	54.02	70.38	57.33	66.34	80.94	71.08	92.98	70.53	93.28	61.99	90.88	54.64	92.54	54.25	102.48	51.71
Zinc	1.15	1.70	1.35	1.77	0.93	1.21	1.19	1.38	3.08	2.70	4.25	3.22	4.98	3.31	4.44	2.67	2.98	1.75	7.82	3.95
Silver	4.46	6.57	3.57	4.69	3.92	5.11	5.90	6.83	6.19	5.44	5.30	4.02	6.58	4.37	6.67	4.01	11.12	6.52	10.85	5.47
Antimony	1.42	2.09	2.18	2.86	2.39	3.11	2.54	2.94	5.46	4.79	5.91	4.48	5.30	3.52	6.40	3.85	6.03	3.54	11.00	5.55
Wolfram	1.49	2.20	2.32	3.05	1.66	2.16	1.16	1.34	1.42	1.25	2.23	1.69	5.11	3.40	7.98	4.80	9.70	5.69	11.14	5.62
Gold	1.58	2.33	2.78	3.65	1.22	1.59	5.36	6.20	1.75	1.54	2.94	2.23	0.56	0.37	0.04	0.02	0.03	0.02	1.50	0.76
Others[6]	6.92	10.20	6.18	8.12	6.06	7.90	7.06	8.17	9.04	7.94	11.12	8.44	15.69	10.43	14.94	8.98	16.50	9.67	22.39	11.30
Hydrocarbons	-	-	-	-	-	-	-	-	-	-	-	-	6.54	4.35	22.85	13.74	24.26	14.22	23.01	11.61
Petroleum[1]		-		-		-		-		-		-	6.54	4.35	22.85	13.74	24.26	14.22	23.01	11.61
Natural gas		-		-		-		-		-		-		-		-		-		-
Propane gas		-		-		-		-		-		-		-		-		-		-
Butane gas		-		-		-		-		-		-		-		-		-		-
Others[2]		-		-		-		-		-		-		-		-		-		-
Non-Traditional Products	**7.96**	**11.73**	**7.43**	**9.76**	**6.55**	**8.53**	**5.88**	**6.80**	**5.99**	**5.26**	**7.10**	**5.39**	**12.43**	**8.26**	**12.13**	**7.29**	**7.42**	**4.35**	**8.01**	**4.04**
Fruits and almonds		-		-		-		-		-		-		-		-		-		-
Almonds and chestnut		-		-		-		-		-		-		-		-		-		-
Quinoa		-		-		-		-		-		-		-		-		-		-
Quinine		-		-		-		-		-		-		-		-		-		-
Coffee		-		-		-		-		-		-		-		-		-		-
Coca leafs		-		-		-		-		-		-		-		-		-		-
Lumber (maderas)		-		-		-		-		-		-		-		-		-		-
Sugar		-		-		-		-		-		-		-		-		-		-
Rubber		-		-		-		-		-		-		-		-		-		-
Leather products		-		-		-		-		-		-		-		-		-		-
Soja (grains, flour, cake)		-		-		-		-		-		-		-		-		-		-

Table 3a: Structure of Exports (millions of current US dollars) continued

	1960	%	1961	%	1962	%	1963	%	1964	%	1965	%	1966	%	1967	%	1968	%	1969	%
Metal-mechanic goods		-		-		-		-		-		-		-		-		-		-
Handicrafts		-		-		-		-		-		-		-		-		-		-
Chestnut (castana)		-		-		-		-		-		-		-		-		-		-
Livestock		-		-		-		-		-		-		-		-		-		-
Meat		-		-		-		-		-		-		-		-		-		-
Cotton		-		-		-		-		-		-		-		-		-		-
Textiles		-		-		-		-		-		-		-		-		-		-
Soja oil		-		-		-		-		-		-		-		-		-		-
Jewelry products		-		-		-		-		-		-		-		-		-		-
Others[3]		-		-		-		-		-		-		-		-		-		-
Total (A)	67.84	100.00	76.14	100.00	76.75	100.00	86.42	100.00	113.87	100.00	131.83	100.00	150.47	100.00	166.33	100.00	170.58	100.00	198.20	100.00
Others[4] (B)		-		-		-		-		-		-		-		-		-		-
Total CIF (A)+(B)	67.84	100.00	76.14	100.00	76.75	100.00	86.42	100.00	113.87	100.00	131.83	100.00	150.47	100.00	166.33	100.00	170.58	100.00	198.20	100.00
Adjustments ©	-		-		-		-		-		-		-		-		-		-	
Realization expenses																				
Others[5]																				
Total FOB (A)+(B)+©	67.84		76.14		76.75		86.42		113.87		131.83		150.47		166.33		170.58		198.20	

Table 3a: Structure of Exports (millions of current US dollars) continued

	1970	%	1971	%	1972	%	1973	%	1974	%	1975	%	1976	%	1977	%	1978	%	1979	%
Minerals	**209.92**	**93.06**	**173.33**	**80.28**	**174.15**	**71.25**	**225.91**	**66.78**	**387.28**	**59.51**	**304.49**	**58.40**	**366.92**	**58.89**	**492.48**	**68.86**	**515.63**	**71.07**	**591.88**	**69.05**
Tin	107.03	47.45	105.88	49.04	113.54	46.45	130.99	38.72	230.12	35.36	171.40	32.87	216.33	34.72	328.79	45.97	374.21	51.58	395.57	46.15
Zinc	14.32	6.35	15.27	7.07	15.44	6.32	25.96	7.67	37.66	5.79	40.33	7.73	39.14	6.28	44.70	6.25	31.53	4.35	42.69	4.98
Silver	10.51	4.66	8.34	3.86	7.59	3.11	12.56	3.71	26.83	4.12	28.54	5.47	24.32	3.90	30.80	4.31	33.76	4.65	58.27	6.80
Antimony	30.98	13.73	9.04	4.19	9.09	3.72	17.35	5.13	29.11	4.47	17.16	3.29	31.39	5.04	18.06	2.53	16.62	2.29	29.72	3.47
Wolfram	17.57	7.79	13.61	6.30	10.28	4.21	11.13	3.29	21.10	3.24	22.30	4.28	34.84	5.59	45.13	6.31	39.47	5.44	35.15	4.10
Gold	0.17	0.08	-	-	-	-	-	-	-	-	-	-	-	-	-	-	-	-	-	-
Others[6]	29.34	13.01	21.19	9.81	18.21	7.45	27.92	8.25	42.46	6.52	24.76	4.75	20.90	3.35	25.00	3.50	20.04	2.76	30.48	3.56
Hydrocarbons	**13.21**	**5.86**	**23.89**	**11.06**	**41.57**	**17.01**	**67.01**	**19.81**	**193.45**	**29.72**	**153.94**	**29.52**	**167.56**	**26.89**	**134.87**	**18.86**	**122.37**	**16.87**	**149.72**	**17.47**
Petroleum[1]	13.21	5.86	23.89	11.06	31.71	12.97	48.90	14.45	163.93	25.19	111.40	21.36	112.60	18.07	67.44	9.43	42.33	5.83	4.19	0.49
Natural gas		-	-	-	9.86	4.03	18.10	5.35	29.19	4.49	42.45	8.14	54.90	8.81	66.80	9.34	78.51	10.82	105.00	12.25
Propane gas		-	-	-	-	-	0.01	0.00	0.22	0.03	-	-	0.04	0.01	0.60	0.08	1.50	0.21	0.70	0.08
Butane gas		-	-	-	-	-	-	-	-	-	-	-	-	-	-	-	-	-	-	-
Others[2]		-	-	-	-	-	-	-	0.11	0.02	0.09	0.02	0.02	0.00	0.03	0.00	0.03	0.00	39.83	4.65
Non-Traditional Products	**2.45**	**1.09**	**18.70**	**8.66**	**28.70**	**11.74**	**45.40**	**13.42**	**70.10**	**10.77**	**63.00**	**12.08**	**88.60**	**14.22**	**87.80**	**12.28**	**87.50**	**12.06**	**115.60**	**13.49**
Fruits and almonds		-	1.20	0.56	1.30	0.53		-		-		-		-		-		-		-
Almonds and chestnut		-		-		-		-		-		-		-		-		-		-
Quinoa		-		-		-		-		-		-		-		-		-		-
Quinine		-		-		-		-		-		-		-		-		-		-
Coffee		-	3.60	1.67	4.70	1.92	5.90	1.74	4.30	0.66	7.00	1.34	13.10	2.10	17.20	2.41	16.70	2.30	19.70	2.30
Coca leafs		-		-		-		-		-		-		-		-		-		-
Lumber (maderas)		-	2.80	1.30	3.70	1.51	7.70	2.28	12.90	1.98	11.10	2.13	10.00	1.60	11.50	1.61	12.60	1.74	21.50	2.51
Sugar		-	0.90	0.42	0.50	0.20	12.40	3.67	21.90	3.36	17.40	3.34	39.70	6.37	27.10	3.79	14.20	1.96	30.80	3.59
Rubber		-	0.80	0.37	0.80	0.33	1.10	0.33	1.90	0.29	2.30	0.44	2.40	0.39	2.30	0.32	2.10	0.29	1.90	0.22
Leather products		-	0.50	0.23	-	-	-	-	0.30	0.05	0.60	0.12	2.50	0.40	3.00	0.42	5.00	0.69	7.20	0.84
Soja (grains, flour, cake)		-		-		-		-		-		-		-		-		-		-

Table 3a: Structure of Exports (millions of current US dollars) continued

	1970	%	1971	%	1972	%	1973	%	1974	%	1975	%	1976	%	1977	%	1978	%	1979	%
Metal-mechanic goods		-		-		-		-		-		-		-	1.60	0.22	1.40	0.19	4.80	0.56
Handicrafts		-	-		-	-	1.50	0.44	2.10	0.32	-	-	-	-	1.30	0.18	1.30	0.18	2.50	0.29
Chestnut (castana)		-	-	-	-	-	-	-	-	-	2.20	0.42	2.20	0.35	2.70	0.38	3.10	0.43	2.80	0.33
Livestock		-	1.80	0.83	1.80	0.74	0.70	0.21	0.30	0.05	0.80	0.15	2.10	0.34	2.20	0.31	2.70	0.37	2.90	0.34
Meat		-	1.90	0.88	2.30	0.94	3.10	0.92	0.20	0.03		-		-		-		-		-
Cotton		-	3.90	1.81	7.90	3.23	11.10	3.28	22.40	3.44	18.10	3.47	12.10	1.94	13.60	1.90	14.80	2.04	10.60	1.24
Textiles		-		-		-		-		-		-		-		-		-		-
Soja oil		-		-		-		-		-		-		-		-		-		-
Jewelry products		-		-		-		-		-		-		-		-		-		-
Others[3]		-	1.30	0.60	5.70	2.33	1.90	0.56	3.80	0.58	3.50	0.67	4.50	0.72	5.30	0.74	13.60	1.87	10.90	1.27
Total (A)	**225.58**	**100.00**	**215.92**	**100.00**	**244.42**	**100.00**	**338.32**	**100.00**	**650.83**	**100.00**	**521.43**	**100.00**	**623.08**	**100.00**	**715.15**	**100.00**	**725.50**	**100.00**	**857.20**	**100.00**
Others[4] (B)		-		-		-		-		-		-		-		-		-		-
Total CIF (A)+(B)	**225.58**	**100.00**	**215.92**	**100.00**	**244.42**	**100.00**	**338.32**	**100.00**	**650.83**	**100.00**	**521.43**	**100.00**	**623.08**	**100.00**	**715.15**	**100.00**	**725.50**	**100.00**	**857.20**	**100.00**
Adjustments ©	-		-		-		-		-		-		-		-		-		-	
Realization expenses																				
Others[5]																				
Total FOB (A)+(B)+©	**225.58**		**215.92**		**244.42**		**338.32**		**650.83**		**521.43**		**623.08**		**715.15**		**725.50**		**857.20**	

Table 3a: Structure of Exports (millions of current US dollars) continued

	1980	%	1981	%	1982	%	1983	%	1984	%	1985	%	1986	%	1987	%	1988	%	1989	%
Minerals	**641.10**	**61.88**	**556.02**	**55.86**	**419.40**	**46.69**	**347.30**	**42.48**	**364.00**	**46.54**	**263.70**	**39.21**	**196.75**	**30.85**	**207.20**	**36.38**	**273.15**	**43.90**	**403.40**	**46.55**
Tin	378.20	36.50	343.10	34.47	278.30	30.98	207.90	25.43	247.70	31.67	186.60	27.75	104.10	16.32	68.90	12.10	77.00	12.38	126.50	14.60
Zinc	36.70	3.54	40.42	4.06	38.40	4.28	33.40	4.09	37.30	4.77	29.50	4.39	28.00	4.39	32.80	5.76	60.15	9.67	132.20	15.25
Silver	118.30	11.42	71.70	7.20	37.10	4.13	58.30	7.13	21.40	2.74	10.20	1.52	27.30	4.28	33.30	5.85	45.10	7.25	58.80	6.78
Antimony	26.40	2.55	34.30	3.45	17.80	1.98	16.30	1.99	22.90	2.93	15.90	2.36	14.50	2.27	22.80	4.00	17.40	2.80	15.80	1.82
Wolfram	47.40	4.58	43.00	4.32	33.80	3.76	20.00	2.45	18.90	2.42	10.30	1.53	6.65	1.04	5.10	0.90	5.30	0.85	6.90	0.80
Gold	-	-	-	-	-	-	-	-	-	-	-	-	7.20	1.13	37.50	6.58	59.80	9.61	44.40	5.12
Others[6]	34.10	3.29	23.50	2.36	14.00	1.56	11.40	1.39	15.80	2.02	11.20	1.67	9.00	1.41	6.80	1.19	8.40	1.35	18.80	2.17
Hydrocarbons	**245.06**	**23.65**	**346.50**	**34.81**	**398.40**	**44.36**	**420.10**	**51.39**	**388.90**	**49.73**	**374.50**	**55.69**	**332.50**	**52.14**	**256.10**	**44.96**	**218.90**	**35.18**	**214.00**	**24.69**
Petroleum[1]	-	-	-	-	-	-	-	-	-	-	-	-	3.40	0.53	-	-	-	-	-	-
Natural gas	220.90	21.32	336.70	33.83	381.60	42.48	378.20	46.26	375.70	48.04	372.60	55.41	328.70	51.54	248.60	43.64	214.90	34.54	213.80	24.67
Propane gas	1.60	0.15	3.10	0.31	5.90	0.66	3.70	0.45	2.30	0.29	0.90	0.13	0.20	0.03	-	-	-	-	-	-
Butane gas	0.06	0.01	3.40	0.34	6.40	0.71	4.00	0.49	2.40	0.31	0.90	0.13	0.20	0.03	-	-	-	-	-	-
Others[2]	22.50	2.17	3.30	0.33	4.50	0.50	34.20	4.18	8.50	1.09	0.10	0.01	-	-	7.50	1.32	4.00	0.64	0.20	0.02
Non-Traditional Products	**149.90**	**14.47**	**92.80**	**9.32**	**80.40**	**8.95**	**50.10**	**6.13**	**29.20**	**3.73**	**34.30**	**5.10**	**108.50**	**17.01**	**106.30**	**18.66**	**119.30**	**19.18**	**226.86**	**26.18**
Fruits and almonds		-		-		-		-		-		-		-		-		-		-
Almonds and chestnut		-		-		-		-		-		-		-		-		-		-
Quinoa		-		-		-		-		-		-		-		-		-		-
Quinine		-		-		-		-		-		-		-		-		-		-
Coffee	20.80	2.01	15.80	1.59	15.50	1.73	12.90	1.58	6.60	0.84	13.80	2.05	13.20	2.07	11.50	2.02	16.90	2.72	12.70	1.47
Coca leafs		-		-		-		-		-		-		-		-		-		-
Lumber (maderas)	31.10	3.00	18.00	1.81	11.60	1.29	7.80	0.95	6.00	0.77	5.80	0.86	22.70	3.56	30.90	5.42	25.50	4.10	44.20	5.10
Sugar	51.20	4.94	5.70	0.57	8.10	0.90	12.30	1.50	6.60	0.84	1.80	0.27	4.80	0.75	8.60	1.51	6.30	1.01	19.30	2.23
Rubber	4.70	0.45	3.20	0.32	4.10	0.46	2.70	0.33	0.80	0.10	0.50	0.07	3.80	0.60	1.90	0.33	2.00	0.32	1.40	0.16
Leather products	4.80	0.46	5.20	0.52	3.20	0.36	0.80	0.10	0.80	0.10	1.40	0.21	6.20	0.97	8.10	1.42	19.50	3.13	17.70	2.04
Soja (grains, flour, cake)	6.10	0.59	3.50	0.35	7.40	0.82	4.50	0.55	1.50	0.19	5.30	0.79	18.70	2.93	19.20	3.37	20.20	3.25	54.30	6.27

Table 3a: Structure of Exports (millions of current US dollars) continued

	1980	%	1981	%	1982	%	1983	%	1984	%	1985	%	1986	%	1987	%	1988	%	1989	%
Metal-mechanic goods	8.80	0.85	8.00	0.80	4.90	0.55	-	-	-	-	-	-	5.80	0.91	-	-	0.10	0.02	0.50	0.06
Handicrafts	-	-	-	-	-	-	-	-	-	-	-	-	-	-	-	-	-	-	-	-
Chestnut (castana)	-	-	-	-	-	-	-	-	-	-	-	-	-	-	-	-	-	-	-	-
Livestock	-	-	-	-	-	-	-	-	-	-	-	-	-	-	-	-	-	-	-	-
Meat		-		-		-		-		-		-		-		-		-		-
Cotton	-	-	-	-	-	-	-	-	-	-	-	-	-	-	-	-	-	-	-	-
Textiles	-	-	-	-	-	-	-	-	-	-	-	-	-	-	-	-	-	-	-	-
Soja oil	-	-	-	-	-	-	-	-	-	-	-	-	-	-	-	-	-	-	-	-
Jewelry products	-	-	-	-	-	-	-	-	-	-	-	-	-	-	-	-	-	-	-	-
Others[3]	22.40	2.16	33.40	3.36	25.60	2.85	9.10	1.11	6.90	0.88	5.70	0.85	33.30	5.22	26.10	4.58	28.80	4.63	76.76	8.86
Total (A)	**1,036.06**	**100.00**	**995.32**	**100.00**	**898.20**	**100.00**	**817.50**	**100.00**	**782.10**	**100.00**	**672.50**	**100.00**	**637.75**	**100.00**	**569.60**	**100.00**	**611.35**	**98.26**	**844.26**	**97.42**
Others[4] (B)		-		-		-		-		-		-		-		-	10.80	1.74	22.40	2.58
Total CIF (A)+(B)	**1,036.06**	**100.00**	**995.32**	**100.00**	**898.20**	**100.00**	**817.50**	**100.00**	**782.10**	**100.00**	**672.50**	**100.00**	**637.75**	**100.00**	**569.60**	**100.00**	**622.15**	**100.00**	**866.66**	**100.00**
Adjustments ©	-		-		-		-		-		-		-		-		-		-	
Realization expenses																				
Others[5]																				
Total FOB (A)+(B)+©	**1,036.06**		**995.32**		**898.20**		**817.50**		**782.10**		**672.50**		**637.75**		**569.60**		**622.15**		**866.66**	

Table 3a: Structure of Exports (millions of current US dollars) continued

	1990	%	1991	%	1992	%	1993	%	1994	%	1995	%	1996	%	1997	%	1998	%	1999	%	2000	%
Minerals	**407.20**	**42.60**	**356.02**	**40.34**	**379.70**	**49.47**	**362.00**	**40.65**	**412.90**	**34.82**	**479.74**	**36.79**	**453.60**	**34.33**	**480.90**	**34.93**	**435.64**	**31.97**	**400.80**	**31.06**	**425.00**	**27.38**
Tin	106.50	11.14	99.70	11.30	107.40	13.99	83.40	9.36	91.10	7.68	88.60	6.79	85.50	6.47	81.00	5.88	64.10	4.70	69.20	5.36	76.00	4.90
Zinc	146.00	15.27	139.72	15.83	172.80	22.51	119.50	13.42	105.30	8.88	151.34	11.61	153.40	11.61	200.00	14.53	156.14	11.46	154.00	11.94	170.60	10.99
Silver	50.80	5.31	43.10	4.88	44.40	5.78	56.00	6.29	62.70	5.29	70.80	5.43	64.20	4.86	59.50	4.32	73.90	5.42	67.70	5.25	74.00	4.77
Antimony	12.80	1.34	10.30	1.17	9.30	1.21	7.80	0.88	12.90	1.09	11.70	0.90	9.30	0.70	8.70	0.63	6.20	0.46	3.60	0.28	1.60	0.10
Wolfram	4.70	0.49	7.70	0.87	5.70	0.74	1.60	0.18	2.40	0.20	4.80	0.37	3.40	0.26	2.70	0.20	2.30	0.17	1.40	0.11	1.90	0.12
Gold	64.60	6.76	39.10	4.43	21.90	2.85	76.30	8.57	119.10	10.04	130.80	10.03	119.70	9.06	110.50	8.03	111.70	8.20	89.10	6.91	88.00	5.67
Others[6]	21.80	2.28	16.40	1.86	18.20	2.37	17.40	1.95	19.40	1.64	21.70	1.66	18.10	1.37	18.50	1.34	21.30	1.56	15.80	1.22	12.90	0.83
Hydrocarbons	**227.00**	**23.75**	**241.70**	**27.39**	**126.30**	**16.45**	**96.50**	**10.84**	**98.20**	**8.28**	**141.80**	**10.87**	**133.10**	**10.07**	**97.70**	**7.10**	**87.70**	**6.44**	**64.59**	**5.01**	**165.90**	**10.69**
Petroleum[1]	-	-	6.40	0.73	1.60	0.21	6.10	0.68	6.60	0.56	48.10	3.69	38.60	2.92	28.20	2.05	30.20	2.22	26.10	2.02	36.30	2.34
Natural gas	225.30	23.57	232.60	26.36	122.80	16.00	90.20	10.13	91.60	7.72	92.40	7.09	94.50	7.15	69.30	5.03	57.40	4.21	35.70	2.77	121.80	7.85
Propane gas	-	-	-	-	-	-		-		-		-		-		-		-		-		-
Butane gas	-	-	-	-	-	-		-		-		-		-		-		-		-		-
Others[2]	1.70	0.18	2.70	0.31	1.90	0.25	0.20	0.02	-	-	1.30	0.10	-	-	0.20	0.01	0.10	0.01	2.79	0.22	7.80	0.50
Non-Traditional Products	**307.22**	**32.14**	**268.22**	**30.40**	**233.98**	**30.48**	**363.82**	**40.85**	**598.33**	**50.45**	**580.33**	**44.50**	**642.48**	**48.62**	**696.47**	**50.59**	**673.46**	**49.43**	**673.05**	**52.16**	**753.55**	**48.56**
Fruits and almonds		-		-		-		-		-		-		-		-		-		-		-
Almonds and chestnut		-		-		-		-		-		-		-		-		-		-		-
Quinoa		-		-		-		-		-		-		-		-		-		-		-
Quinine		-		-		-		-		-		-		-		-		-		-		-
Coffee	14.30	1.50	7.20	0.82	6.80	0.89	3.70	0.42	15.00	1.26	16.90	1.30	16.40	1.24	26.50	1.92	14.40	1.06	13.80	1.07	10.40	0.67
Coca leafs		-		-		-		-		-		-		-		-		-		-		-
Lumber (maderas)	49.90	5.22	48.80	5.53	49.90	6.50	52.30	5.87	82.10	6.92	72.00	5.52	78.90	5.97	73.40	5.33	51.40	3.77	32.00	2.48	28.20	1.82
Sugar	31.70	3.32	30.80	3.49	25.30	3.30	18.50	2.08	45.40	3.83	17.90	1.37	29.40	2.22	22.10	1.61	24.70	1.81	8.80	0.68	7.20	0.46
Rubber	2.00	0.21	1.00	0.11	0.70	0.09	1.30	0.15	0.10	0.01	0.10	0.01	-	-	-	-	-	-	-	-	-	-
Leather products	26.50	2.77	12.50	1.42	10.30	1.34	12.20	1.37	10.50	0.89	10.10	0.77	8.80	0.67	14.80	1.07	9.40	0.69	10.30	0.80	21.20	1.37
Soja (grains, flour, cake)	48.20	5.04	69.30	7.85	51.50	6.71	68.90	7.74	99.40	8.38	115.50	8.86	162.30	12.28	184.70	13.42	150.80	11.07	163.00	12.63	185.80	11.97

Table 3a: Structure of Exports (millions of current US dollars) continued

	1990	%	1991	%	1992	%	1993	%	1994	%	1995	%	1996	%	1997	%	1998	%	1999	%	2000	%
Metal-mechanic goods	0.40	0.04	0.50	0.06	-	-		-		-		-		-		-		-		-		-
Handicrafts	-	-	7.70	0.87	8.10	1.06	7.90	0.89	7.90	0.67	8.50	0.65	8.30	0.63	8.00	0.58	7.10	0.52	7.00	0.54	5.30	0.34
Chestnut (castana)	-	-	11.50	1.30	11.30	1.47	14.90	1.67	15.50	1.31	18.80	1.44	28.70	2.17	31.50	2.29	31.00	2.28	32.70	2.53	33.70	2.17
Livestock	-	-	14.90	1.69	-	-	0.40	0.04	4.40	0.37	-	-	-	-	40.00	2.91	1.00	0.07	0.90	0.07	-	-
Meat		-		-		-		-		-		-		-		-		-		-		-
Cotton	-	-	13.10	1.48	6.50	0.85	10.30	1.16	14.90	1.26	32.00	2.45	32.80	2.48	40.70	2.96	17.50	1.28	20.70	1.60	9.60	0.62
Textiles	-	-	6.80	0.77	6.60	0.86	8.30	0.93	12.80	1.08	13.20	1.01	15.20	1.15	13.20	0.96	16.60	1.22	15.80	1.22	20.70	1.33
Soja oil	-	-	7.40	0.84	3.90	0.51	7.30	0.82	21.80	1.84	37.40	2.87	41.50	3.14	60.00	4.36	64.30	4.72	88.80	6.88	44.00	2.84
Jewelry products	-	-	-	-	5.90	0.77	58.00	6.51	141.70	11.95	78.30	6.00	39.90	3.02	19.30	1.40	3.70	0.27	16.10	1.25	31.10	2.00
Others[3]	134.22	14.04	36.72	4.16	47.18	6.15	99.82	11.21	126.83	10.69	159.63	12.24	180.28	13.64	162.27	11.79	281.56	20.66	263.15	20.40	356.35	22.96
Total (A)	**941.42**	**98.48**	**865.94**	**98.13**	**739.98**	**96.40**	**822.32**	**92.33**	**1,109.43**	**93.55**	**1,201.87**	**92.16**	**1,229.18**	**93.02**	**1,275.07**	**92.61**	**1,196.80**	**87.84**	**1,138.44**	**88.23**	**1,344.45**	**86.63**
Others[4] (B)	**14.50**	**1.52**	**16.50**	**1.87**	**27.60**	**3.60**	**68.30**	**7.67**	**76.50**	**6.45**	**102.20**	**7.84**	**92.20**	**6.98**	**101.70**	**7.39**	**165.70**	**12.16**	**151.80**	**11.77**	**207.50**	**13.37**
Total CIF (A)+(B)	**955.92**	**100.00**	**882.44**	**100.00**	**767.58**	**100.00**	**890.62**	**100.00**	**1,185.93**	**100.00**	**1,304.07**	**100.00**	**1,321.38**	**100.00**	**1,376.77**	**100.00**	**1,362.50**	**100.00**	**1,290.24**	**100.00**	**1,551.95**	**100.00**
Adjustments ©	-		-		-		-		-		-		-		-		-		-		-	
Realization expenses																	-		-		-	
Others[5]																	-		-		-	
Total FOB (A)+(B)+©	**955.92**		**882.44**		**767.58**		**890.62**		**1,185.93**		**1,304.07**		**1,321.38**		**1,376.77**		**1,362.50**		**1,290.24**		**1,551.95**	

Table 3a: Structure of Exports (millions of current US dollars) continued

	2001	%	2002	%	2003	%	2004	%	2005	%	2006	%	2007	%	2008	%	2009	%	2010[p]	%	2011[p]	%
Minerals	**334.50**	**21.07**	**347.70**	**22.38**	**369.30**	**19.55**	**455.80**	**18.69**	**544.30**	**17.21**	**1,061.30**	**22.98**	**1,384.85**	**26.92**	**1,938.10**	**25.97**	**1,847.10**	**32.02**	**2,397.81**	**34.18**	**3,439.51**	**37.39**
Tin	56.00	3.53	57.80	3.72	73.30	3.88	145.40	5.96	124.90	3.95	144.40	3.13	214.10	4.16	281.70	3.77	233.50	4.05	353.81	5.04	460.98	5.01
Zinc	120.60	7.60	111.90	7.20	124.20	6.58	151.60	6.22	200.10	6.33	548.40	11.88	692.75	13.46	740.80	9.93	689.60	11.95	888.12	12.66	941.16	10.23
Silver	52.70	3.32	68.50	**4.41**	75.90	4.02	91.20	3.74	92.40	2.92	172.10	3.73	225.30	4.38	525.80	7.05	610.60	10.58	797.60	11.37	1,373.67	14.93
Antimony	1.80	0.11	3.30	0.21	6.30	0.33	9.20	0.38	17.90	0.57	27.10	0.59	25.90	0.50	24.60	0.33	16.40	0.28	41.93	0.60	56.74	0.62
Wolfram	4.00	0.25	1.60	0.10	2.10	0.11	2.60	0.11	7.40	0.23	16.40	0.36	22.00	0.43	22.80	0.31	17.80	0.31	21.34	0.30	19.90	0.22
Gold	86.20	5.43	89.70	5.77	71.80	3.80	33.70	1.38	77.80	2.46	126.10	2.73	123.00	2.39	142.20	1.91	116.50	2.02	95.25	1.36	272.46	2.96
Others[6]	13.20	0.83	14.90	0.96	15.70	0.83	22.10	0.91	23.80	0.75	26.80	0.58	81.80	1.59	200.20	2.68	162.70	2.82	199.76	2.85	314.60	3.42
Hydrocarbons	**289.30**	**18.23**	**330.80**	**21.30**	**490.90**	**25.99**	**838.80**	**34.40**	**1,427.50**	**45.15**	**2,043.20**	**44.25**	**2,263.30**	**43.99**	**3,519.40**	**47.16**	**2,089.20**	**36.22**	**3,014.85**	**42.98**	**4,096.54**	**44.53**
Petroleum[1]	47.30	2.98	62.30	4.01	95.80	5.07	171.50	7.03	313.70	9.92	344.80	7.47	268.00	5.21	324.30	4.35	118.70	2.06	186.64	2.66	227.56	2.47
Natural gas	236.90	14.92	265.60	17.10	389.60	20.63	619.70	25.41	1,085.80	34.34	1,669.10	36.15	1,971.20	38.31	3,159.10	42.33	1,967.60	34.11	2,797.77	39.89	3,832.75	41.66
Propane gas		-		-		-		-		-		-		-		-		-		-		-
Butane gas		-		-		-		-		-		-		-		-		-		-		-
Others[2]	5.10	0.32	2.90	0.19	5.50	0.29	47.60	1.95	28.00	0.89	29.30	0.63	24.10	0.47	36.00	0.48	2.90	0.05	30.44	0.43	36.23	0.39
Non-Traditional Products	**732.03**	**46.12**	**694.22**	**44.69**	**825.22**	**43.69**	**966.27**	**39.62**	**949.59**	**30.03**	**1,141.72**	**24.73**	**1,212.33**	**23.56**	**1,600.70**	**21.45**	**1,515.90**	**26.28**	**1,517.92**	**21.64**	**1,596.10**	**17.35**
Fruits and almonds		-		-		-		-		-		-		-		-		-		-		-
Almonds and chestnut		-		-		-		-		-		-		-		-		-		-		-
Quinoa		-		-		-		-		-		-		-		-		-		-		-
Quinine		-		-		-		-		-		-		-		-		-		-		-
Coffee	5.80	0.37	6.20	0.40	6.30	0.33	9.40	0.39	11.30	0.36	13.90	0.30	13.70	0.27	13.90	0.19	14.60	0.25	15.33	0.22	26.25	0.29
Coca leafs		-		-		-		-		-		-		-		-		-		-		-
Lumber (maderas)	24.30	1.53	23.70	1.53	26.30	1.39	32.50	1.33	39.80	1.26	58.20	1.26	68.70	1.34	73.00	0.98	64.00	1.11	95.98	1.37	73.69	0.80
Sugar	10.00	0.63	15.50	1.00	23.70	1.25	30.40	1.25	18.30	0.58	18.10	0.39	32.30	0.63	49.70	0.67	75.10	1.30	44.01	0.63	0.85	0.01
Rubber	-	-	-	-	-	-	-	-	-	-	-	-	-	-	-	-	-	-	-	-	-	-
Leather products	20.80	1.31	22.80	1.47	19.60	1.04	20.40	0.84	19.20	0.61	28.60	0.62	29.40	0.57	22.90	0.31	12.30	0.21	35.04	0.50	52.64	0.57

Table 3a: Structure of Exports (millions of current US dollars) continued

	2001	%	2002	%	2003	%	2004	%	2005	%	2006	%	2007	%	2008	%	2009	%	2010[p]	%	2011[p]	%
Soja (grains, flour, cake)	164.90	10.39	179.40	11.55	223.00	11.81	276.30	11.33	189.90	6.01	167.10	3.62	185.50	3.61	232.80	3.12	337.30	5.85	548.21	7.82	653.80	7.11
Metal-mechanic goods		-		-		-		-		-		-		-		-		-		-		-
Handicrafts	5.50	0.35	5.60	0.36	5.10	0.27	5.80	0.24	6.80	0.22	7.40	0.16	7.30	0.14	15.10	0.20	18.50	0.32		-		-
Chestnut (castana)	26.60	1.68	27.30	1.76	37.70	2.00	55.40	2.27	66.40	2.10	65.20	1.41	70.50	1.37	83.50	1.12	64.20	1.11		-		-
Livestock	-	-	-	-	-	-	-	-	-	-	-	-	-	-	-	-	-	-	-	-	-	-
Meat		-		-		-		-		-		-		-		-		-		-		-
Cotton	3.00	0.19	2.20	0.14	1.90	0.10	4.10	0.17	3.80	0.12	3.40	0.07	3.80	0.07	2.10	0.03	0.50	0.01	-	-		-
Textiles	20.00	1.26	18.90	1.22	33.70	1.78	41.10	1.69	43.20	1.37	41.90	0.91	31.50	0.61	30.50	0.41	24.80	0.43	54.88	0.78	31.59	0.34
Soja oil	56.70	3.57	64.40	4.15	91.30	4.83	110.30	4.52	73.90	2.34	69.70	1.51	91.60	1.78	106.80	1.43	143.50	2.49		-		-
Jewelry products	27.70	1.75	41.50	2.67	41.50	2.20	44.50	1.82	49.30	1.56	51.20	1.11	54.70	1.06	23.70	0.32	2.10	0.04	17.62	0.25	24.40	0.27
Others[3]	366.73	23.10	286.72	18.46	315.12	16.68	336.07	13.78	427.69	13.53	617.02	13.36	623.33	12.12	946.70	12.68	759.00	13.16	706.85	10.08	732.88	7.97
Total (A)	**1,355.83**	**85.42**	**1,372.72**	**88.37**	**1,685.42**	**89.23**	**2,260.87**	**92.71**	**2,921.39**	**92.40**	**4,246.22**	**91.96**	**4,860.48**	**94.47**	**7,058.20**	**94.57**	**5,452.20**	**94.52**	**6,930.58**	**98.81**	**9,132.15**	**99.27**
Others[4] (B)	**231.50**	**14.58**	**180.60**	**11.63**	**203.50**	**10.77**	**177.80**	**7.29**	**240.40**	**7.60**	**371.40**	**8.04**	**284.60**	**5.53**	**405.00**	**5.43**	**316.40**	**5.48**	**83.69**	**1.19**	**67.36**	**0.73**
Total CIF (A)+(B)	**1,587.33**	**100.00**	**1,553.32**	**100.00**	**1,888.92**	**100.00**	**2,438.67**	**100.00**	**3,161.79**	**100.00**	**4,617.62**	**100.00**	**5,145.08**	**100.00**	**7,463.20**	**100.00**	**5,768.60**	**100.00**	**7,014.27**	**100.00**	**9,199.51**	**100.00**
Adjustments ©	-		**-73.90**		**-87.50**		**-114.90**		**-130.30**		**-371.80**		**-402.00**		**-531.50**		**-535.10**		**-666.10**		-	
Realization expenses	-		-73,9		-84,0		-108,1		-127,8		-297,3		-398,8		-531,5		-535,1		-666,1			
Others[5]	-		-		-3,5		-6,8		-2,5		-74,5		-3,2		-		-		-			
Total FOB (A)+(B)+©	**1,587.33**		**1,479.42**		**1,801.42**		**2,323.77**		**3,031.49**		**4,245.82**		**4,743.08**		**6,931.70**		**5,233.50**		**6,348.17**		**9,199.51**	

Notes: Values in table reflect author's own estimations based on data from the National Institute of Statistics (NIS), Central Bank of Bolivia (CBB), and Customs Department.
Between 1946 and 1970, there is no disaggregated data for non-traditional exports.The figure for non-traditional exports is derived by substracting total exports from traditional exports; between 1946 and 1965, there is no reliable information on petroleum exports, hence the subcategory of hydrocarbon exports is empty during this period.

(1)Starting in 1991, this petroleum category includes diesel oil.

(2) Liquid gas (gasoline), fuel oil.

(3) It includes flowers, palmetto, alcohol, cocoa beans, wooden products, personal effects, beverages, and others.

(4) It includes re-exportation, intermediate products for transformation and reparation, certain fuels, and lubricants.

(5) Airplane leasings.

(6) Until 1985, it includes gold.

(p) preliminary estimates.

Table 4a: Yearly Exports of Minerals (thousands of current US dollars)

Year	Tin			Wolfram	Antimony	Lead	Zinc	Copper	Silver	Bismuth	Sulfur	Gold	Alloy	Others[1]	Total
	Concentrated	Metallic	Total												
1929	37,373	-	37,373	573	526	1,323	171	1,944	2,578	432	-	-	-	-	44,920
1930	26,940	-	26,940	247	137	814	453	807	2,070	103	-	-	-	-	31,571
1931	16,243	-	16,243	57	127	281	776	310	1,254	37	-	-	-	-	19,085
1932	8,085	-	8,085	56	100	144	499	165	721	2	-	-	-	-	9,772
1933	12,083	-	12,083	49	174	320	840	207	1,430	3	-	-	-	-	15,106
1934	26,657	-	26,657	492	229	555	661	219	2,034	140	-	-	-	-	30,987
1935	28,003	-	28,003	682	645	687	594	307	3,519	24	-	-	-	-	34,461
1936	24,654	-	24,654	796	1,056	1,251	998	610	4,262	138	-	-	-	-	33,765
1937	21,953	-	21,953	1,548	1,256	2,011	1,260	973	3,740	-	-	142	-	65	32,948
1938	17,344	-	17,344	1,835	1,134	951	714	551	2,446	-	-	346	-	46	25,367
1939	22,437	-	22,437	2,198	1,628	1,017	543	844	2,908	-	-	308	-	32	31,915
1940	35,514	-	35,514	3,264	2,308	1,343	1,666	1,649	2,086	-	-	412	-	22	48,264
1941	42,820	-	42,820	5,373	2,515	2,068	829	1,796	2,582	-	-	311	-	35	58,329
1942	43,933	-	43,933	7,773	3,703	1,609	1,455	1,642	3,043	-	-	206	-	49	63,413
1943	54,988	-	54,988	10,079	3,839	1,460	2,811	1,567	3,116	-	-	152	-	51	78,063
1944	53,113	-	53,113	10,064	1,581	1,166	2,177	1,598	2,946	-	-	160	-	168	72,973
1945	60,275	-	60,275	3,296	1,175	1,227	2,797	1,579	3,355	-	-	111	-	42	73,857
1946	52,000	-	52,000	1,533	2,084	1,088	2,563	1,626	4,349	-	-	96	-	56	65,395
1947	54,652	-	54,652	2,830	4,705	3,541	1,950	2,705	4,344	-	-	276	-	230	75,233
1948	80,183	-	80,183	2,896	6,233	10,093	2,814	3,124	5,477	-	-	141	-	195	111,156
1949	72,865	-	72,865	2,254	4,185	8,524	2,359	2,182	4,653	-	-	1,812	-	202	99,036
1950	63,586	-	63,586	2,681	2,091	9,190	5,288	2,159	4,769	-	-	61	-	194	90,019
1951	93,355	-	93,355	11,292	7,479	11,753	12,180	2,690	6,321	-	-	43	-	476	145,589
1952	84,783	-	84,783	14,221	4,229	11,356	13,152	2,918	5,957	-	-	288	-	850	137,754
1953	72,329	-	72,329	13,746	1,794	7,075	5,562	2,900	5,262	-	-	36	-	1,269	109,973
1954	54,913	-	54,913	14,156	1,708	5,621	4,735	2,371	4,366	-	-	7,529	-	766	96,165
1955	57,291	-	57,291	15,674	1,888	6,333	5,727	2,673	4,983	-	-	2,583	-	618	97,770
1956	59,208	-	59,208	14,425	1,529	7,594	5,019	3,956	6,721	-	-	844	-	716	100,012
1957	57,389	-	57,389	6,387	1,668	8,441	5,407	2,557	4,785	-	-	1,643	-	184	88,461

Table 4a: Yearly Exports of Minerals (thousands of current US dollars) continued

Year	Tin			Wolfram	Antimony	Lead	Zinc	Copper	Silver	Bismuth	Sulfur	Gold	Alloy	Others[1]	Total
	Concentrated	Metallic	Total												
1958	36,285	-	36,285	1,198	1,253	5,938	3,228	1,520	5,306	-	-	664	-	337	55,729
1959	52,877	-	52,877	1,319	1,482	4,954	858	1,489	4,084	-	-	1,223	-	609	68,895
1960	42,859	-	42,859	1,485	1,416	4,843	1,154	1,479	4,463	-	-	1,575	-	599	59,873
1961	50,332	-	50,332	2,317	2,175	4,122	1,346	1,272	3,567	-	-	2,784	-	789	68,704
1962	54,022	-	54,022	1,655	2,386	3,458	929	1,476	3,924	-	-	1,218	-	1,122	70,190
1963	57,331	-	57,331	1,162	2,535	4,234	1,188	1,848	5,896	-	125	5,356		852	80,527
1964	80,935	-	80,935	1,419	5,463	4,907	3,076	3,153	6,194	855	123	1,750	-	6	107,881
1965	92,983	-	92,983	2,229	5,912	5,667	4,250	3,519	5,300	1,447	189	2,943	-	298	124,737
1966	93,276	-	93,276	5,106	5,288	6,369	4,975	6,189	6,584	1,384	1,169	552	-	575	131,467
1967	90,879	-	90,879	7,971	6,411	4,922	4,441	6,401	6,669	1,849	1,480	39	-	283	131,345
1968	92,537	-	92,537	9,699	6,034	5,133	2,978	7,729	11,199	1,962	1,553	26	-	119	138,969
1969	102,477	-	102,477	11,143	10,999	6,844	7,818	10,957	10,848	2,805	1,573	1,497	-	206	167,167
1970	107,032	-	107,032	17,568	30,978	7,808	14,319	12,498	10,508	7,958	476	170	-	600	209,915
1971	82,004	23,874	105,878	13,610	9,040	5,949	15,270	8,297	8,342	5,792	310	-	-	837	173,325
1972	88,927	24,614	113,541	10,284	9,087	5,776	15,438	8,770	7,593	2,646	526	-	-	490	174,151
1973	98,667	32,326	130,993	11,128	17,353	8,347	25,963	13,440	12,561	4,378	1,155	-	-	602	225,920
1974	174,470	55,647	230,117	21,096	29,114	11,495	37,657	16,018	26,834	12,700	1,024	-	-	1,224	387,279
1975	120,019	51,379	171,398	22,298	17,159	7,706	40,332	7,263	28,542	7,528	722	-	-	1,545	304,493
1976	142,078	74,251	216,329	34,844	31,393	8,436	39,139	6,519	24,323	3,697	789	-	-	1,458	366,927
1977	192,864	135,921	328,785	45,132	18,054	12,404	44,745	4,099	30,843	5,168	356	-	-	3,082	492,668
1978	172,703	201,508	374,211	39,472	16,616	10,683	31,527	3,968	33,764	635	793	-	-	3,956	515,625
1979	167,563	228,004	395,567	35,148	29,720	17,995	42,687	3,296	58,267	287	706	-	-	8,191	591,864
1980	139,349	238,800	378,149	47,369	26,433	14,450	36,679	3,536	118,328	2,670	587	-	-	12,926	641,127
1981	77,199	265,896	343,095	42,955	34,306	11,459	40,423	4,402	71,693	9	530	-	-	7,174	556,046
1982	41,015	237,328	278,343	33,776	17,769	6,540	38,395	3,126	37,067	-	308	-	-	4,025	419,349
1983	32,442	175,464	207,906	20,008	16,317	4,007	33,372	2,978	58,264	-	162	-	-	4,302	347,316
1984	56,975	190,773	247,748	18,941	22,932	1,007	37,278	1,837	21,441	-	173	-	-	12,683	364,040
1985	52,721	133,927	186,648	10,292	15,928	537	29,486	1,709	10,192	-	266	-	-	8,700	263,758
1986	48,808	55,292	104,100	6,649	14,499	5,010	28,010	777	27,293	235	476	7,182	2,253	336	196,820

Table 4a: Yearly Exports of Minerals (thousands of current US dollars) continued

Year	Tin			Wolfram	Antimony	Lead	Zinc	Copper	Silver	Bismuth	Sulfur	Gold	Alloy	Others[1]	Total
	Concentrated	Metallic	Total												
1987	56,234	12,638	68,872	5,094	22,768	4,259	32,798	12	33,348	-	776	37,477	1,489	274	207,167
1988	33,433	43,461	76,894	5,264	17,356	5,920	60,149	142	45,057	129	599	59,755	1,248	545	273,058
1989	45,079	81,432	126,511	6,895	15,783	11,161	132,202	-	58,818	694	731	44,456	2,865	3,318	403,434
1990	23,547	82,952	106,499	4,692	12,826	15,272	145,991	1,133	50,803	797	151	64,577	1,880	2,521	407,142
1991	19,667	80,018	99,685	7,753	10,313	10,888	139,724	58	43,123	-	207	39,147	999	4,198	356,095
1992	20,363	87,059	107,422	5,737	9,292	10,923	172,781	213	44,417	-	-	21,885	596	6,404	379,670
1993	8,762	74,590	83,352	1,602	7,769	9,798	119,498	245	55,979	498	-	76,310	843	6,587	362,481
1994	7,796	83,341	91,137	2,407	12,853	12,022	105,335	155	62,665	-	-	119,056	879	5,762	412,271
1995	8,210	80,388	88,598	4,843	11,681	12,544	151,342	332	70,841	-	-	130,811	2,141	6,672	479,805
1996	12,737	72,803	85,540	3,432	9,250	10,898	153,367	220	64,213	-	-	119,658	1,359	5,631	453,568
1997	10,887	70,097	80,984	2,738	8,697	11,339	200,036	389	59,455	-	-	110,490	868	5,874	480,870
1998	7,456	56,621	64,077	2,350	6,183	9,520	156,137	78	73,901	-	-	111,749	686	10,908	435,589
1999	5,340	63,867	69,207	1,428	3,637	4,776	153,993	387	67,706	-	-	89,074	300	10,442	400,950
2000	10,293	65,702	75,995	1,916	1,616	4,529	170,589	448	74,040	-	-	87,970	429	7,828	425,360
2001	5,161	50,805	55,966	4,024	1,790	4,048	120,621	252	52,744	-	-	86,160	262	8,884	334,751
2002	9,294	48,501	57,795	1,578	3,279	4,405	111,934	204	68,472	-	-	89,652	474	9,845	347,638
2003	15,339	57,947	73,286	2,148	6,346	4,321	124,180	286	75,857	-	-	71,841	1,436	9,611	369,312
2004	30,742	114,610	145,352	2,554	9,246	9,313	151,643	354	91,224	-	-	33,692	2,050	10,343	455,771
2005	23,855	101,043	124,898	7,427	17,936	10,752	200,148	131	92,361	-	-	77,773	1,283	11,595	544,304
2006	27,918	116,505	144,423	16,388	27,150	14,703	548,427	1,271	172,131	-	-	126,122	1,748	9,053	1,061,416
2007	37,871	176,266	214,137	21,983	25,941	60,958	692,748	4,678	225,256	-	-	123,007	3,344	12,814	1,384,866
2008	55,295	226,401	281,696	22,796	24,619	170,255	740,753	5,527	525,763	-	-	142,203	9,734	14,704	1,938,050
2009	31,529	202,008	233,537	17,829	16,401	138,676	689,635	3,700	610,593	-	-	116,456	3,643	16,714	1,847,184
2010[p]	60,625	293,180	353,805	21,336	10,300	156,760	888,120	8,750	684,180	-	-	95,250	3,241	199,760	2,421,502
2011[p]	68,460	392,520	460,980	19,900	6,450	240,620	941,160	11,170	1,081,910	-	-	272,460	-	314,600	3,349,250

Notes: Values in table reflect author's own estimations based on data from the National Institute of Statistics (NIS), Customs Department, and Ministry of Mining.
(1) It includes salt, plaster (yeso), cadmium, iron, ulexite, calcite, manganese, barite, tantalite, and other non-traditional minerals; from 1972 and before, it also includes gold and alloy.
(p) Preliminary estimates.

Table 5a: Yearly Exports of Hydrocarbons (thousands of current US dollars)

Year	Petroleum		Gasoline and others		Natural Gas		Propane Gas		Butane Gas		Total Value
	Volume (000s of barrels)	Dollar value	Volume (000s of barrels)	Dollar value	Volume (millions of M^3)	Dollar value	Volume (MT)	Dollar Value	Volume (MT)	Dollar Value	
1940		9.00									9.00
1941		52.00									52.00
1942		86.00									86.00
1943		99.00									99.00
1944		140.00									140.00
1945		141.00									141.00
1966		6,538.00	-	-	-	-	-	-	-	-	6,538.00
1967		22,853.20	-	-	-	-	-	-	-	-	22,853.20
1968		24,262.00	-	-	-	-	-	-	-	-	24,262.00
1969		23,011.60	-	-	-	-	-	-	-	-	23,011.60
1970		13,209.70	-	-	-	-	-	-	-	-	13,209.70
1971	8,447.20	23,892.20	-	-	-	-	-	-	-	-	23,892.20
1972	10,944.80	31,711.90	-	-	1,005.10	9,863.80	-	-	-	-	41,575.70
1973	11,844.10	48,860.60	-	-	1,570.20	18,101.20	90.00	4.50	-	-	66,966.30
1974	10,798.40	163,928.20	5.70	112.80	1,546.10	29,188.20	395.00	22.30	-	-	193,251.50
1975	8,282.60	111,428.80	4.60	89.60	1,556.70	42,453.30	-	-	-	-	153,971.70
1976	8,064.90	112,571.20	1.30	25.00	1,571.20	54,896.30	199.60	30.90	-	-	167,523.40
1977	4,489.40	67,442.40	1.70	31.30	1,639.10	66,802.60	3,873.00	600.90	-	-	134,877.20
1978	2,862.80	42,325.40	1.90	34.30	1,581.40	78,505.80	9,868.00	1,461.70	-	-	122,327.20
1979	182.20	4,190.80	1,181.20	39,825.60	1,726.40	104,981.60	3,107.00	670.10	-	-	149,668.10
1980	-	-	651.10	22,574.40	2,039.70	220,869.40	5,887.50	1,630.20	195.80	55.80	245,129.80
1981	-	-	89.20	3,318.70	2,195.70	336,664.90	10,067.10	3,090.50	9,724.10	3,419.60	346,493.70
1982	-	-	164.10	4,495.70	2,296.90	381,625.80	19,061.60	5,856.20	19,061.60	6,430.90	398,408.60
1983	1,039.10	29,303.90	154.60	4,888.00	2,227.10	378,154.50	11,618.40	3,732.80	11,618.40	3,981.00	420,060.20
1984	310.00	8,370.00	5.50	99.00	2,210.30	375,720.40	7,682.00	2,281.20	7,682.00	2,436.00	388,906.60
1985	-	-	4.00	71.40	2,216.10	372,573.80	3,524.90	925.10	3,524.90	941.20	374,511.50
1986	270.00	3,375.00	-	-	2,214.60	328,667.60	1,066.80	238.00	1,066.80	238.00	332,518.60

Table 5a: Yearly Exports of Hydrocarbons (thousands of current US dollars) continued

Year	Petroleum		Gasoline and others		Natural Gas		Propane Gas		Butane Gas		Total Value
	Volume (000s of barrels)	Dollar value	Volume (000s of barrels)	Dollar value	Volume (millions of M^3)	Dollar value	Volume (MT)	Dollar Value	Volume (MT)	Dollar Value	
1987	50.00	810.00	330.00	6,683.00	2,119.90	248,566.00	-	-	-	-	256,059.00
1988	-	-	208.90	3,975.90	2,228.50	214,948.30	-	-	-	-	218,924.20
1989	-	-	7.00	214.00	2,209.70	213,787.50	-	-	-	-	214,001.50
1990	-	-	-	1,669.20	2,202.90	225,270.50	-	-	-	-	226,939.70
1991	397.60	6,373.70	-	2,208.30	2,177.70	232,627.20	-	-	-	-	241,209.20
1992	125.60	1,584.70	-	1,856.30	2,125.70	122,811.00	-	-	-	-	126,252.00
1993	467.10	6,054.70	-	238.00	2,091.70	90,203.00	-	-	-	-	96,495.70
1994	499.70	6,576.60	-	-	2,167.70	91,621.70	-	-	-	-	98,198.30
1995	2,973.20	48,109.00	36.90	1,289.70	2,052.60	92,407.50	-	-	-	-	141,806.20
1996	1,446.00	38,617.00	-	-	2,055.00	94,538.90	-	-	-	-	133,155.90
1997	1,444.00	28,241.00	16.00	222.30	1,627.90	69,300.00	-	-	-	-	97,763.30
1998	2,225.00	30,182.00	6.70	147.00	1,632.90	57,365.00	-	-	-	-	87,694.00
1999	1,678.50	26,088.50	7.10	3,010.90	1,035.10	35,691.50	-	-	-	-	64,790.90
2000	1,195.40	36,255.40	39.70	7,760.30	2,116.30	121,775.10	-	-	-	-	165,790.80
2001	1,606.20	47,338.90	34.80	5,089.80	3,882.60	236,894.10	-	-	-	-	289,322.80
2002	2,198.60	62,337.40	103.50	2,940.40	4,912.30	265,567.00	-	-	-	-	330,844.80
2003	2,912.90	95,815.80	134.10	5,486.30	5,549.40	389,562.10	-	-	-	-	490,864.20
2004	3,829.30	171,494.30	1,112.00	47,640.20	8,414.10	619,720.10	-	-	-	-	838,854.60
2005	4,870.00	313,702.70	451.10	28,042.60	10,392.60	1,085,757.40	-	-	-	-	1,427,502.70
2006	4,676.50	344,758.60	400.90	29,301.70	11,179.90	1,669,102.90	-	-	-	-	2,043,163.20
2007	3,205.90	267,950.50	320.90	24,065.30	11,866.00	1,971,238.50	-	-	-	-	2,263,254.30
2008	2,854.40	324,291.50	321.30	35,959.20	12,089.80	3,159,086.00	-	-	-	-	3,519,336.70
2009	1,657.00	118,720.60	37.80	2,926.70	9,604.80	1,967,574.10	-	-	-	-	2,089,221.40
2010p	1,527.90	186,640.00	29.00	30,440.00	11,588.60	2,797,774.10	-	-	-	-	3,014,854.10
2011p		227,560.00		36,230.00		3,832,750.00	-	-	-	-	4,096,540.00

Notes: Values in table reflect author's own estimations based on data from the National Institute of Statistics (NIS), Central Bank of Bolivia (CBB), and Customs Department.
(p) Preliminary estimates.

Table 6a: Exports of Non-Traditional Products (thousands of current US dollars)

Year	Sugar	Fruits and Almonds	Almonds and Chestnut	Quinoa	Quinine	Coca leafs	Meat	Cotton	Coffee	Chestnut	Leather	Livestock	Rubber	Lumber (maderas)	handicrafts	Metal mechanic products	Jewelry	Soybeans[1]	Soybean oil[3]	Other[2]	TOTAL
1929	-	-	80.00	70.00	-	390.00	-	-	-	-	310.00	240.00	1,050.00	-	-	-	-	-	-	3,930.00	6,070.00
1930	-	-	180.00	140.00	-	400.00	-	-	-	-	220.00	340.00	620.00	-	-	-	-	-	-	3,080.00	4,980.00
1931	-	-	80.00	90.00	-	340.00	-	-	-	-	160.00	90.00	240.00	-	-	-	-	-	-	260.00	1,260.00
1932	-	-	120.00	80.00	-	180.00	-	-	-	-	90.00	30.00	70.00	-	-	-	-	-	-	320.00	890.00
1933	-	-	130.00	80.00	-	120.00	-	-	-	-	110.00	30.00	250.00	-	-	-	-	-	-	610.00	1,330.00
1934	-	-	210.00	180.00	-	140.00	-	-	-	-	180.00	50.00	140.00	-	-	-	-	-	-	4,870.00	5,770.00
1935	-	-	180.00	240.00	-	300.00	-	-	-	-	330.00	80.00	130.00	-	-	-	-	-	-	210.00	1,470.00
1936	-	-	570.00	340.00	-	530.00	-	-	-	-	660.00	160.00	870.00	-	-	-	-	-	-	390.00	3,520.00
1937	-	-	630.00	410.00	-	380.00	-	-	-	-	540.00	180.00	550.00	-	-	-	-	-	-	1,800.00	4,490.00
1938	-	-	640.00	380.00	-	370.00	-	-	-	-	250.00	450.00	290.00	-	-	-	-	-	-	750.00	3,130.00
1939	-	-	420.00	330.00	-	270.00	-	-	-	-	240.00	230.00	370.00	-	-	-	-	-	-	900.00	2,760.00
1940	-	-	320.00	320.00	-	230.00	-	-	-	-	170.00	20.00	390.00	6.00	-	-	-	-	-	4.00	1,460.00
1941	-	-	440.00	220.00	3.00	210.00	-	-	-	-	210.00	450.00	660.00	61.00	-	-	-	-	-	32.00	2,286.00
1942	-	-	190.00	120.00	46.00	230.00	-	-	-	-	250.00	90.00	1,300.00	10.00	-	-	-	-	-	2.70	2,238.70
1943	-	-	0.88	410.00	120.00	190.00	-	-	-	-	180.00	100.00	2,020.00	20.00	-	-	-	-	-	4,000.00	7,040.88
1944	-	-	-	360.00	280.00	250.00	-	-	-	-	180.00	200.00	2,910.00	38.00	-	-	-	-	-	4,710.00	8,928.00
1945	-	-	-	340.00	290.00	320.00	-	-	-	-	270.00	110.00	3,690.00	30.00	-	-	-	-	-	1,390.00	6,440.00
1971	900.00	1,200.00	-	-	-	-	1,900.00	3,900.00	3,600.00	-	500.00	1,800.00	800.00	2,800.00	-	-	-	-	-	1,300.00	18,700.00
1972	500.00	1,300.00	-	-	-	-	2,300.00	7,900.00	4,700.00		-	1,800.00	800.00	3,700.00	-		-	-	-	5,700.00	28,700.00
1973	12,400.00	-	-	-	-	-	3,100.00	11,100.00	5,900.00	-	-	700.00	1,100.00	7,700.00	1,500.00	-	-	-	-	1,900.00	45,400.00
1974	21,900.00	-	-	-	-	-	200.00	22,400.00	4,300.00	-	300.00	300.00	1,900.00	12,900.00	2,100.00	-	-	-	-	3,800.00	70,100.00
1975	17,400.00	-	-	-	-	-	-	18,100.00	7,000.00	2,200.00	600.00	800.00	2,300.00	11,100.00	-	-	-	-	-	3,500.00	63,000.00
1976	39,700.00	-	-	-	-	-	-	12,100.00	13,100.00	2,200.00	2,500.00	2,100.00	2,400.00	10,000.00	-	-	-	-	-	4,500.00	88,600.00
1977	27,100.00	-	-	-	-	-	-	13,600.00	17,200.00	2,700.00	3,000.00	2,200.00	2,300.00	11,500.00	1,300.00	1,600.00	-	-	-	5,300.00	87,800.00
1978	14,200.00	-	-	-	-	-	-	14,800.00	16,700.00	3,100.00	5,000.00	2,700.00	2,100.00	12,600.00	1,300.00	1,400.00	-	-	-	13,600.00	87,500.00
1979	30,820.00	-	-	-	-	-	-	-	19,698.00	2,820.00	7,228.00	2,902.00	1,903.00	21,651.00	2,527.00	4,783.00	-	-	-	21,335.90	115,667.90
1980	51,226.00	-	-	-	-	-	-	-	20,794.00	2,862.00	4,854.00	1,279.00	4,700.00	31,080.00	4,204.00	8,814.00	-	6,102.00	-	13,888.20	149,803.20
1981	5,683.00	-	-	-	-	-	-	-	15,825.00	2,541.00	5,155.00	917.00	3,240.00	17,986.00	4,768.00	7,989.00	-	3,562.00	-	25,114.30	92,780.30
1982	8,068.00	-	-	-	-	-	-	-	15,520.00	2,243.00	3,176.00	588.00	4,150.00	11,604.00	1,068.00	4,925.00	-	7,444.00	-	21,656.40	80,442.40
1983	12,291.00	-	-	-	-	-	-	-	12,922.00	1,756.00	816.00	1,249.00	2,709.00	7,760.00	628.00	-	-	4,550.00	-	5,442.80	50,123.80
1984	6,649.00	-	-	-	-	-	-	-	6,570.00	2,322.00	764.00	1,536.00	753.00	5,975.00	145.00	-	-	1,527.00	-	2,912.40	29,153.40
1985	1,765.00	-	-	-	-	-	-	-	13,780.00	1,437.00	1,415.00	1,166.00	510.00	5,822.00	298.00	-	-	5,309.00	-	2,728.50	34,230.50
1986	4,853.00	-	-	-	-	-	-	-	13,231.00	3,465.00	6,191.00	13,427.00	3,757.00	22,656.00	4,850.00	5,843.00	-	18,741.00	-	11,397.40	108,411.40
1987	8,565.00	-	-	-	-	-	-	-	11,522.00	6,655.00	8,119.00	6,754.00	1,850.00	30,882.00	1,010.00	17.00	-	19,204.00	-	11,796.00	106,374.00
1988	6,292.00	-	-	-	-	-	-	-	16,911.00	5,559.00	19,543.00	514.00	2,023.00	25,496.00	2,142.00	65.00	-	20,233.00	-	20,589.80	119,367.80
1989	19,287.00	-	-	-	-	-	-	-	12,699.00	11,101.00	17,679.00	6,179.00	1,361.00	44,186.00	4,265.00	459.00	-	54,280.00	-	55,328.50	226,824.50
1990	31,710.00	-	-	-	-	-	-	-	14,309.00	15,630.00	27,008.00	49,449.00	1,973.00	50,105.00	5,190.00	413.00	-	48,168.00	-	63,383.30	307,338.30
1991	30,807.00	-	-	-	-	-	-	-	7,155.00	11,502.00	12,453.00	14,939.00	1,039.00	48,778.00	7,736.00	519.00	-	69,324.00	-	64,383.80	268,635.80
1992	25,261.00	-	-	-	-	-	-	-	6,841.00	11,321.00	10,319.00	-	686.00	49,892.00	8,148.00	-	-	51,503.00	-	70,087.00	234,058.00

Table 6a: Exports of Non-Traditional Products (thousands of current US dollars) continued

Year	Sugar	Fruits and Almonds	Almonds and Chestnut	Quinoa	Quinine	Coca leafs	Meat	Cotton	Coffee	Chestnut	Leather	Livestock	Rubber	Lumber (maderas)	handicrafts	Metal mechanic products	Jewelry	Soybeans[1]	Soybean oil[3]	Other[2]	TOTAL
1993	18,486.00	-	-	-	-	-	-	-	3,693.00	14,881.00	12,214.00	418.00	1,334.00	52,269.00	7,891.00	-	-	68,917.00	-	183,240.30	363,343.30
1994	45,415.00	-	-	-	-	-	-	-	15,021.00	15,506.00	10,489.00	4,390.00	97.00	82,148.00	7,868.00	-	-	99,387.00	-	318,639.70	598,960.70
1995	17,901.00	-	-	-	-	-	-	-	16,869.00	18,766.00	10,114.00	402.00	136.00	71,955.00	8,476.00	-	-	115,493.00	-	320,146.80	580,258.80
1996	29,398.00	-	-	-	-	-	-	-	16,448.00	28,726.00	8,837.00	515.00	9.00	78,894.00	8,259.00	-	-	162,251.00	-	309,119.10	642,456.10
1997	22,054.00	-	-	-	-	-	-	-	26,528.00	31,532.00	14,804.00	156.00	-	73,374.00	7,999.00	-	19,273.00	184,684.00	-	316,032.70	696,436.70
1998	24,710.00	-	-	-	-	-	-	-	14,435.00	31,023.00	9,366.00	1,477.00	-	51,395.00	7,052.00	-	3,705.00	150,785.00	-	379,569.00	673,517.00
1999	8,834.00	-	-	-	-	-	-	-	13,775.00	32,706.00	10,250.00	890.00	-	32,045.00	6,957.00	-	16,109.00	162,968.00	-	388,165.10	672,699.10
2000	7,221.00	-	-	-	-	-	-	-	10,337.00	33,732.00	21,248.00	-	-	28,218.00	5,309.00	-	31,104.00	185,819.00	43,980.00	386,331.20	753,299.20
2001	9,988.00	-	-	-	-	-	-	-	5,823.00	26,562.00	20,711.00	-	-	24,287.00	5,547.00	-	27,671.00	164,917.00	56,721.00	389,528.90	731,755.90
2002	15,462.00	-	-	-	-	-	-	-	6,166.00	27,312.00	22,769.00	-	-	23,733.00	5,589.00	-	41,456.00	179,399.00	64,433.00	307,918.20	694,237.20
2003	23,669.00	-	-	-	-	-	-	-	6,340.00	37,675.00	19,616.00	-	-	26,310.00	5,126.00	-	41,512.00	223,047.00	91,262.00	350,686.80	825,243.80
2004	30,431.00	-	-	-	-	-	-	-	9,352.00	55,446.00	20,437.00	-	-	32,535.00	5,800.00	-	44,537.00	276,310.00	110,293.00	381,103.40	966,244.40
2005	18,276.00	-	-	-	-	-	-	-	11,276.00	66,357.00	19,183.00	-	-	39,775.00	6,842.00	-	49,274.00	189,914.00	73,888.00	474,798.30	949,583.30
2006	18,093.00	-	-	-	-	-	-	-	13,938.00	65,240.00	28,553.00	-	-	58,197.00	7,408.00	-	51,167.00	167,098.00	69,662.00	662,284.80	1,141,640.80
2007	32,325.00	-	-	-	-	-	-	-	13,744.00	70,466.00	29,366.00	-		68,745.00	7,318.00	-	54,681.00	185,513.00	91,615.00	658,586.70	1,212,359.70
2008	49,744.00	-	-	-	-	-	-	-	13,914.00	83,530.00	22,881.00	-	-	72,958.00	15,099.00	-	23,746.00	232,841.00	106,780.00	979,320.30	1,600,813.30
2009	75,096.00	-	-	-	-	-	-	-	14,628.00	64,243.00	12,342.00	-	-	64,047.00	18,567.00	-	2,101.00	337,310.00	143,485.00	783,975.60	1,515,794.60
2010p	41,099.00	-	-	-	-	-	-	-	15,325.00	91,806.00	25,554.00	-	-	69,967.00	13,394.00	-	17,620.00	317,369.00	178,610.00	747,179.90	1,517,923.90
2011p	850.00	-	-	-	-	-	-	-	26,250.00	-	52,640.00	-	-	73,690.00	-	-	24,400.00	392,280.00	261,520.00	764,430.00	1,596,060.00

Notes: Values in table reflect author's own estimations based on data from the CBB, NIS, and Customs Department.
(1) It includes grains, flour, and cake.
(2) It includes flowers, cotton, alcohol, cocoa, wooden products, personal effects, beverages, and others.
(3) Until 1999 this category included soja oil, sunflower oil, and oil from other oleaginous. Since 2000, it only includes soja oil.
(p) Preliminary estimates.

Table 7a: Structure of Imports (millions of current US dollars)

Type of good	1962	%	1963	%	1964	%	1965	%	1966	%	1967	%	1968	%	1969	%	1970	%	1971	%	1972	%
Consumer goods	**27.29**	**28.15**	**27.99**	**27.10**	**27.46**	**26.74**	**33.47**	**25.01**	**34.70**	**25.07**	**35.56**	**23.56**	**31.28**	**20.33**	**32.44**	**19.66**	**32.30**	**20.29**	**34.20**	**20.17**	**34.80**	**20.12**
Perishable	17.76	18.32	18.50	17.91	17.54	17.08	20.07	14.99	20.80	15.03	21.23	14.06	18.93	12.30	21.28	12.89	22.50	14.13	24.70	14.56	26.60	15.38
Non-perishable	9.53	9.83	9.49	9.19	9.92	9.66	13.40	10.01	13.90	10.04	14.33	9.49	12.35	8.03	11.16	6.76	9.80	6.16	9.50	5.60	8.20	4.74
Intermediate goods	**44.81**	**46.23**	**45.03**	**43.60**	**46.72**	**45.49**	**56.89**	**42.50**	**56.02**	**40.47**	**64.66**	**42.83**	**61.90**	**40.24**	**63.66**	**38.57**	**68.70**	**43.15**	**79.60**	**46.93**	**65.70**	**37.98**
Fuels and oil lubricants	3.07	3.17	1.39	1.35	1.32	1.29	1.23	0.92	1.59	1.15	1.17	0.78	1.57	1.02	1.43	0.87	1.10	0.69	1.20	0.71	1.70	0.98
For agricultural purposes	0.56	0.58	0.42	0.41	0.71	0.69	0.87	0.65	1.09	0.79	1.89	1.25	1.63	1.06	1.88	1.14	2.40	1.51	2.10	1.24	2.10	1.21
For industry purposes	37.22	38.40	38.87	37.64	40.43	39.36	43.57	32.55	44.67	32.27	52.92	35.06	46.68	30.34	45.98	27.86	56.40	35.43	60.90	35.91	47.40	27.40
For construction purposes	3.96	4.09	4.35	4.21	4.26	4.15	11.22	8.38	8.67	6.26	8.68	5.75	12.02	7.81	14.37	8.71	8.80	5.53	15.40	9.08	14.50	8.38
Parts and accessories for transport equipment[1]	-	-	-	-	-	-	-	-	-	-	-	-	-	-	-	-	-	-	-	-	-	-
Capital goods	**24.58**	**25.36**	**29.43**	**28.50**	**28.01**	**27.27**	**43.16**	**32.25**	**47.19**	**34.09**	**50.00**	**33.12**	**59.87**	**38.92**	**68.37**	**41.43**	**57.40**	**36.06**	**55.60**	**32.78**	**70.40**	**40.69**
For agricultural purposes	0.45	0.46	0.63	0.61	1.72	1.67	3.06	2.29	1.54	1.11	2.67	1.77	4.64	3.02	3.40	2.06	3.20	2.01	2.90	1.71	4.20	2.43
For industry purposes	15.81	16.31	15.82	15.32	15.12	14.72	24.09	18.00	27.17	19.63	26.83	17.77	34.11	22.17	32.05	19.42	26.40	16.58	31.30	18.46	31.70	18.32
Transport equipment	8.32	8.58	12.98	12.57	11.17	10.88	16.01	11.96	18.48	13.35	20.50	13.58	21.12	13.73	32.92	19.95	27.80	17.46	21.40	12.62	34.50	19.94
Diverse goods	**0.25**	**0.26**	**0.82**	**0.79**	**0.52**	**0.51**	**0.33**	**0.25**	**0.52**	**0.38**	**0.74**	**0.49**	**0.79**	**0.51**	0.57	0.35	0.80	0.50	0.20	0.12	2.10	1.21
Personal effect goods	-	-	-	-	-	-	-	-	-	-	-	-	-	-	-	-	-	-	-	-	-	-
CIF Total Value	**96.93**	**100.00**	**103.27**	**100.00**	**102.71**	**100.00**	**133.85**	**100.00**	**138.43**	**100.00**	**150.96**	**100.00**	**153.84**	**100.00**	**165.04**	**100.00**	**159.20**	**100.00**	**169.60**	**100.00**	**173.00**	**100.00**
Adjustments[2]																	-		**0.10**		**12.40**	
Adjusted CIF Total Value	**96.93**		**103.27**		**102.71**		**133.85**		**138.43**		**150.96**		**153.84**		**165.04**		**159.20**		**169.70**		**185.40**	
Deduction for shipping, insurance, and other expenses																	-24,00		-25,20		-32,30	
Compensation for contraband																	31.00		37.00		42.60	
FOB Total Value	**96.93**		**103.27**		**102.71**		**133.85**		**138.43**		**150.96**		**153.84**		**165.04**		**166.20**		**181.50**		**195.70**	

Table 7a: Structure of Imports (millions of current US dollars) continued

Type of good	1973	%	1974	%	1975	%	1976	%	1977	%	1978	%	1979	%	1980	%	1981	%	1982	%	1983	%
Consumer goods	**40.80**	**20.02**	**90.40**	**23.18**	**127.80**	**22.91**	**118.70**	**21.40**	**126.70**	**20.50**	**160.90**	**20.70**	**170.50**	**19.80**	**168.90**	**25.38**	**233.60**	**25.47**	**96.00**	**17.33**	**65.60**	**11.38**
Perishable	31.00	15.21	52.70	13.51	67.50	12.10	62.70	11.31	64.90	10.50	97.90	12.60	92.10	10.70	104.60	15.72	115.90	12.64	56.80	10.25	46.40	8.05
Non-perishable	9.80	4.81	37.70	9.67	60.30	10.81	56.00	10.10	61.80	10.00	63.00	8.11	78.40	9.11	64.30	9.66	117.70	12.83	39.20	7.07	19.20	3.33
Intermediate goods	**78.00**	**38.27**	**139.40**	**35.74**	**223.80**	**40.11**	**221.30**	**39.90**	**248.40**	**40.20**	**251.80**	**32.40**	**309.10**	**35.90**	**250.50**	**37.65**	**341.90**	**37.28**	**248.40**	**44.83**	**282.30**	**48.95**
Fuels and oil lubricants	2.00	0.98	4.00	1.03	7.20	1.29	6.10	1.10	6.20	1.00	7.00	0.90	12.00	1.39	1.70	0.26	13.90	1.52	9.00	1.62	4.10	0.71
For agricultural purposes	2.40	1.18	12.30	3.15	21.20	3.80	18.90	3.41	21.60	3.50	8.50	1.09	11.20	1.30	11.20	1.68	14.70	1.60	7.30	1.32	11.20	1.94
For industry purposes	56.70	27.82	103.30	26.49	170.80	30.61	170.80	30.80	191.50	30.99	195.90	25.21	224.70	26.10	205.60	30.90	264.00	28.79	196.60	35.48	223.70	38.79
For construction purposes	16.90	8.29	19.80	5.08	24.60	4.41	25.50	4.60	29.10	4.71	40.40	5.20	61.20	7.11	32.00	4.81	49.30	5.38	35.50	6.41	43.30	7.51
Parts and accessories for transport equipment[1]	-	-	-	-	-	-	-	-	-	-	-	-		-	-	-	-	-	-	-	-	-
Capital goods	**83.00**	**40.73**	**157.40**	**40.36**	**199.10**	**35.69**	**210.20**	**37.90**	**238.50**	**38.60**	**351.30**	**45.20**	**377.90**	**43.90**	**242.50**	**36.44**	**334.80**	**36.51**	**198.60**	**35.84**	**222.20**	**38.53**
For agricultural purposes	4.90	2.40	6.00	1.54	7.20	1.29	8.30	1.50	9.90	1.60	15.60	2.01	18.90	2.20	13.60	2.04	20.40	2.22	5.10	0.92	7.30	1.27
For industry purposes	36.90	18.11	70.40	18.05	92.60	16.60	98.20	17.71	111.20	18.00	219.90	28.29	227.30	26.40	148.00	22.24	195.30	21.30	138.90	25.07	156.30	27.10
Transport equipment	41.20	20.22	81.00	20.77	99.30	17.80	103.70	18.70	117.40	19.00	115.80	14.90	131.70	15.30	80.90	12.16	119.10	12.99	54.60	9.85	58.60	10.16
Diverse goods	**2.00**	**0.98**	**2.80**	**0.72**	**7.20**	**1.29**	**4.40**	**0.79**	**4.30**	**0.70**	**13.20**	**1.70**	**3.40**	**0.39**	**3.50**	**0.53**	**6.80**	**0.74**	**11.10**	**2.00**	**6.60**	**1.14**
Personal effect goods	-	-	-	-	-	-	-	-	-	-	-	-	-	-	-	-	-	-		-		-
CIF Total Value	**203.80**	**100.00**	**390.00**	**100.00**	**557.90**	**100.00**	**554.60**	**100.00**	**617.90**	**100.00**	**777.20**	**100.00**	**860.90**	**100.00**	**665.40**	**100.00**	**917.10**	**100.00**	**554.10**	**100.00**	**576.70**	**100.00**
Adjustments[2]	**25.60**						**33.00**		**48.00**		-		-		**13.00**		**58.30**		**23.40**		**12.40**	
Adjusted CIF Total Value	**229.40**		**390.00**		**557.90**		**587.60**		**665.90**		**777.20**		**860.90**		**678.40**		**975.40**		**577.50**		**589.10**	
Deduction for shipping, insurance, and other expenses	-36,10		-66,00		-88,00		-75,30		-86,90		-113,10		-119,20		-104,00		-147,70		-81,50		-93,1	
Compensation for contraband	42.00		40.00		45.00		50.00		65.00													
FOB Total Value	**235.30**		**364.00**		**514.90**		**562.30**		**644.00**		**664.10**		**741.70**		**574.40**		**827.70**		**496.00**		**496.00**	

Table 7a: Structure of Imports (millions of current US dollars) continued

Type of good	1984	%	1985	%	1986	%	1987	%	1988	%	1989	%	1990	%	1991	%	1992	%	1993	%	1994	%
Consumer goods	**94.90**	**19.43**	**133.80**	**19.37**	**133.70**	**19.84**	**190.30**	**24.83**	**128.30**	**21.73**	**137.50**	**22.50**	**152.90**	**22.25**	**206.00**	**21.25**	**204.80**	**18.78**	**224.10**	**19.04**	**282.40**	**23.61**
Perishable	42.00	8.60	46.10	6.67	61.90	9.18	92.80	12.11	57.40	9.72	70.20	11.49	63.30	9.21	96.30	9.93	88.90	8.15	109.60	9.31	133.90	11.19
Non-perishable	52.90	10.83	87.70	12.69	71.80	10.65	97.50	12.72	70.90	12.01	67.30	11.01	89.60	13.04	109.70	11.32	115.90	10.63	114.50	9.73	148.50	12.41
Intermediate goods	**203.10**	**41.58**	**278.80**	**40.35**	**235.30**	**34.91**	**306.50**	**40.00**	**251.60**	**42.61**	**274.80**	**44.98**	**272.50**	**39.65**	**370.70**	**38.24**	**415.60**	**38.12**	**478.00**	**40.61**	**512.10**	**42.81**
Fuels and oil lubricants	1.50	0.31	2.40	0.35	2.70	0.40	2.00	0.26	4.80	0.81	2.60	0.43	3.50	0.51	7.80	0.80	12.00	1.10	51.70	4.39	57.40	4.80
For agricultural purposes	17.50	3.58	18.40	2.66	15.80	2.34	11.20	1.46	8.30	1.41	9.70	1.59	10.90	1.59	21.80	2.25	13.10	1.20	18.10	1.54	15.90	1.33
For industry purposes	152.40	31.20	231.70	33.54	183.20	27.18	256.10	33.42	185.70	31.45	199.30	32.62	194.10	28.25	263.40	27.17	307.30	28.18	321.90	27.35	350.70	29.32
For construction purposes	31.70	6.49	26.30	3.81	33.60	4.99	37.20	4.85	29.50	5.00	37.40	6.12	45.00	6.55	58.20	6.00	52.30	4.80	51.20	4.35	48.90	4.09
Parts and accessories for transport equipment[1]	-	-	-	-	-	-		-	23.30	3.95	25.80	4.22	19.00	2.76	19.50	2.01	30.90	2.83	35.10	2.98	39.20	3.28
Capital goods	**185.10**	**37.89**	**253.80**	**36.73**	**281.60**	**41.78**	**262.50**	**34.26**	**208.50**	**35.31**	**195.00**	**31.91**	**251.80**	**36.64**	**364.10**	**37.56**	**438.60**	**40.23**	**455.80**	**38.73**	**387.50**	**32.39**
For agricultural purposes	13.50	2.76	27.40	3.97	40.10	5.95	24.20	3.16	13.40	2.27	13.90	2.27	16.00	2.33	24.60	2.54	18.60	1.71	13.30	1.13	18.50	1.55
For industry purposes	103.40	21.17	137.10	19.84	151.70	22.51	133.80	17.46	137.40	23.27	127.60	20.88	169.20	24.62	252.30	26.02	301.50	27.65	273.90	23.27	224.10	18.73
Transport equipment	68.20	13.96	89.30	12.93	89.80	13.32	104.50	13.64	57.70	9.77	53.50	8.76	66.60	9.69	87.20	8.99	118.50	10.87	168.60	14.32	144.90	12.11
Diverse goods	**5.40**	**1.11**	**24.50**	**3.55**	**23.40**	**3.47**	**7.00**	**0.91**	**2.10**	**0.36**	**3.70**	**0.61**	**10.00**	**1.46**	**28.70**	**2.96**	**31.30**	**2.87**	**19.10**	**1.62**	**14.20**	**1.19**
Personal effect goods	-	-	-	-	-	-	-	-		-		-		-		-		-		-		-
CIF Total Value	**488.50**	**100.00**	**690.90**	**100.00**	**674.00**	**100.00**	**766.30**	**100.00**	**590.50**	**100.00**	**611.00**	**100.00**	**687.20**	**100.00**	**969.50**	**100.00**	**1,090.30**	**100.00**	**1,177.00**	**100.00**	**1,196.20**	**100.00**
Adjustments[2]	**3.10**								-		**9.00**		**15.50**		**24.20**		**40.20**		-		-	
Adjusted CIF Total Value	**491.60**		**690.90**		**674.00**		**766.30**		**590.50**		**620.00**		**702.70**		**993.70**		**1,130.50**		**1,177.00**		**1,196.20**	
Deduction for shipping, insurance, and other expenses	-79,30		-125,80		-110,10		-120,00		-85,9		-98,4		-83,3		-110,8		-125,9		-132,8		-131,9	
Compensation for contraband																						
FOB Total Value	**412.30**		**565.10**		**563.90**		**646.30**		**504.60**		**521.60**		**619.40**		**882.90**		**1,004.60**		**1,044.20**		**1,064.30**	

Table 7a: Structure of Imports (millions of current US dollars) continued

Type of good	1995	%	1996	%	1997	%	1998	%	1999	%	2000	%	2001	%	2002	%	2003	%	2004	%
Consumer goods	**282.30**	**19.69**	**339.60**	**20.50**	**386.60**	**20.41**	**505.40**	**21.17**	**412.00**	**22.22**	**466.00**	**23.57**	**400.20**	**23.44**	**373.80**	**20.41**	**359.10**	**21.22**	**402.80**	**20.97**
Perishable	137.90	9.62	173.20	10.46	183.20	9.67	213.10	8.93	223.40	12.05	293.40	14.84	274.40	16.07	239.90	13.10	226.50	13.39	249.90	13.01
Non-perishable	144.40	10.07	166.40	10.04	203.40	10.74	292.30	12.25	188.60	10.17	172.60	8.73	125.80	7.37	133.90	7.31	132.60	7.84	152.90	7.96
Intermediate goods	**604.10**	**42.14**	**615.60**	**37.16**	**730.10**	**38.54**	**891.80**	**37.36**	**719.80**	**38.82**	**903.10**	**45.68**	**890.50**	**52.15**	**926.00**	**50.55**	**862.20**	**50.96**	**997.40**	**51.93**
Fuels and oil lubricants	67.00	4.67	52.20	3.15	135.10	7.13	99.10	4.15	59.30	3.20	94.90	4.80	106.30	6.22	81.30	4.44	114.60	6.77	122.50	6.38
For agricultural purposes	27.40	1.91	32.10	1.94	44.50	2.35	43.20	1.81	42.80	2.31	52.90	2.68	59.30	3.47	54.20	2.96	69.10	4.08	95.70	4.98
For industry purposes	416.30	29.04	445.30	26.88	467.40	24.67	639.00	26.77	482.30	26.01	621.20	31.42	603.60	35.35	549.90	30.02	551.10	32.57	617.10	32.13
For construction purposes	50.60	3.53	48.70	2.94	51.50	2.72	72.70	3.05	101.40	5.47	81.60	4.13	63.80	3.74	185.50	10.13	79.40	4.69	106.40	5.54
Parts and accessories for transport equipment[1]	42.80	2.99	37.30	2.25	31.60	1.67	37.80	1.58	34.00	1.83	52.50	2.66	57.50	3.37	55.10	3.01	48.00	2.84	55.70	2.90
Capital goods	**534.90**	**37.31**	**659.20**	**39.79**	**733.70**	**38.73**	**944.10**	**39.55**	**693.30**	**37.39**	**594.30**	**30.06**	**398.30**	**23.32**	**523.80**	**28.59**	**457.60**	**27.04**	**503.60**	**26.22**
For agricultural purposes	17.40	1.21	19.30	1.17	16.20	0.86	15.90	0.67	12.80	0.69	12.50	0.63	14.80	0.87	18.80	1.03	25.40	1.50	50.30	2.62
For industry purposes	313.80	21.89	368.90	22.27	455.10	24.02	465.40	19.50	531.90	28.68	406.00	20.54	352.40	20.64	405.80	22.15	322.70	19.07	346.70	18.05
Transport equipment	203.70	14.21	271.00	16.36	262.40	13.85	462.80	19.39	148.60	8.01	175.80	8.89	31.10	1.82	99.20	5.42	109.50	6.47	106.60	5.55
Diverse goods	**12.20**	**0.85**	**42.20**	**2.55**	**44.20**	**2.33**	**45.60**	**1.91**	**29.30**	**1.58**	**13.50**	**0.68**	**18.70**	**1.10**	**8.20**	**0.45**	**11.50**	**0.68**	**15.50**	**0.81**
Personal effect goods		-	-	-	-	-	-	-	-	-	-	-	-	-	-	-	1.60	0.09	1.20	0.06
CIF Total Value	**1,433.50**	**100.00**	**1,656.60**	**100.00**	**1,894.60**	**100.00**	**2,386.90**	**100.00**	**1,854.40**	**100.00**	**1,976.90**	**100.00**	**1,707.70**	**100.00**	**1,831.80**	**100.00**	**1,692.00**	**100.00**	**1,920.50**	**100.00**
Adjustments[2]	-		**-119,2**		**-43,7**		**-403,8**		**-99,4**		**-147**		-		**-57,1**		**-76,2**		**-43,6**	
Adjusted CIF Total Value	**1,433.50**		**1,537.40**		**1,850.90**		**1,983.10**		**1,755.00**		**1,829.90**		**1,707.70**		**1,774.70**		**1,615.80**		**1,876.90**	
Deduction for shipping, insurance, and other expenses	-161,7		-173,3		-206,1		-223,7		-163,9		-157,9		-127,7		-132,6		-118,2		-127,4	
Compensation for contraband																				
FOB Total Value	**1,271.80**		**1,364.10**		**1,644.80**		**1,759.40**		**1,591.10**		**1,672.00**		**1,580.00**		**1,642.10**		**1,497.60**		**1,749.50**	

Table 7a: Structure of Imports (millions of current US dollars) continued

Type of good	2005	%	2006	%	2007	%	2008	%	2009	%	2010p	%	2011p	%
Consumer goods	**524.20**	**21.48**	**490.20**	**16.75**	**836.70**	**23.32**	**1,118.70**	**21.93**	**927.90**	**20.27**	**1,132.60**	**21.00**	**1,354.41**	**17.79**
Perishable	297.20	12.18	336.50	11.50	417.90	11.65	554.00	10.86	516.90	11.29	641.50	11.89	470.99	6.19
Non-perishable	227.00	9.30	153.70	5.25	418.80	11.67	564.70	11.07	411.00	8.98	491.10	9.11	883.42	11.60
Intermediate goods	**1,281.40**	**52.51**	**1,466.80**	**50.13**	**1,769.90**	**49.33**	**2,599.10**	**50.96**	**2,305.10**	**50.36**	**2,709.50**	**50.24**	**3,997.13**	**52.51**
Fuels and oil lubricants	239.50	9.81	272.30	9.31	280.40	7.81	555.40	10.89	470.20	10.27	615.20	11.41	512.51	6.73
For agricultural purposes	113.70	4.66	108.60	3.71	146.70	4.09	210.90	4.14	218.30	4.77	240.70	4.46	512.51	6.73
For industry purposes	729.10	29.88	830.40	28.38	1,024.10	28.54	1,393.50	27.32	1,204.20	26.31	1,414.80	26.23	1,160.22	15.24
For construction purposes	122.00	5.00	166.80	5.70	205.60	5.73	309.00	6.06	295.50	6.46	313.10	5.81	1,160.22	15.24
Parts and accessories for transport equipment[1]	77.10	3.16	88.70	3.03	113.10	3.15	130.30	2.55	116.90	2.55	125.70	2.33	651.67	8.56
Capital goods	**611.40**	**25.06**	**945.70**	**32.32**	**952.50**	**26.55**	**1,315.10**	**25.79**	**1,273.90**	**27.83**	**1,495.40**	**27.73**	**2,248.46**	**29.54**
For agricultural purposes	39.00	1.60	39.00	1.33	65.80	1.83	97.30	1.91	77.30	1.69	101.50	1.88	625.75	8.22
For industry purposes	441.80	18.11	588.80	20.12	653.90	18.22	902.10	17.69	852.50	18.62	1,046.00	19.39	625.75	8.22
Transport equipment	130.60	5.35	317.90	10.87	232.80	6.49	315.70	6.19	344.10	7.52	347.90	6.45	996.96	13.10
Diverse goods	**22.00**	**0.90**	**20.00**	**0.68**	**24.10**	**0.67**	**61.80**	**1.21**	**64.30**	**1.40**	**49.20**	**0.91**	**4.58**	**0.06**
Personal effect goods	**1.20**	**0.05**	**3.10**	**0.11**	**4.80**	**0.13**	**5.50**	**0.11**	**6.10**	**0.13**	**6.60**	**0.12**	**7.98**	**0.10**
CIF Total Value	**2,440.20**	**100.00**	**2,925.80**	**100.00**	**3,588.00**	**100.00**	**5,100.20**	**100.00**	**4,577.30**	**100.00**	**5,393.30**	**100.00**	**7,612.55**	**100.00**
Adjustments[2]	**-9,2**		**-10,0**		**-2,3**		**-18,8**		**-32,4**		**-9,6**			
Adjusted CIF Total Value	**2,431.00**		**2,915.80**		**3,585.70**		**5,081.40**		**4,544.90**		**5,383.70**		**7,612.55**	
Deduction for shipping, insurance, and other expenses	-154,2		-180,2		-219,3		-317,3		-296,7		-376,9			
Compensation for contraband														
FOB Total Value	**2,276.80**		**2,735.60**		**3,366.40**		**4,764.10**		**4,248.20**		**5,006.80**		**7,612.55**	

Notes: Values in table reflect author's own estimations based on data from CBB, NIS, Customs Department.
(1) According to UN methodology for recording national accounts.
(2) Adjustments for leasing of airplanes y nationalization of imported vehicles during previous fiscal years.
(p) Preliminary estimates.

Table 1b: Bolivia: Monthly Consumer Price Index (CPI), 1937–2012 (base month: January 2000)

	January	February	March	April	May	June	July	August	September	October	November	December	Inflation[1]
1937	0.0000000500	0.0000000512	0.0000000540	0.0000000503	0.0000000494	0.0000000512	0.0000000528	0.0000000528	0.0000000524	0.0000000537	0.0000000565	0.0000000562	12.35
1938	0.0000000592	0.0000000608	0.0000000614	0.0000000654	0.0000000651	0.0000000725	0.0000000744	0.0000000725	0.0000000710	0.0000000731	0.0000000740	0.0000000753	27.08
1939	0.0000000691	0.0000000722	0.0000000734	0.0000000753	0.0000000771	0.0000000818	0.0000000910	0.0000000916	0.0000000929	0.0000000944	0.0000000981	0.0000001058	53.13
1940	0.0000001077	0.0000001077	0.0000001077	0.0000001092	0.0000001111	0.0000001111	0.0000001132	0.0000001145	0.0000001169	0.0000001228	0.0000001240	0.0000001237	14.90
1941	0.0000001237	0.0000001290	0.0000001311	0.0000001370	0.0000001416	0.0000001453	0.0000001469	0.0000001499	0.0000001570	0.0000001577	0.0000001604	0.0000001672	35.16
1942	0.0000001712	0.0000001820	0.0000001808	0.0000001820	0.0000001851	0.0000001857	0.0000001876	0.0000001876	0.0000001882	0.0000001907	0.0000002138	0.0000002163	26.31
1943	0.0000002187	0.0000002298	0.0000002277	0.0000002277	0.0000002329	0.0000002348	0.0000002366	0.0000002342	0.0000002332	0.0000002336	0.0000002342	0.0000002345	7.19
1944	0.0000002397	0.0000002413	0.0000002502	0.0000002508	0.0000002440	0.0000002443	0.0000002447	0.0000002447	0.0000002447	0.0000002508	0.0000002524	0.0000002524	5.28
1945	0.0000002533	0.0000002533	0.0000002542	0.0000002511	0.0000002511	0.0000002518	0.0000002616	0.0000002663	0.0000002635	0.0000002693	0.0000002715	0.0000002718	7.31
1946	0.0000002690	0.0000002696	0.0000002696	0.0000002703	0.0000002718	0.0000002737	0.0000002755	0.0000002829	0.0000002820	0.0000002826	0.0000002949	0.0000003153	17.20
1947	0.0000003227	0.0000003230	0.0000003249	0.0000003249	0.0000003277	0.0000003329	0.0000003357	0.0000003409	0.0000003459	0.0000003474	0.0000003489	0.0000003653	13.19
1948	0.0000003678	0.0000003702	0.0000003718	0.0000003739	0.0000003749	0.0000003758	0.0000003764	0.0000003764	0.0000003782	0.0000003810	0.0000003847	0.0000003847	4.61
1949	0.0000003878	0.0000003937	0.0000003974	0.0000003974	0.0000004011	0.0000004017	0.0000004011	0.0000004020	0.0000004039	0.0000004116	0.0000004140	0.0000004221	8.83
1950	0.0000004248	0.0000004285	0.0000004319	0.0000004529	0.0000004850	0.0000004912	0.0000004989	0.0000005143	0.0000005202	0.0000005467	0.0000005627	0.0000005732	34.93
1951	0.0000005954	0.0000006062	0.0000006211	0.0000006390	0.0000006386	0.0000006494	0.0000006605	0.0000006843	0.0000006858	0.0000006923	0.0000007059	0.0000007275	22.18
1952	0.0000007537	0.0000007587	0.0000007633	0.0000007741	0.0000007858	0.0000007948	0.0000007926	0.0000008136	0.0000008349	0.0000008651	0.0000008818	0.0000009521	26.32
1953	0.0000010194	0.0000010514	0.0000010709	0.0000011480	0.0000015216	0.0000017299	0.0000018351	0.0000018373	0.0000019165	0.0000020045	0.0000022269	0.0000024015	135.59
1954	0.0000025317	0.0000025891	0.0000026585	0.0000031994	0.0000033725	0.0000037692	0.0000039127	0.0000040617	0.0000042774	0.0000043313	0.0000046695	0.0000047707	88.44
1955	0.0000033000	0.0000034187	0.0000039408	0.0000043749	0.0000044455	0.0000045880	0.0000046389	0.0000046494	0.0000047648	0.0000049481	0.0000050681	0.0000054312	64.58
1956	0.0000066971	0.0000078013	0.0000082348	0.0000086396	0.0000090561	0.0000099705	0.0000103503	0.0000108116	0.0000124232	0.0000161838	0.0000181983	0.0000312259	366.26
1957	0.0000315617	0.0000287413	0.0000294128	0.0000284055	0.0000256523	0.0000251822	0.0000251822	0.0000243092	0.0000244435	0.0000257866	0.0000263909	0.0000269282	-14.68
1958	0.0000271968	0.0000269282	0.0000269952	0.0000269280	0.0000263236	0.0000267937	0.0000263908	0.0000266594	0.0000266594	0.0000294798	0.0000312929	0.0000319644	17.53
1959	0.0000316958	0.0000327702	0.0000323673	0.0000327031	0.0000327031	0.0000328374	0.0000331732	0.0000337775	0.0000337775	0.0000339790	0.0000344490	0.0000351877	11.02
1960	0.0000355044	0.0000358239	0.0000361464	0.0000364717	0.0000367999	0.0000371311	0.0000374653	0.0000378025	0.0000381427	0.0000384860	0.0000388324	0.0000389482	9.70
1961	0.0000386125	0.0000387468	0.0000386796	0.0000396198	0.0000393512	0.0000395526	0.0000398884	0.0000397541	0.0000401570	0.0000417686	0.0000425073	0.0000418358	8.35
1962	0.0000419029	0.0000415000	0.0000427088	0.0000425745	0.0000422387	0.0000423058	0.0000425073	0.0000420372	0.0000421715	0.0000425073	0.0000429774	0.0000431788	3.04
1963	0.0000433947	0.0000436117	0.0000438297	0.0000440489	0.0000442691	0.0000444905	0.0000447129	0.0000449365	0.0000451612	0.0000453870	0.0000456139	0.0000425073	-2.04
1964	0.0000459992	0.0000464693	0.0000461335	0.0000462678	0.0000461335	0.0000463350	0.0000463350	0.0000464693	0.0000464020	0.0000464692	0.0000464692	0.0000469392	2.04
1965	0.0000481480	0.0000478794	0.0000480808	0.0000480808	0.0000472750	0.0000468049	0.0000468721	0.0000468721	0.0000474765	0.0000480808	0.0000486180	0.0000492224	2.23
1966	0.0000498343	0.0000498085	0.0000496793	0.0000505770	0.0000507288	0.0000512519	0.0000518784	0.0000522724	0.0000537385	0.0000560119	0.0000553176	0.0000536707	7.70
1967	0.0000553079	0.0000564591	0.0000533058	0.0000540066	0.0000535561	0.0000566093	0.0000553580	0.0000558084	0.0000559586	0.0000569597	0.0000572088	0.0000574591	3.89
1968	0.0000578094	0.0000577594	0.0000577093	0.0000574090	0.0000582098	0.0000589106	0.0000598615	0.0000596113	0.0000592109	0.0000590607	0.0000594111	0.0000594611	2.86
1969	0.0000596613	0.0000593110	0.0000589106	0.0000588105	0.0000590607	0.0000592109	0.0000596113	0.0000606123	0.0000607124	0.0000610628	0.0000616634	0.0000613631	2.85
1970	0.0000613631	0.0000615633	0.0000615633	0.0000613130	0.0000616634	0.0000621139	0.0000626144	0.0000626644	0.0000626644	0.0000630648	0.0000635153	0.0000638657	4.08
1971	0.0000634652	0.0000632150	0.0000633651	0.0000630148	0.0000631649	0.0000641660	0.0000651169	0.0000658677	0.0000662681	0.0000659178	0.0000659178	0.0000659678	3.94
1972	0.0000660179	0.0000659678	0.0000655674	0.0000655674	0.0000655674	0.0000661180	0.0000665684	0.0000663682	0.0000666185	0.0000670690	0.0000829353	0.0000815338	23.50
1973	0.0000813336	0.0000814838	0.0000830354	0.0000839863	0.0000844869	0.0000847872	0.0000877402	0.0000908934	0.0000933960	0.0001017546	0.0001033563	0.0001098629	35.08
1974	0.0001274310	0.0001431972	0.0001457999	0.0001468009	0.0001481023	0.0001514557	0.0001519062	0.0001523566	0.0001492034	0.0001480522	0.0001514557	0.0001526569	19.80
1975	0.0001546090	0.0001545139	0.0001544638	0.0001543187	0.0001550894	0.0001578773	0.0001615381	0.0001640929	0.0001643884	0.0001639376	0.0001634567	0.0001620190	4.79
1976	0.0001640077	0.0001660215	0.0001633815	0.0001622143	0.0001634016	0.0001658812	0.0001671736	0.0001680303	0.0001680854	0.0001685212	0.0001693127	0.0001709257	4.22
1977	0.0001764110	0.0001755443	0.0001718374	0.0001725337	0.0001726840	0.0001789958	0.0001808192	0.0001836896	0.0001836997	0.0001864548	0.0001873214	0.0001888042	7.03
1978	0.0001896458	0.0001872814	0.0001873866	0.0001877973	0.0001863847	0.0001933377	0.0002008418	0.0002037473	0.0002053202	0.0002131549	0.0002132501	0.0002142670	12.98
1979	0.0002159101	0.0002204536	0.0002194617	0.0002178137	0.0002233090	0.0002272864	0.0002341443	0.0002386978	0.0002415782	0.0002455858	0.0002563409	0.0003116447	44.34

Table 1b: Bolivia: Monthly Consumer Price Index (CPI), 1937–2012 (base month: January 2000) continued

	January	February	March	April	May	June	July	August	September	October	November	December	Inflation[1]
1980	0.0003171701	0.0003183673	0.0003236522	0.0003264625	0.0003363110	0.0003549109	0.0003601257	0.0003721382	0.0003634569	0.0003682910	0.0003725089	0.0003862397	21.78
1981	0.0004342748	0.0004425754	0.0004413430	0.0004417889	0.0004515522	0.0004521583	0.0004586705	0.0004861421	0.0004837576	0.0004871340	0.0004864527	0.0004832767	11.28
1982	0.0004955347	0.0005751240	0.0006220170	0.0007004842	0.0007286270	0.0007629314	0.0009275803	0.0010934565	0.0013063259	0.0014974896	0.0017783866	0.0019164155	286.74
1983	0.0019278169	0.0021254678	0.0023765939	0.0025754620	0.0028137892	0.0029038381	0.0031961415	0.0040250968	0.0047193694	0.0052262003	0.0065213553	0.0082116165	325.95
1984	0.0089968497	0.0110667132	0.0134061123	0.0218480309	0.0321208296	0.0334277616	0.0351581732	0.0404304500	0.0555220246	0.0883513334	0.1162309156	0.1869975769	1,978.48
1985	0.3155779825	0.8923666343	1.1149291225	1.2462994274	1.6908292673	3.0174822528	5.0181661044	8.3532851373	13.0727901785	12.8300294096	13.2406946483	15.4656722313	4,800.75
1986	20.5636997906	22.1988004808	22.2134155965	23.0116763558	23.2344054768	24.2241065134	24.6560475944	24.8132406777	25.3785298543	25.5281795597	25.5011619347	25.6673632138	24.82
1987	26.2960137580	26.6194940316	26.8047329990	27.2316734279	27.3242611195	27.2646152629	27.2500506368	27.5206879673	27.6795673945	28.2575874215	28.1772674464	28.4040432997	8.02
1988	28.2758733693	28.8258526118	29.0680369942	30.4446197170	30.8749270528	31.5101187894	32.7684797065	33.5544543399	33.4302212557	34.1245238954	34.0599026541	34.5122513435	22.06
1989	34.6790643152	34.8694214602	35.1624712755	35.2020455241	35.4219581207	35.3583387590	35.5216451519	36.6347335109	37.9982917975	38.7882739498	39.4650436946	40.2284760343	16.00
1990	40.6487645732	40.6106931443	40.7524591234	40.8852081851	41.1116329996	41.9361800016	42.6850850855	43.1543154483	43.6626692136	45.1594462051	46.4505998855	47.4736693522	16.79
1991	50.2446682570	50.3799721121	50.6998723037	50.9488394120	51.3505931761	51.7396731616	52.1752403659	52.7111458232	52.9315593596	53.4433696100	53.3870019458	54.3670025151	8.20
1992	55.7626209541	57.0130748886	57.3115367108	57.4613537272	57.8591375562	58.2362574438	58.6753690512	59.2126354543	59.2519895100	59.5501016745	59.8579039340	60.0554361722	7.70
1993	61.0763845566	61.6566135142	61.6257850471	61.6997363897	62.1686570517	62.7281781109	63.4244647771	64.5343990502	64.8764332237	65.2073048108	65.3311993550	65.6447907779	7.48
1994	66.1896454625	66.5470714344	66.4938334845	66.8196549907	67.2272570445	67.5499495522	68.1815448567	69.0201821539	69.4412073909	69.9738241598	71.1464513618	71.2389421897	7.63
1995	71.8302283164	72.2324795488	72.9006332279	74.0305984740	74.3785439155	74.8917583007	75.1838375061	75.5747952956	75.9602285428	77.3913258267	78.7766368122	80.1946226006	11.64
1996	81.4376446560	83.6853333070	83.5012248122	83.3175213410	83.6382951396	84.0815799606	85.0317057576	85.9160391623	86.0535053920	85.9846996079	86.4257719509	86.5701229026	6.30
1997	86.5614667040	86.7259497384	86.5182117494	86.9943182242	87.6245512420	88.4487021624	89.5654612427	90.1541404741	89.2105223109	89.5524757081	89.6606887795	92.3963157170	6.74
1998	93.6877808773	94.4660010336	94.6600340392	94.9279843733	95.2236536994	95.4454057067	95.6579180331	95.6856370385	95.6394387116	96.5818847083	96.6096036705	96.4525293427	2.95
1999	96.5962441419	96.9637296093	96.5579523320	96.4083741377	96.4911105029	96.8479861365	97.0399273685	97.5424468760	98.1213570551	98.8299963642	98.8966453174	99.4752661309	2.98
2000	100.0000000000	100.4152112300	101.0270857365	102.0019467721	100.7286588676	100.9250237271	101.6500020127	102.0536740839	103.9317737060	105.3281129561	102.6398838821	102.8673846305	2.87
2001	103.0987339546	103.0712678436	102.8314958537	103.0525476301	102.8692372535	103.6286044561	104.8733042256	104.1820353330	103.9063488207	103.9835010096	103.7489611590	103.8168529852	0.70
2002	103.8064727015	104.0295753373	103.7100333499	103.6820667779	103.7235039276	103.8376170726	104.2632682533	104.4916660238	104.9714059769	105.5402183030	106.1112144722	106.3603763159	2.46
2003	106.7805083750	106.5518236291	106.6156417357	106.9559967980	106.9751404775	107.1899906761	107.8281542177	108.5194965958	108.7744435327	110.1361822416	109.5724690702	110.5541794540	3.53
2004	111.2385118148	111.4477904001	111.1511718274	111.1732833078	111.6331901269	112.4612435925	113.0549217066	113.4507059480	113.4219624288	114.3351440284	114.9708332402	115.6617976466	3.98
2005	117.2509611947	117.3053579490	117.4923815646	117.0497425521	117.8362468849	119.6562020297	119.1013362503	119.5175835818	119.6972787109	120.1431970020	120.6666034468	121.3390961296	3.49
2006	121.8289363941	122.2086112429	121.8695125933	122.0403638273	123.0611805189	123.8279077155	124.5246257231	124.7593580546	124.8612080388	125.4440473972	126.3870504435	127.3395378352	4.52
2007	129.1662790127	130.2433333349	130.6293567445	130.2958717142	130.8871874883	131.9938917594	135.5267934216	137.6825539391	137.9437899393	139.6636029817	141.3785863566	142.2719943174	10.15
2008	143.8232974696	147.5924573676	149.0314952506	150.1319104583	152.9342628953	154.8574459367	155.5717710625	156.5883106648	157.9620128438	158.2504903063	158.4565456270	159.1296596839	10.64
2009	159.7066145952	159.5967184135	158.8137081695	158.1268570818	157.8246425974	158.1405941010	157.8246426043	158.8137081753	158.9785524370	159.4868222424	159.1846077603	159.5555073392	-0.09
2010	159.8302477703	160.0912511882	159.8989328798	160.0500401216	160.0225660758	160.2423584305	161.2314239899	162.9348146849	164.1848836590	166.1904888338	168.0449867610	171.5754013389	7.35
2011	173.2238439374	176.0948814774	177.6609019574	177.7021130153	178.0592755859	178.3065419792	179.2543964835	179.9412475622	180.4907284277	181.3424237814	181.9331157173	182.8122851030	5.54
2012	183.3755029897	184.2821464278	184.8178902677	185.1063677258	186.0130111626								

Notes: Values in table reflect author's calculations based on data from Central Bank of Bolivia (CBB) and National Institute of Statistics (NIS).
First Index: From January 1937 through August 1956 (Base month: December 1936; Coverage: La Paz).
Second Index: From September 1956 through December 1965 (Base month: January 1956; Coverage: La Paz).
Third Index: From January 1966 through January 1967 (Base month: January 1957; Coverage: La Paz).
Fourth Index: From February 1967 through January 1992 (Base year: 1966; Coverage: La Paz y El Alto).
Fifth Index: From February 1992 through March 2008 (Base year: 1980; Coverage: La Paz, Cochabamba, Santa Cruz and El Alto).
Sixth Index: From April 2008 through present (Base year: 2007; Coverage: nine Department's capitals).
(1) Inflation is calculated between December and January of each year.

Table 2b: Bolivia: Monthly Industrial Production Index (IPI), 1986–2011 (base month: January 2000)

	January	February	March	April	May	June	July	August	September	October	November	December	Inflation[1]
1986	37.4414531480	37.5987072512	37.3138685599	38.5153751275	38.3887839192	39.1488818408	41.6191762850	42.3475118700	42.4110331378	42.8224201592	43.9614965355	45.3243029281	21.05
1987	43.6784483525	43.6784483525	43.7745409388	45.0089829933	45.4815773147	45.4499269478	46.6543500119	46.6870080569	46.8457438843	48.0824715228	47.1961586837	49.1595188850	12.55
1988	49.7936766786	50.1123562093	50.7437718975	52.4538370105	52.8944492414	53.5291826323	54.2571795161	55.0167800293	55.6494729996	55.8720708916	55.9055941342	56.5373273479	13.54
1989	58.0242590571	58.9120302207	59.8958611254	61.4172159980	61.7672941292	62.0205400351	63.3477795919	64.6147351837	66.5144083981	67.4988216424	68.3560566772	69.1489869347	19.17
1990	69.5293063628	69.5107343517	75.1132995404	79.1168384059	77.9817193892	77.2608426560	77.3226513301	77.3249710097	80.1859949370	82.7599653745	79.3721633864	76.4073445256	9.89
1991	71.2382831731	71.4591218510	76.8685773751	84.8475357066	84.2196752991	82.7423719901	81.1964096792	81.2532471660	85.2671575760	88.2344546596	84.1516725425	78.9952677581	10.89
1992	74.2053131653	73.5106267458	78.8327961222	86.2982619149	86.1618827035	84.2228070928	83.1217681191	80.9553959680	84.6793441825	88.8370999818	84.8235913727	80.9544765824	9.10
1993	76.5623741745	76.0182949240	83.2096256238	91.8218218759	91.2538205194	88.7625908445	86.0745830263	83.7481346740	86.9640630454	91.3035697914	88.1340303967	84.6784425683	10.60
1994	81.4781061362	80.7063255274	87.3888092811	92.1689771488	92.8971120682	91.3521587395	91.2203333635	91.5578485969	94.7165943735	95.5122137663	90.9198528136	86.5713963174	6.25
1995	84.5273800825	84.5208664896	93.6406679839	97.2177415009	97.3635681131	94.7637942101	94.2220848171	93.5799442414	98.0437075817	100.6810833156	95.7879245667	92.5501363016	9.49
1996	87.7774035664	87.8037367875	96.6982553241	102.9159531414	102.7494663647	100.1016113519	99.1922996680	97.4911374316	101.2055497677	104.9299139992	100.4268579114	94.8150749123	8.02
1997	92.4307208294	91.1013201991	101.8330557186	108.9104530910	108.3277485722	105.9575941217	103.7829527164	101.4339627566	104.3856910728	109.2605028459	105.6440760430	101.3269551110	9.62
1998	97.7954914490	97.8932869404	108.9160710499	114.3836578166	114.1053446308	110.6176817102	108.3130124035	105.5770005735	110.1696000984	113.0890945010	109.7714868852	105.7050863389	8.09
1999	98.6887432589	98.5839304063	109.5760386466	114.6932396514	112.1338511415	109.2406996814	107.0368850879	105.0840997102	109.3715309783	115.5947710910	112.7776705589	109.0682352127	10.52
2000	100.0000000000	101.7300000000	111.6079830000	119.7888481539	117.4673825605	115.1435825967	108.4590781989	106.2449323312	110.0485009087	118.3021384769	115.5608853899	110.0549469627	10.05
2001	100.3957926626	100.0530858829	112.8598808759	121.2115120607	118.2260663696	116.1346871349	110.7445597739	108.5077075933	113.9005406607	122.2038900749	120.0968247680	112.5017167827	12.06
2002	102.8928996467	100.7671929383	113.9475417747	125.7069280858	121.9777261974	121.6097903874	115.7052311164	112.3452596879	117.5805487893	124.1650595215	119.1341603427	114.7627311323	11.54
2003	104.5148859669	104.9956544423	118.6555890853	130.7940558487	125.7861914260	124.5687199583	117.0509115635	112.1798022789	119.4939253874	126.8428017988	124.8487669738	118.5084882486	13.39
2004	105.9243105618	110.0871359669	126.5671802211	134.8446738076	129.1194741793	134.6070518319	130.8906592098	121.4912926444	127.3714712084	132.3389585856	126.2799677002	131.1291184599	23.80
2005	114.5697560012	116.2539314144	136.2379822245	146.8372972416	138.4834875632	136.2182080336	130.4289375233	129.0118383580	134.8044699003	135.6806989547	131.3710579975	144.0220908826	25.71
2006	119.6386457596	121.0384179150	142.6316716710	146.3258319673	149.0621250251	142.4675704138	139.0749465935	135.2937118615	142.5183960750	145.8390747035	138.7057210964	147.8880398330	23.61
2007	126.0592724675	121.6738087365	145.2663602505	151.7742931898	155.0677953520	148.9412494515	147.7407095189	141.8962865033	149.5444963458	151.7727093414	148.3659637034	158.6922347772	25.89
2008	134.7837561819	131.1920525095	152.7600259421	162.4908395946	165.2206856998	159.4434166953	159.3423410204	151.8267961244	159.0385689404	161.7740323261	154.2470179630	162.0827664755	20.25
2009	138.7214767770	135.9439237742	156.4578618718	165.5950010051	165.9593100073	166.3742082823	163.2642159586	157.4141290569	166.6228556068	168.2724218773	162.0023094552	169.9728230804	22.53
2010	142.9064342811	139.1546576158	162.9640195339	169.7270263445	174.6491101085	172.3948612823	168.1858792082	162.4556732759	174.7352000000	177.4149000000	169.8171070000	181.2848560000	26.86
2011	152.7613150000	148.4737630000	169.2496970000	178.8495400000	181.4820260000	179.3461640000	175.9728420000	171.8585970000	183.5549490000	184.9973240000	180.1342990000	191.1686060000	25.14

Notes: Values in table reflect author's calculations based on data from Banco Central de Bolivia and Instituto Nacional de Estadística.
From January 1986 through December 1989, values represent an Index of Prices for Industrial Production, or Indice de Precios de Produccion Industrial (IPPI).
From January 1990 through 2011, values represent the Index of Global Economic Activity, or Indice Global de Actividad Economica (IGAE).
(1) Inflation is calculated between December and January of each year.

Table 3b: Yearly Exchange Rate, Bs/$ and Bs/British Pound, 1886-2012		
Year	Bs/$	Bs/£
1886	1.52	7.39
1887	1.68	8.14
1888	1.70	8.28
1889	1.79	8.73
1890	1.59	7.74
1891	1.65	8.00
1892	1.76	8.57
1893	2.10	10.21
1894	2.49	12.15
1895	2.31	11.29
1896	2.40	11.71
1897	2.67	13.01
1898	2.76	13.39
1899	2.49	12.12
1900	2.26	10.98
1901	2.64	12.87
1902	2.89	14.07
1903	2.86	13.91
1904	2.56	12.47
1905	2.49	12.10
1906	2.48	12.04
1907	2.50	12.16
1908	2.78	13.52
1909	2.63	12.80
1910	2.54	12.33
1911	2.56	12.43
1912	2.63	12.80
1913	2.70	13.15
1914	2.91	14.33
1915	3.18	15.12
1916	2.78	13.24
1917	2.78	13.24
1918	2.43	11.57
1919	2.81	12.43
1920	3.08	11.29
1921	3.79	14.60
1922	3.44	15.24

Table 3b: Yearly Exchange Rate, Bs/$ and Bs/British Pound, 1886-2012 continued		
Year	Bs/$	Bs/£
1923	3.22	14.71
1924	3.17	14.02
1925	2.82	13.64
1926	2.82	13.71
1927	2.74	13.33
1928	2.79	13.33
1929	2.78	13.52
1930	2.82	13.51
1931	3.08	13.50
1932	4.71	16.10
1933	5.04	19.55
1934	4.19	20.18
1935	4.25	20.26
1936	8.69	32.00
1937	17.35	80.42
1938	29.53	141.40
1939	32.33	141.40
1940	39.07	140.78
1941	43.36	169.49
1942	46.46	186.54
1943	42.91	172.29
1944	42.42	170.32
1945	42.42	170.32
1946	42.42	170.32
1947	42.42	170.59
1948	42.42	170.85
1949	42.42	157.82
1950	56.06	156.89
1951	60.60	169.61
1952	60.60	169.68
1953	148.13	414.65
1954	191.90	536.94
1955	191.90	532.52
1956	191.90	531.56
1957	8,190.83	22,105.69
1958	9,595.83	27,195.10
1959	11,885.00	33,661.81

Table 3b: Yearly Exchange Rate, Bs/$ and Bs/British Pound, 1886-2012 continued		
Year	Bs/$	Bs/£
1960	11,885.00	33,582.50
1961	11,885.00	33,416.25
1962	11,885.00	33,416.25
1963	11,885.00	33,416.25
1964	11,885.00	33,400.81
1965	11,885.00	33,298.38
1966	11,885.00	33,347.33
1967	11,885.00	32,594.62
1968	11,885.00	28,736.92
1969	11,885.00	28,489.42
1970	11,885.00	28,633.67
1971	11,885.00	28,987.25
1972	13,918.75	34,709.17
1973	20,020.00	49,222.50
1974	20,020.00	46,922.00
1975	20,020.00	44,422.50
1976	20,020.00	36,143.33
1977	20,020.00	35,023.33
1978	20,020.00	38,630.00
1979	20,771.67	44,307.50
1980	24,530.00	57,251.67
1981	24,530.00	49,382.50
1982	67,090.00	113,521.67
1983	246,670.00	370,612.50
1984	2,720,170.00	3,466,954.17
1985	446,467,580.00	691,494,592.50
1986	1,916,664,330.00	2,773,440,000.00
1987	2.06	3.42
1988	2.35	4.20
1989	2.69	4.40
1990	3.17	5.72
1991	3.56	6.33
1992	3.91	6.85
1993	4.27	6.42
1994	4.63	7.10

Table 3b: Yearly Exchange Rate, Bs/$ and Bs/British Pound, 1886-2012 continued		
Year	Bs/$	Bs/£
1995	4.81	7.59
1996	5.08	7.98
1997	5.26	8.61
1998	5.52	9.16
1999	5.82	9.38
2000	6.19	9.38
2001	6.62	9.54
2002	7.18	10.85
2003	7.67	12.61
2004	7.95	14.53
2005	8.09	14.58
2006	8.06	14.75
2007	7.90	15.59
2008	7.29	13.27
2009	7.07	10.85
2010	7.07	10.74
2011	6.99	11.10

Notes: Exchange rates refer to the yearly average, official selling (spot) exchange rates between Bolivian currency and the foreign currencies.

1) The unit of account (Boliviano) changed on July 13, 1962 (Supreme Decree 6161). It becomes 'Peso Boliviano' and this new unit of account is worth 1 Peso Boliviano = 1000 Bolivianos. Values above do not reflect this change–they continue utilizing Bolivianos.

2) Until December 1986, the official exchange rate was Pesos Bolivianos per US Dollar or British Pound (since values in table always reflect Bolivianos, until December 1986, exchange rates in table reflect 'old' Bolivianos per foreign currency). From January 1, 1987 (Law 901, November 28 1986), a new unit of account, the 'Boliviano' is introduced. The exchange rate between the new (Boliviano) and the old currency (Pesos Bolivianos) is 1 Boliviano = 1 million Pesos Bolivianos. Since values in table until December 1986 always reflect 'old' bolivianos, the correct exchange rate between the old currency (old Bolivianos) and new currency (Bolivianos) is 1 Boliviano = 1,000,000,000 old Bolivianos.

Starting on 1987, the exchange rates reflect the price of foreign currencies (Dollar and British Pound) in terms of the 'new' Boliviano.

Values in table reflect author's calculations based on data from Banco Central de Bolivia and Instituto Nacional de Estadística.

Table 4b: Monthly Exchange Rates Bs/$ on the Official Market[1]

Month	1982	1983	1984	1985	1986	1987	1988	1989		1990		1991	
	Selling	Selling	Selling	Selling	Selling	Selling	Selling	Buying[3]	Selling	Buying	Selling	Buying	Selling
January	24.51	196.00	500.00	8,571.00	2,062,839.00	1.9260	2.2165	na	2.4761	2.9865	2.9965	3.4294	3.4394
February	43.18	196.00	500.00	45,000.00	1,836,571.00	1.9416	2.2400	na	2.5043	3.0246	3.0346	3.4621	3.4721
March	43.18	196.00	500.00	45,000.00	1,888,194.00	1.9836	2.2684	2.5203	2.5303	3.0603	3.0703	3.4919	3.5019
April	43.18	196.00	2,000.00	45,000.00	1,904,600.00	2.0058	2.3003	2.5497	2.5597	3.0903	3.1003	3.5157	3.5257
May	43.18	196.00	2,000.00	67,000.00	1,904,323.00	2.0334	2.3374	2.5816	2.5916	3.1174	3.1274	3.5374	3.5474
June	43.18	196.00	2,000.00	67,000.00	1,904,933.00	2.0634	2.3660	2.6167	2.6267	3.1377	3.1477	3.5640	3.5740
July	43.18	196.00	2,000.00	67,000.00	1,904,161.00	2.0710	2.4033	2.6500	2.6600	3.1610	3.1710	3.5887	3.5987
August	43.18	196.00	2,000.00	67,000.00	1,909,355.00	2.0861	2.4019	2.7565	2.7665	3.1877	3.1977	3.6081	3.6181
September	43.18	196.00	2,000.00	1,044,567.00	1,915,133.00	2.1077	2.3977	2.8257	2.8357	3.2310	3.2410	3.6327	3.6427
October	43.18	196.00	2,000.00	1,102,839.00	1,921,129.00	2.1210	2.4000	2.8723	2.8823	3.2748	3.2848	3.6626	3.6726
November	196.00	500.00	8,571.00	1,209,067.00	1,924,967.00	2.1527	2.4210	2.9043	2.9143	3.3147	3.3247	3.6910	3.7010
December	196.00	500.00	8,571.00	1,589,567.00	1,923,767.00	2.1858	2.4503	2.9416	2.9516	3.3648	3.3748	3.7158	3.7258
Yearly Avg	**67.09**	**246.67**	**2,720.17**	**446,467.58**	**1,916,664.33**	**2.0565**	**2.3502**	**2.7219**	**2.6916**	**3.1626**	**3.1726**	**3.5750**	**3.5850**

Table 4b: Monthly Exchange Rates Bs/$ on the Official Market[1] continued

Month	1992		1993		1994		1995		1996		1997		1998	
	Buying	Selling	Buying	Selling	Buying	Selling	Buying	Selling	Buying	Selling	Buying	Selling	Buying	Selling
January	3.7484	3.7584	4.0977	4.1077	4.4794	4.4894	4.7103	4.7203	4.9494	4.9594	5.1894	5.1994	5.3674	5.3774
February	3.7676	3.7776	4.1246	4.1346	4.5114	4.5214	4.7207	4.7307	4.9710	4.9810	5.2032	5.2132	5.3946	5.4046
March	3.7871	3.7971	4.1545	4.1645	4.5535	4.5635	4.7390	4.7490	4.9935	5.0035	5.2184	5.2284	5.4274	5.4374
April	3.8063	3.8163	4.1830	4.1930	4.5820	4.5920	4.7607	4.7707	5.0207	5.0307	5.2253	5.2353	5.4627	5.4727
May	3.8319	3.8419	4.2126	4.2226	4.6097	4.6197	4.7568	4.7668	5.0510	5.0610	5.2158	5.2258	5.4813	5.4913
June	3.8597	3.8697	4.2433	4.2533	4.6450	4.6550	4.7777	4.7877	5.0567	5.0667	5.2173	5.2273	5.5000	5.5100
July	3.8942	3.9042	4.2732	4.2832	4.6445	4.6545	4.7948	4.8048	5.0845	5.0945	5.2316	5.2416	5.5216	5.5316
August	3.9387	3.9487	4.3000	4.3100	4.6590	4.6690	4.8184	4.8284	5.1097	5.1197	5.2555	5.2655	5.5365	5.5465
September	3.9833	3.9933	4.3273	4.3373	4.6703	4.6803	4.8417	4.8517	5.1333	5.1433	5.2713	5.2813	5.5577	5.5677
October	4.0135	4.0235	4.3616	4.3716	4.6606	4.6706	4.8532	4.8632	5.1658	5.1758	5.2948	5.3048	5.5842	5.5942
November	4.0417	4.0517	4.4020	4.4120	4.6760	4.6860	4.8723	4.8813	5.1667	5.1767	5.3173	5.3273	5.6033	5.6133
December	4.0745	4.0845	4.4426	4.4526	4.6948	4.7048	4.9087	4.9187	5.1684	5.1784	5.3452	5.3552	5.6261	5.6361
Yearly Avg	**3.8956**	**3.9056**	**4.2602**	**4.2702**	**4.6155**	**4.6255**	**4.7962**	**4.8061**	**5.0726**	**5.0826**	**5.2488**	**5.2588**	**5.5052**	**5.5152**

Table 4b: Monthly Exchange Rates Bs/$ on the Official Market[1] continued														
Month	1999		2000		2001		2002		2003		2004		2005	
	Buying	Selling	Buying	Selling	Buying	Selling	Buying	Selling	Buying	Selling	Buying	Selling	Buying	Selling
January	5.6410	5.6574	5.9955	6.0155	6.3971	6.4171	6.8513	6.8713	7.5106	7.5306	7.8310	7.8510	8.0455	8.0655
February	5.6632	5.6832	6.0279	6.0479	6.4207	6.4407	6.9282	6.9482	7.5400	7.5600	7.8414	7.8614	8.0543	8.0743
March	5.6929	5.7129	6.0635	6.0835	6.4561	6.4761	6.9861	7.0061	7.5668	7.5868	7.8748	7.8948	8.0719	8.0919
April	5.7230	5.7430	6.0957	6.1157	6.4897	6.5097	7.0353	7.0553	7.5890	7.6090	7.8823	7.9023	8.0800	8.1000
May	5.7539	5.7739	6.1277	6.1477	6.5184	6.5384	7.0500	7.0700	7.5974	7.6174	7.8961	7.9161	8.0800	8.1000
June	5.7787	5.7987	6.1573	6.1773	6.5613	6.5813	7.1190	7.1390	7.6260	7.6460	7.9080	7.9280	8.0800	8.1000
July	5.8177	5.8377	6.1868	6.2068	6.6129	6.6329	7.1813	7.2013	7.6587	7.6787	7.9216	7.9416	8.0632	8.0948
August	5.8513	5.8713	6.2181	6.2381	6.6648	6.6848	7.2477	7.2677	7.6916	7.7116	7.9445	7.9645	8.0300	8.0900
September	5.8863	5.9063	6.2507	6.2707	6.7020	6.7220	7.3053	7.3253	7.7217	7.7417	7.9720	7.9920	8.0240	8.0840
October	5.9203	5.9403	6.2819	6.3019	6.7445	6.7645	7.3603	7.3813	7.7403	7.7603	7.9965	8.0165	8.0161	8.0800
November	5.9470	5.9670	6.3163	6.3363	6.7897	6.8097	7.4027	7.4227	7.7553	7.7753	8.0173	8.0373	8.0000	8.0800
December	5.9703	5.9903	6.3587	6.3787	6.8058	6.8258	7.4523	7.4723	7.7926	7.8126	8.0297	8.0497	8.0000	8.0800
Yearly Avg	**5.8038**	**5.8235**	**6.1733**	**6.1933**	**6.5969**	**6.6169**	**7.1600**	**7.1800**	**7.6492**	**7.6692**	**7.9263**	**7.9463**	**8.0454**	**8.0867**

Table 4b: Monthly Exchange Rates Bs/$ on the Official Market[1] continued

Month	2006		2007		2008		2009		2010		2011		2012	
	Buying	Selling	Buying	Selling	Buying	Selling	Buying	Selling	Buying	Selling	Buying	Selling	Buying	Selling
January	8.0000	8.0800	7.9155	8.0155	7.5532	7.6532	6.9700	7.0700	6.9700	7.0700	6.9400	7.0400	6.8600	6.9600
February	7.9936	8.0736	7.9050	8.0050	7.4948	7.5948	6.9700	7.0700	6.9700	7.0700	6.9264	7.0264	6.8600	6.9600
March	7.9752	8.0700	7.8900	7.9900	7.4516	7.5516	6.9700	7.0700	6.9700	7.0700	6.9071	7.0071	6.8600	6.9600
April	7.9690	8.0690	7.8900	7.9900	7.3540	7.4540	6.9700	7.0700	6.9700	7.0700	6.8927	6.9927	6.8600	6.9600
May	7.9600	8.0600	7.8771	7.9771	7.2458	7.3458	6.9700	7.0700	6.9700	7.0700	6.8900	6.9900		
June	7.9600	8.0600	7.8600	7.9600	7.1680	7.2680	6.9700	7.0700	6.9700	7.0700	6.8810	6.9810		
July	7.9600	8.0600	7.8100	7.9100	7.0787	7.1787	6.9700	7.0700	6.9700	7.0700	6.8761	6.9761		
August	7.9558	8.0558	7.7377	7.8377	7.0135	7.1135	6.9700	7.0700	6.9700	7.0700	6.8700	6.9700		
September	7.9500	8.0500	7.7100	7.8100	6.9900	7.0900	6.9700	7.0700	6.9700	7.0700	6.8700	6.9700		
October	7.9500	8.0500	7.6984	7.7984	6.9719	7.0719	6.9700	7.0700	6.9700	7.0700	6.8700	6.9700		
November	7.9500	8.0500	7.6533	7.7533	6.9700	7.0700	6.9700	7.0700	6.9677	7.0677	6.8600	6.9600		
December	7.9384	8.0384	7.5945	7.6945	6.9700	7.0700	6.9700	7.0700	6.9477	7.0477	6.8600	6.9600		
Yearly Avg	**7.9635**	**8.0597**	**7.7951**	**7.8951**	**7.1885**	**7.2885**	**6.9700**	**7.0700**	**6.9680**	**7.0680**	**6.8869**	**6.9869**	**6.8600**	**6.9600**

Notes: (1) Monthly average is estimated by considering daily quotations throughtout the month; Yearly average is estimated as an average of all monthly averages for each year.
(2) Until 1986, exchange rate is expressed in Pesos Bolivianos per US Dollar ($). From 1987 onwards, the exchange rate is expressed in Bolivianos per Dollar. 1 Boliviano = 1,000,000 Pesos Bolivianos.
(3) The official Buying price was established by Supreme Resolution 042-051/89 and Decree 22139, dated February 21, 1989.
Values in table reflect author's own estimations based on data from the CBB and the NIS.

Table 5b: Monthly Exchange Rates Bs/$ on the Parallel Market[1]														
Month	1982		1983		1984		1985		1986		1987		1988	
	Buying	Selling	Buying	Selling	Buying	Selling	Buying	Selling	Buying	Selling	Buying	Selling	Buying	Selling
January	-	-	362.00	390.00	1,850.00	1,900.00	63,322.00	68,229.00	2,234,032.00	2,310,857.00	1.9281	1.9429	2.2200	2.2494
February	-	-	450.00	500.00	2,000.00	2,100.00	119,642.00	132,856.00	1,855,000.00	1,912,500.00	1.9354	1.9455	2.2293	2.2531
March	-	-	475.00	500.00	2,450.00	2,780.00	121,290.00	126,451.00	1,948,871.00	1,965,484.00	1.9761	1.9935	2.2635	2.2835
April	78.12	79.00	395.00	420.00	3,420.00	3,560.00	156,767.00	162,700.00	1,915,833.00	1,926,700.00	2.0220	2.0278	2.2947	2.3170
May	87.50	89.00	345.00	380.00	3,390.00	3,480.00	231,290.00	250,000.00	1,945,967.00	1,963,548.00	2.0224	2.0485	2.3403	2.3503
June	101.68	103.00	360.00	390.00	3,280.00	3,330.00	445,830.00	470,330.00	1,931,333.00	1,944,300.00	2.0670	2.0873	2.3660	2.3807
July	150.81	152.00	550.00	600.00	3,420.00	3,500.00	801,290.00	847,419.00	1,922,000.00	1,932,742.00	2.0690	2.0906	2.4023	2.4192
August	179.54	180.00	750.00	780.00	6,890.00	7,330.00	1,093,870.00	1,149,354.00	1,923,000.00	1,933,323.00	2.0787	2.0984	2.4019	2.4216
September	229.17	233.00	755.00	785.00	13,090.00	13,515.00	1,030,833.00	1,065,166.00	1,914,833.00	1,924,400.00	2.1127	2.1330	2.3953	2.4077
October	225.09	230.00	945.00	1,050.00	14,970.00	15,160.00	1,107,740.00	1,118,225.00	1,922,419.00	1,932,581.00	2.1203	2.1435	2.4000	2.4200
November	240.00	250.00	1,200.00	1,350.00	17,683.00	18,394.00	1,298,722.00	1,333,333.00	1,925,000.00	1,935,500.00	2.1547	2.1753	2.4190	2.4390
December	275.00	290.00	1,180.00	1,200.00	22,323.00	23,381.00	1,690,654.00	1,724,193.00	1,938,710.00	1,952,903.00	2.1997	2.2268	2.4510	2.4739
Yearly Avg	**174.10**	**178.44**	**647.25**	**695.42**	**7,897.17**	**8,202.50**	**680,104.17**	**704,021.33**	**1,948,083.17**	**1,969,569.83**	**2.0572**	**2.0761**	**2.3486**	**2.3680**

Table 5b: Monthly Exchange Rates Bs/$ on the Parallel Market[1] continued

Month	1989		1990		1991		1992		1993		1994		1995	
	Buying	Selling	Buying	Selling	Buying	Selling	Buying	Selling	Buying	Selling	Buying	Selling	Buying	Selling
January	2.4768	2.5087	2.9916	3.0219	3.4313	3.4813	3.7500	3.7823	4.0969	4.1177	4.4794	4.4994	4.7103	4.7303
February	2.5043	2.5243	3.0246	3.0446	3.4621	3.4786	3.7676	3.7962	4.1246	4.1446	4.5114	4.5314	4.7207	4.7407
March	2.5303	2.5403	3.0603	3.0803	3.4919	3.5019	3.7871	3.8071	4.1545	4.1745	4.5535	4.5735	4.7390	4.7590
April	2.5597	2.5697	3.0903	3.1103	3.5157	3.5357	3.8063	3.8263	4.1830	4.2030	4.5820	4.6020	4.7607	4.7807
May	2.5916	2.6016	3.1174	3.1374	3.5374	3.5574	3.8319	3.8519	4.2126	4.2326	4.6097	4.6297	4.7568	4.7768
June	2.6267	2.6367	3.1377	3.1577	3.5640	3.5840	3.8597	3.8797	4.2433	4.2633	4.6450	4.6650	4.7777	4.7977
July	2.6621	2.6737	3.1610	3.1810	3.5887	3.6087	3.8942	3.9142	4.2732	4.2932	4.6445	4.6645	4.7948	4.8148
August	2.7655	2.8147	3.1877	3.2077	3.6081	3.6297	3.9387	3.9587	4.3000	4.3200	4.6590	4.6790	4.8184	4.8384
September	2.8358	2.8523	3.2310	3.2510	3.6327	3.6528	3.9833	4.0033	4.3273	4.3473	4.6703	4.6903	4.8417	4.8617
October	2.8795	2.8995	3.2748	3.2948	3.6626	3.6826	4.0135	4.0335	4.3616	4.3816	4.6606	4.6806	4.8532	4.8732
November	2.9043	2.9243	3.3147	3.3347	3.6910	3.7110	4.0417	4.0617	4.4020	4.4220	4.6760	4.6960	4.8723	4.8923
December	2.9516	2.9758	3.3648	3.3916	3.7158	3.7358	4.0745	4.0945	4.4426	4.4626	4.6948	4.7148	4.9087	4.9287
Yearly Avg	**2.6907**	**2.7101**	**3.1630**	**3.1844**	**3.5751**	**3.5966**	**3.8957**	**3.9175**	**4.2601**	**4.2802**	**4.6155**	**4.6355**	**4.7962**	**4.8162**

Table 5b: Monthly Exchange Rates Bs/$ on the Parallel Market[1] continued

Month	1996		1997		1998		1999		2000		2001	
	Buying	Selling	Buying	Selling	Buying	Selling	Buying	Selling	Buying	Selling	Buying	Selling
January	4.9494	4.9694	5.1894	5.2094	5.3674	5.3874	5.6410	5.6674	5.9955	6.0255	6.3971	6.4271
February	4.9710	4.9910	5.2032	5.2232	5.3946	5.4146	5.6632	5.6932	6.0279	6.0579	6.4207	6.4507
March	4.9935	5.0135	5.2184	5.2384	5.4274	5.4474	5.6929	5.7229	6.0635	6.0935	6.4561	6.4861
April	5.0207	5.0407	5.2253	5.2453	5.4627	5.4827	5.7230	5.7530	6.0957	6.1257	6.4897	6.5197
May	5.0510	5.0710	5.2158	5.2358	5.4813	5.5013	5.7539	5.7839	6.1277	6.1577	6.5184	6.5484
June	5.0567	5.0767	5.2173	5.2373	5.5000	5.5200	5.7787	5.8087	6.1573	6.1873	6.5613	6.5913
July	5.0845	5.1045	5.2316	5.2516	5.5216	5.5416	5.8177	5.8477	6.1868	6.2168	6.6129	6.6429
August	5.1097	5.1297	5.2555	5.2755	5.5365	5.5565	5.8513	5.8813	6.2181	6.2481	6.6648	6.6948
September	5.1333	5.1533	5.2713	5.2913	5.5577	5.5777	5.8863	5.9163	6.2507	6.2807	6.7020	6.7320
October	5.1658	5.1858	5.2943	5.3148	5.5840	5.6042	5.9203	5.9503	6.2819	6.3119	6.7445	6.7745
November	5.1657	5.1867	5.3173	5.3390	5.6033	5.6233	5.9470	5.9770	6.3163	6.3463	6.7897	6.8197
December	5.1684	5.1884	5.3447	5.3652	5.6261	5.6461	5.9703	6.0003	6.3587	6.3887	6.8058	6.8358
Yearly Avg	**5.0725**	**5.0926**	**5.2487**	**5.2689**	**5.5052**	**5.5252**	**5.8038**	**5.8335**	**6.1733**	**6.2033**	**6.5969**	**6.6269**

Table 5b: Monthly Exchange Rates Bs/$ on the Parallel Market[1] continued

Month	2002		2003		2004		2005		2006		2007	
	Buying	Selling	Buying	Selling	Buying	Selling	Buying	Selling	Buying	Selling	Buying	Selling
January	6.8513	6.8813	7.5106	7.5406	7.8310	7.8610	8.0455	8.0755	7.9828	8.0606	7.9017	7.9812
February	6.9282	6.9582	7.5400	7.5700	7.8414	7.8714	8.0543	8.0843	7.9763	8.0554	7.8872	7.9835
March	6.9861	7.0161	7.5668	7.5968	7.8748	7.9048	8.0719	8.1019	7.9604	8.0481	7.8731	7.9535
April	7.0353	7.0653	7.5890	7.6190	7.8823	7.9123	8.0800	8.1100	7.9537	8.0452	7.8730	7.9568
May	7.0500	7.0800	7.5974	7.6274	7.8961	7.9261	8.0800	8.1100	7.9447	8.0257	7.8588	7.9449
June	7.1190	7.1490	7.6260	7.6560	7.9080	7.9380	8.0803	8.1126	7.9449	8.0299	7.8417	7.9142
July	7.1813	7.2113	7.6587	7.6887	7.9216	7.9516	8.0620	8.1034	7.9436	8.0333	7.7893	7.8819
August	7.2477	7.2777	7.6916	7.7216	7.9445	7.9745	8.0211	8.0779	7.9392	8.0170	7.7158	7.8024
September	7.3053	7.3353	7.7217	7.7517	7.9720	8.0020	8.0083	8.0672	7.9348	8.0102	7.6885	7.7683
October	7.3603	7.3913	7.7403	7.7703	7.9965	8.0265	8.0034	8.0601	7.9342	8.0108	7.6754	7.7566
November	7.4027	7.4327	7.7553	7.7853	8.0173	8.0473	7.9903	8.0525	7.9360	8.0134	7.6301	7.7095
December	7.4523	7.4823	7.7926	7.8226	8.0297	8.0597	7.9760	8.0581	7.9219	8.0000	7.5785	7.6562
Yearly Avg	**7.1600**	**7.1900**	**7.6492**	**7.6792**	**7.9263**	**7.9563**	**8.0394**	**8.0845**	**7.9477**	**8.0291**	**7.7761**	**7.8591**

Table 5b: Monthly Exchange Rates Bs/$ on the Parallel Market[1] continued

Month	2008		2009		2010		2011		2012	
	Buying	Selling	Buying	Selling	Buying	Selling	Buying	Selling	Buying	Selling
January	7.5339	7.6129	6.9815	7.0830	7.0276	7.0762	6.9617	7.0310	6.8902	6.9514
February	7.4680	7.5660	6.9805	7.0839	7.0173	7.0754	6.9626	7.0240	6.8863	6.9504
March	7.4228	7.5242	6.9878	7.0828	7.0318	7.0752	6.9353	7.0024	6.8967	6.9587
April	7.3259	7.4154	6.9810	7.0777	7.0302	7.0702	6.9135	6.9828	6.9016	6.9590
May	7.2152	7.3179	6.9880	7.0765	7.0296	7.0729	6.8959	6.9771		
June	7.1377	7.2338	6.9869	7.0762	7.0307	7.0742	6.8838	6.9631		
July	7.0436	7.1436	6.9993	7.0762	7.0347	7.0710	6.8720	6.9538		
August	6.9908	7.0636	6.9986	7.0763	7.0310	7.0724	6.8647	6.9355		
September	6.9690	7.0855	6.9963	7.0758	7.0346	7.0697	6.8660	6.9387		
October	6.9613	7.0849	7.0018	7.0755	7.0382	7.0709	6.8662	6.9385		
November	6.9687	7.0879	7.0086	7.0763	7.0020	7.0659	6.8573	6.9243		
December	6.9815	7.0913	7.0113	7.0755	6.9414	7.0345	6.8621	6.9306		
Yearly Avg	**7.1682**	**7.2689**	**6.9935**	**7.0780**	**7.0208**	**7.0690**	**6.8951**	**6.9668**	**6.8937**	**6.9549**

Notes: (1) Monthly average is estimated by considering daily quotations throughtout the month; Yearly average is estimated as an average of all monthly averages for each year.
(2) Until 1986, exchange rate is expressed in Pesos Bolivianos per US Dollar ($). From 1987 onwards, the exchange rate is expressed in Bolivianos per Dollar. 1 Boliviano = 1,000,000 Pesos Bolivianos.
Values in table reflect author's own estimations based on data from the CBB and the NIS.

Table 6b: Yearly Nominal Interest Rates in the Financial System (%)						
	Time Deposits and Credits in Bolivianos (Bs) (181-360 Days)		Savings Accounts		Time Deposits and Credits in US Dollars ($) (181-360 Days)	
At the end of:	Lending Rate	Savings Rate	Savings Rate Bs	Savings Rate $	Lending Rate	Savings Rate
1976	15.00	10.75	10.00	-	-	9.00
1977	15.00	10.75	10.00	-	-	9.00
1978	15.00	10.75	10.00	-	-	9.00
1979	19.00	11.75	15.00	-	-	9.00
1980	20.88	18.00	17.00	-	-	11.00
1981	30.00	23.00	22.00	-	-	20.00
1982	38.00	32.00	30.00	-	-	-
1983	62.00	45.00	43.00	-	-	-
1984	150.00	140.00	110.00	-	-	-
1985	231.10	110.00	99.60	-	16.80	11.20
1986	64.78	33.39	29.57	-	22.01	14.97
1987	38.77	29.10	22.45	-	26.03	15.56
1988	34.58	24.87	20.15	7.10	22.27	14.12
1989	33.56	18.98	16.65	7.88	22.06	15.06
1990	33.45	18.95	17.67	8.58	20.33	13.64
1991	32.20	17.60	18.53	7.84	17.78	10.99
1992	43.73	21.78	19.71	8.00	17.43	11.17
1993	43.53	18.40	19.72	7.57	16.36	9.83
1994	42.68	15.68	15.40	6.70	16.30	10.17
1995	43.98	23.50	15.76	6.94	17.40	11.71
1996	47.99	17.04	15.06	6.96	17.32	9.94
1997	40.88	13.70	12.47	6.06	16.56	8.92
1998	33.13	11.60	11.04	5.50	15.81	8.71
1999	25.73	15.48	9.92	5.34	15.58	9.40
2000	35.77	10.88	8.11	4.17	14.76	8.70
2001	21.18	13.83	5.90	2.19	13.04	5.78
2002	35.02	14.90	6.04	1.09	10.95	5.59
2003	24.25	6.19	4.18	0.53	10.09	3.51
2004	9.71	7.47	3.51	0.53	8.04	3.50
2005	9.26	6.38	2.78	0.45	9.75	4.50
2006	9.29	5.16	2.33	1.17	10.14	4.74
2007	11.16	5.78	2.32	1.57	8.96	4.72
2008	12.23	6.06	2.71	3.57	10.60	6.61
2009	6.36	1.02	0.29	0.37	5.98	0.98
2010	5.97	0.98	0.58	0.14	5.50	0.78
2011	7.31	1.44	0.69	0.12	6.47	1.01

Notes: Lending and saving rates for Bolivianos (Bs) and for US Dollars ($) are end-of-year nominal rates for loans with maturities between 181–360 days.

From 1976 to 1994, interest rates percentages are nominal rates reported for Bolivian currency and US Dollars, without distinction or reference to maturity.

Information on interest rates by maturity only begins to be available on March 21, 1994.

Values in table reflect author's own estimations based on data from the Central Bank of Bolivia (CBB), and the National Institute of Statistics (NIS).

Table 1c: Yearly Gross Domestic Product (GDP), Current US Dollars, 1940-2013		
Year	GDP	GDP per Capita
1940	287,171,850.00	116.05
1941	375,497,600.00	150.35
1942	463,206,200.00	183.78
1943	484,024,800.00	190.30
1944	534,067,800.00	208.10
1945	589,638,000.00	227.72
1946	644,784,000.00	246.82
1947	851,344,500.00	323.06
1948	1,283,376,850.00	482.79
1949	1,415,038,300.00	527.76
1950	248,000,000.00	91.71
1951	285,700,000.00	103.35
1952	314,700,000.00	111.40
1953	292,200,000.00	101.28
1954	309,900,000.00	105.21
1955	386,600,000.00	128.62
1956	357,300,000.00	116.20
1957	345,400,000.00	109.86
1958	282,900,000.00	88.04
1959	322,100,000.00	98.13
1960	563,110,051.99	167.85
1961	612,518,907.15	178.57
1962	669,722,540.43	190.95
1963	721,142,960.44	201.05
1964	812,543,073.81	221.49
1965	908,874,535.94	242.18
1966	994,044,552.92	258.88
1967	1,084,059,817.95	275.90
1968	908,874,535.94	226.00
1969	964,615,702.56	234.29
1970	1,017,171,717.17	241.23
1971	1,095,454,545.45	253.60
1972	1,257,615,644.98	284.14
1973	1,263,018,490.75	278.47
1974	2,100,249,875.06	451.92
1975	2,404,697,651.17	505.05
1976	2,732,083,958.02	560.17
1977	3,227,436,281.86	646.11
1978	3,758,220,889.56	734.85

Table 1c: Yearly Gross Domestic Product (GDP), Current US Dollars, 1940-2013 continued		
Year	GDP	GDP per Capita
1979	4,421,343,606.18	844.80
1980	4,537,487,842.82	847.71
1981	5,891,606,677.69	1,076.87
1982	5,594,118,400.64	1,000.87
1983	5,422,656,261.90	949.91
1984	6,169,481,549.38	1,058.08
1985	5,377,277,407.53	902.64
1986	3,958,338,767.71	650.16
1987	4,323,623,592.64	694.72
1988	4,597,615,614.04	722.50
1989	4,715,978,705.93	724.60
1990	4,867,582,765.48	731.04
1991	5,343,259,488.69	784.18
1992	5,643,864,513.50	809.25
1993	5,734,703,516.15	803.38
1994	5,981,218,963.40	818.87
1995	6,715,164,449.93	898.84
1996	7,396,952,017.82	968.49
1997	7,925,733,799.38	1,015.56
1998	8,497,499,275.78	1,066.02
1999	8,285,061,590.60	1,017.97
2000	8,397,858,205.83	1,010.91
2001	8,141,513,227.14	960.46
2002	7,905,485,150.07	914.28
2003	8,082,396,474.24	916.80
2004	8,773,451,753.44	976.68
2005	9,549,196,301.70	1,044.01
2006	11,451,297,465.95	1,230.44
2007	13,120,517,443.16	1,386.43
2008	16,675,015,771.13	1,733.65
2009	17,339,992,191.23	1,774.20
2010	19,649,724,655.58	1,979.02
2011	20,533,962,265.08	2,023.56
2012	21,457,990,567.01	2,069.10
2013	22,423,600,142.53	2,115.67

Notes: All values in current US Dollars, converted from Bolivianos at yearly average official exchange rate (Bs/$).
Values for 2010 and 2011 are preliminary estimates; values for 2012 and 2013 are forecasts.
Values in table reflect author's own estimations based on data from the Central Bank of Bolivia (CBB), and the National Institute of Statistics (NIS).

Table 2c: GDP by Economic Activity, 1958-2010						
	US Dollars from 1958					
	1958	1959	1960	1961	1962	1963
GDP AT MARKET PRICES	350,000,000.00	348,958,333.33	363,958,333.33	371,562,500.00	392,291,666.67	417,500,000.00
GOODS	205,937,500.00	212,500,000.00	214,479,166.67	218,125,000.00	227,083,333.33	244,791,666.67
Agriculture and livestock	111,041,666.67	112,916,666.67	112,916,666.67	118,437,500.00	117,291,666.67	123,854,166.67
Crude oil and natural gas	13,958,333.33	13,125,000.00	14,375,000.00	13,645,833.33	14,583,333.33	15,937,500.00
Metallic and non-metallic minerals	29,166,666.67	33,854,166.67	29,895,833.33	31,875,000.00	33,437,500.00	37,604,166.67
Manufacturing industries	39,062,500.00	39,479,166.67	42,604,166.67	42,291,666.67	46,458,333.33	49,479,166.67
Construction and public works	12,708,333.33	13,125,000.00	14,687,500.00	11,875,000.00	15,312,500.00	17,916,666.67
BASIC UTILITIES	35,104,166.67	34,166,666.67	35,937,500.00	36,458,333.33	38,645,833.33	41,354,166.67
Electricity, gas, and water	5,416,666.67	4,791,666.67	5,104,166.67	5,416,666.67	5,937,500.00	6,354,166.67
Transportation, storage, and telecommunications	29,687,500.00	29,375,000.00	30,833,333.33	31,041,666.67	32,708,333.33	35,000,000.00
OTHER SERVICES	108,958,333.33	102,291,666.67	113,541,666.67	116,979,166.67	126,562,500.00	131,354,166.67
Commerce	44,791,666.67	45,416,666.67	47,291,666.67	47,500,000.00	50,104,166.67	53,645,833.33
Financial and real estate services	37,187,500.00	29,062,500.00	37,708,333.33	37,916,666.67	40,312,500.00	40,312,500.00
Public administration	26,979,166.67	27,812,500.00	28,541,666.67	31,562,500.00	36,145,833.33	37,395,833.33
IMPORT DUTIES, VAT, IT AND OTHER INDIRECT TAXES	-	-	-	-	-	-

Table 2c: GDP by Economic Activity, 1958-2010 continued									
	US Dollars from 1968				US Dollars from 1970				
	1964	1965	1966	1967	1968	1969	1970	1971	1972
GDP AT MARKET PRICES	660,723,296.89	693,187,552.57	742,893,187.55	789,823,380.99	923,348,758.94	965,586,874.21	1,040,807,740.85	1,091,796,381.99	1,155,153,554.90
GOODS	330,950,378.47	358,116,063.92	380,656,013.46	403,364,171.57	464,282,709.30	470,256,626.00	489,188,052.17	513,420,277.66	550,357,593.61
Agriculture and livestock	143,397,813.29	151,387,720.77	156,938,603.87	152,312,867.96	169,962,137.15	154,648,716.87	188,472,864.96	199,663,441.31	211,358,855.70
Crude oil and natural gas	6,896,551.72	5,971,404.54	10,933,557.61	31,118,587.05	32,898,611.70	31,468,237.27	9,928,481.28	19,604,543.54	26,756,415.65
Metallic and non-metallic minerals	68,040,370.06	68,208,578.64	75,525,651.81	76,366,694.70	91,712,242.32	101,472,444.26	97,181,320.99	94,068,153.13	97,770,298.70
Manufacturing industries	88,393,608.07	96,551,724.14	108,494,533.22	112,952,060.56	128,481,278.92	138,409,760.20	150,610,012.62	155,994,951.62	168,615,902.40
Construction and public works	24,222,035.32	35,996,635.83	28,763,666.95	30,613,961.31	41,228,439.21	44,257,467.40	42,995,372.32	44,089,188.05	45,856,121.16
BASIC UTILITIES	67,703,952.90	69,217,830.11	74,936,921.78	78,216,989.07	92,385,359.70	99,453,092.13	92,385,359.70	99,284,812.79	106,184,265.88
Electricity, gas, and water	9,083,263.25	10,092,514.72	12,531,539.11	13,456,686.29	16,070,677.32	17,080,353.39	14,051,325.20	15,061,001.26	15,986,537.65
Transportation, storage, and telecommunications	58,620,689.66	59,125,315.39	62,405,382.67	64,760,302.78	76,314,682.37	82,372,738.75	78,334,034.50	84,223,811.53	90,197,728.23
OTHER SERVICES	262,068,965.52	265,853,658.54	287,300,252.31	308,242,220.35	366,680,689.95	395,877,156.08	470,256,626.00	490,618,426.59	511,653,344.55
Commerce	84,104,289.32	86,543,313.71	96,215,306.98	106,980,656.01	125,872,949.10	132,099,284.81	183,592,763.99	188,472,864.96	192,679,848.55
Financial and real estate services	128,763,666.95	121,530,698.07	127,838,519.76	135,744,322.96	166,512,410.60	184,602,440.05	203,702,145.56	210,517,458.98	219,183,845.18
Public administration	49,201,009.25	57,779,646.76	63,246,425.57	65,517,241.38	74,295,330.25	79,175,431.22	82,961,716.45	91,628,102.65	99,789,650.82
IMPORT DUTIES, VAT, IT AND OTHER INDIRECT TAXES	-	-	-	-	-	-	-11,022,297.01	-11,527,135.04	-13,041,649.14

Table 2c: GDP by Economic Activity, 1958-2010 continued

	US Dollars from 1970					US Dollars from 1980			
	1973	1974	1975	1976	1977	1978	1979	1980	1981
GDP AT MARKET PRICES	1,232,309,633.99	1,295,750,946.57	1,381,320,992.85	1,465,544,804.38	1,527,219,183.85	5,075,010,191.60	5,081,777,415.41	5,012,066,856.91	5,058,418,263.35
GOODS	600,504,838.03	620,698,359.28	650,988,641.14	685,065,208.25	702,061,421.96	2,779,942,927.03	2,723,073,787.20	2,628,006,522.63	2,573,664,900.12
Agriculture and livestock	221,119,057.64	229,280,605.81	247,202,355.91	259,570,887.67	257,888,094.24	876,070,118.22	907,541,785.57	919,812,474.52	911,292,295.15
Crude oil and natural gas	36,095,919.23	31,720,656.29	24,905,342.87	26,335,717.29	20,025,241.90	284,386,465.55	261,842,641.66	274,276,396.25	288,300,040.77
Metallic and non-metallic minerals	118,889,356.33	111,737,484.22	112,663,020.61	112,663,020.61	115,355,490.11	577,415,409.70	532,205,462.70	516,877,293.11	532,694,659.60
Manufacturing industries	177,029,869.58	197,055,111.49	209,087,084.56	226,503,996.63	242,238,115.27	769,710,558.50	757,358,336.73	732,735,426.01	675,947,819.00
Construction and public works	47,370,635.25	50,904,501.47	57,130,837.19	59,991,586.03	66,554,480.44	272,360,375.05	264,125,560.54	184,304,932.74	165,430,085.61
BASIC UTILITIES	113,756,836.35	129,827,513.67	145,393,352.97	161,884,728.65	183,087,925.96	300,856,094.58	338,809,620.87	331,308,601.71	370,199,755.40
Electricity, gas, and water	17,753,470.76	19,520,403.87	19,941,102.23	21,539,755.99	23,979,806.48	29,107,215.65	29,922,543.82	32,857,725.23	36,975,132.49
Transportation, storage, and telecommunications	96,003,365.59	110,307,109.80	125,452,250.74	140,344,972.65	159,108,119.48	271,748,878.92	308,887,077.05	298,450,876.48	333,224,622.91
OTHER SERVICES	533,024,821.20	560,454,354.23	604,291,123.26	641,649,137.57	667,564,156.50	1,847,900,529.96	1,887,892,376.68	1,918,711,781.49	1,961,557,276.80
Commerce	198,737,904.92	204,880,100.97	221,623,895.67	232,646,192.68	238,451,830.04	541,500,203.83	555,320,016.31	540,603,342.85	587,770,077.46
Financial and real estate services	228,102,650.40	239,040,807.74	257,551,535.55	275,641,565.00	291,039,124.95	853,974,724.83	872,604,973.50	850,591,112.92	835,955,972.28
Public administration	106,184,265.88	116,533,445.52	125,115,692.05	133,361,379.89	138,073,201.51	452,425,601.30	459,967,386.87	527,517,325.72	537,831,227.07
IMPORT DUTIES, VAT, IT AND OTHER INDIRECT TAXES	-14,976,861.59	-15,229,280.61	-19,352,124.53	-23,054,270.09	-25,494,320.57	146,310,640.03	132,001,630.66	134,039,951.08	152,996,331.02

Table 2c: GDP by Economic Activity, 1958–2010 continued

	US Dollars from 1980							
	1982	1983	1984	1985	1986	1987	1988	1989
GDP AT MARKET PRICES	4,837,912,759.89	4,622,013,860.58	4,594,211,170.00	4,549,857,317.57	4,436,526,702.00	4,551,936,404.40	4,686,628,618.02	4,819,445,576.84
GOODS	2,513,452,914.80	2,289,930,697.11	2,351,406,441.09	2,301,467,590.71	2,162,576,437.02	2,218,181,818.18	2,390,052,996.33	2,496,697,920.91
Agriculture and livestock	974,317,162.66	806,685,690.99	960,171,218.92	1,034,325,315.94	997,880,146.76	1,032,898,491.64	1,057,929,066.45	1,043,783,122.71
Crude oil and natural gas	304,769,669.79	292,539,747.25	285,976,355.48	284,264,166.33	279,127,598.86	283,326,538.93	293,069,710.56	305,870,362.82
Metallic and non-metallic minerals	491,235,222.18	445,821,443.13	362,291,072.16	295,067,264.57	216,836,526.70	220,179,372.20	310,517,733.39	389,115,368.94
Manufacturing industries	592,376,681.61	593,477,374.64	599,551,569.51	549,653,485.53	560,211,985.32	574,276,396.25	605,462,698.74	626,742,763.96
Construction and public works	150,754,178.56	151,406,441.09	143,416,225.03	138,157,358.34	108,520,179.37	107,501,019.16	123,073,787.20	131,186,302.49
BASIC UTILITIES	355,849,979.62	358,377,496.94	387,117,814.92	401,916,021.20	424,174,480.23	441,133,306.16	445,128,414.19	455,727,680.39
Electricity, gas, and water	37,912,759.89	38,768,854.46	41,785,568.69	40,195,678.76	43,171,626.58	40,603,342.85	42,845,495.31	45,046,881.37
Transportation, storage, and telecommunications	317,937,219.73	319,608,642.48	345,332,246.23	361,720,342.44	381,002,853.65	400,529,963.31	402,282,918.87	410,680,799.02
OTHER SERVICES	1,924,174,480.23	1,950,387,280.88	1,812,963,717.90	1,793,232,776.19	1,769,017,529.56	1,799,836,934.37	1,776,966,979.21	1,793,192,009.78
Commerce	548,878,923.77	651,569,506.73	539,869,547.49	542,845,495.31	602,038,320.42	651,202,609.05	625,764,370.16	627,231,960.86
Financial and real estate services	814,798,206.28	756,135,344.48	752,221,769.26	759,518,956.38	754,504,688.14	726,090,501.43	734,977,578.48	744,598,450.88
Public administration	560,497,350.18	542,682,429.68	520,872,401.14	490,868,324.50	412,474,520.99	422,543,823.89	416,225,030.57	421,361,598.04
IMPORT DUTIES, VAT, IT AND OTHER INDIRECT TAXES	44,435,385.24	23,318,385.65	42,723,196.09	53,240,929.47	80,758,255.20	92,784,345.70	74,480,228.29	73,827,965.76

Table 2c: GDP by Economic Activity, 1958-2010 continued								
	Thousands of US Dollars from 1990							
	1990	1991	1992	1993	1994	1995	1996	1997
GDP AT MARKET PRICES	4,882,433.45	5,139,567.50	5,224,190.64	5,447,226.68	5,701,463.17	5,968,193.80	6,228,487.51	6,537,059.44
GOODS	2,227,832.75	2,361,823.59	2,352,213.09	2,460,819.16	2,585,619.03	2,715,466.65	2,830,583.94	2,942,420.49
Agriculture and livestock	749,629.15	823,541.89	788,663.93	821,342.40	876,145.43	883,444.20	948,007.90	991,187.48
Crude oil and natural gas	209,877.33	211,421.75	213,393.93	218,475.50	237,211.82	245,084.41	250,586.15	285,992.41
Metallic and non-metallic minerals	290,253.24	299,920.64	304,760.04	330,003.16	330,116.66	363,607.97	346,073.66	346,845.40
Manufacturing industries	828,208.35	868,127.73	868,805.25	904,253.24	953,192.22	1,017,949.73	1,067,467.28	1,089,034.78
Construction and public works	149,864.69	158,811.57	176,589.95	186,744.86	188,952.89	200,380.34	218,448.94	229,360.42
BASIC UTILITIES	533,515.97	568,831.81	595,164.08	631,133.42	674,165.98	717,209.61	762,067.34	826,767.63
Electricity, gas, and water	78,538.41	84,059.12	87,966.17	101,634.84	113,075.25	122,878.60	127,000.95	132,979.77
Transportation, storage, and telecommunications	454,977.55	484,772.68	507,197.91	529,498.58	561,090.74	594,331.01	635,066.39	693,787.86
OTHER SERVICES	1,716,494.78	1,775,852.04	1,834,479.29	1,899,642.74	1,967,097.38	2,021,761.62	2,104,420.17	2,205,647.49
Commerce	433,430.29	461,926.65	465,283.59	478,795.13	498,740.12	512,902.62	540,601.33	567,280.43
Financial and real estate services	792,182.74	818,996.21	854,145.12	890,317.10	923,460.64	950,464.75	996,808.41	1,044,770.47
Public administration	490,881.76	494,929.18	515,050.58	530,530.51	544,896.62	558,394.25	567,010.43	593,596.59
IMPORT DUTIES, VAT, IT AND OTHER INDIRECT TAXES	404,589.95	433,060.07	442,334.18	455,631.36	474,580.78	513,755.93	531,416.06	562,223.84

TTable 2c: GDP by Economic Activity, 1958-2010 continued								
	Thousands of US Dollars from 1990							
	1998	1999	2000	2001	2002	2003	2004	2005
GDP AT MARKET PRICES	6,865,830.86	6,895,140.37	7,068,057.22	7,187,069.24	7,365,708.19	7,565,417.96	7,881,145.12	8,229,604.49
GOODS	3,042,753.71	3,016,286.12	3,100,704.08	3,139,152.39	3,200,707.56	3,307,948.47	3,452,656.97	3,665,192.54
Agriculture and livestock	947,285.80	971,035.41	1,004,782.48	1,039,556.75	1,044,206.77	1,135,187.16	1,138,000.32	1,194,705.03
Crude oil and natural gas	322,831.17	309,049.00	345,043.63	344,873.54	361,143.85	393,162.50	488,292.44	559,531.77
Metallic and non-metallic minerals	345,215.62	328,526.72	333,429.66	323,187.16	323,481.50	325,366.74	297,940.25	329,609.55
Manufacturing industries	1,116,096.43	1,148,747.71	1,169,311.41	1,200,734.11	1,203,743.60	1,249,561.81	1,319,294.97	1,358,929.81
Construction and public works	311,324.69	258,927.28	248,136.90	230,800.82	268,131.84	204,670.25	209,128.99	222,416.38
BASIC UTILITIES	878,996.52	879,658.55	899,365.48	923,114.13	959,983.24	995,722.42	1,034,436.29	1,064,367.06
Electricity, gas, and water	136,327.85	142,773.32	145,342.71	146,315.52	149,579.20	153,961.11	158,716.09	163,027.82
Transportation, storage, and telecommunications	742,668.67	736,885.24	754,022.76	776,798.61	810,404.05	841,761.30	875,720.20	901,339.23
OTHER SERVICES	2,321,327.85	2,441,479.29	2,491,263.99	2,532,608.60	2,562,607.97	2,600,840.97	2,667,205.82	2,710,873.22
Commerce	576,284.54	575,413.53	597,913.69	601,437.24	614,374.01	629,510.59	654,135.00	674,244.39
Financial and real estate services	1,129,222.26	1,236,515.02	1,253,450.84	1,275,146.06	1,271,412.58	1,271,226.37	1,289,165.35	1,286,457.16
Public administration	615,821.06	629,550.74	639,899.46	656,025.29	676,821.37	700,104.02	723,905.47	750,171.67
IMPORT DUTIES, VAT, IT AND OTHER INDIRECT TAXES	622,752.77	557,716.41	576,723.68	592,194.12	642,409.42	660,906.10	726,846.03	789,171.67

Table 2c: GDP by Economic Activity, 1958-2010 continued

	Thousands of US Dollars from 1990				
	2006	2007	2008	2009	2010[p]
GDP AT MARKET PRICES	8,624,379.07	9,018,029.09	9,572,502.69	9,893,851.41	10,302,143.53
GOODS	3,892,120.77	4,075,577.93	4,420,450.52	4,552,582.67	4,654,544.42
Agriculture and livestock	1,245,593.11	1,239,293.08	1,271,700.60	1,318,523.55	1,302,990.52
Crude oil and natural gas	585,284.22	615,958.27	628,528.30	543,798.61	619,651.28
Metallic and non-metallic minerals	351,578.56	386,653.18	604,179.89	663,977.55	636,931.71
Manufacturing industries	1,468,901.04	1,558,365.79	1,615,404.36	1,693,115.40	1,736,955.74
Construction and public works	240,763.83	275,307.62	300,637.37	333,167.56	358,015.18
BASIC UTILITIES	1,106,246.92	1,146,357.89	1,191,638.63	1,259,104.33	1,358,425.86
Electricity, gas, and water	169,603.22	176,916.85	183,244.07	194,438.19	208,704.08
Transportation, storage, and telecommunications	936,643.69	969,441.04	1,008,394.56	1,064,666.14	1,149,721.78
OTHER SERVICES	2,789,849.19	2,907,652.86	3,010,650.33	3,150,926.97	3,277,392.35
Commerce	700,183.05	739,308.25	774,547.58	812,527.98	844,729.05
Financial and real estate services	1,312,113.18	1,359,211.19	1,396,017.39	1,443,847.30	1,505,545.68
Public administration	777,552.96	809,133.42	840,085.36	894,551.69	927,117.61
IMPORT DUTIES, VAT, IT AND OTHER INDIRECT TAXES	836,162.19	888,440.40	949,763.20	931,237.43	1,011,780.90

Notes: Values in table reflect author's own estimations based on data from the Central Bank of Bolivia (CBB) and the National Institute of Statistics (NIS).
Between 1974 and 1977, 'Other services' includes: financial intermediaries, real estate, and for-profit and not-for-profit private services.
(p) preliminary.

Table 3c: GDP Growth, by Economic Activity (in %)

	1959	1960	1961	1962	1963	1964	1965	1966	1967	1968	1969	1970	1971
GDP AT MARKET PRICES	-0.30	4.30	2.09	5.58	6.43	4.82	4.91	7.17	6.32	8.53	4.57	7.79	4.90
GOODS	3.19	0.93	1.70	4.11	7.80	4.09	8.21	6.29	5.97	5.86	1.29	4.03	4.95
Agriculture and livestock	1.69	-	4.89	-0.97	5.60	2.02	5.57	3.67	-2.95	6.07	-9.01	21.87	5.94
Crude oil and natural gas	-5.97	9.52	-5.07	6.87	9.29	5.88	-13.41	83.10	184.62	-0.54	-4.35	-68.45	97.46
Metallic and non-metallic minerals	16.07	-11.69	6.62	4.90	12.46	8.31	0.25	10.73	1.11	5.73	10.64	-4.23	-3.20
Manufacturing industries	1.07	7.92	-0.73	9.85	6.50	6.11	9.23	12.37	4.11	2.53	7.73	8.81	3.58
Construction and public works	3.28	11.90	-19.15	28.95	17.01	2.33	48.61	-20.09	6.43	23.90	7.35	-2.85	2.54
BASIC UTILITIES	-2.67	5.18	1.45	6.00	7.01	4.79	2.24	8.26	4.38	8.82	7.65	-7.11	7.47
Electricity, gas, and water	-11.54	6.52	6.12	9.62	7.02	-	11.11	24.17	7.38	11.25	6.28	-17.73	7.19
Transportation, storage, and telecommunications	-1.05	4.96	0.68	5.37	7.01	5.65	0.86	5.55	3.77	8.31	7.94	-4.90	7.52
OTHER SERVICES	-6.12	11.00	3.03	8.19	3.79	6.19	1.44	8.07	7.29	11.95	7.96	18.79	4.33
Commerce	1.40	4.13	0.44	5.48	7.07	3.69	2.90	11.18	11.19	7.86	4.95	38.98	2.66
Financial and real estate services	-21.85	29.75	0.55	6.32	-	11.89	-5.62	5.19	6.18	17.66	10.86	10.35	3.35
Public administration	3.09	2.62	10.58	14.52	3.46	3.62	17.44	9.46	3.59	6.80	6.57	4.78	10.45
IMPORT DUTIES, VAT, IT AND OTHER INDIRECT TAXES	-	-	-	-	-	-	-	-	-	-	-	-	4.58

Table 3c: GDP Growth, by Economic Activity (in %) continued													
	1972	1973	1974	1975	1976	1977	1978	1979	1980	1981	1982	1983	1984
GDP AT MARKET PRICES	5.80	6.68	5.15	6.60	6.10	4.21	3.36	0.13	-1.37	0.92	-4.36	-4.46	-0.60
GOODS	7.19	9.11	3.36	4.88	5.23	2.48	0.87	-2.05	-3.49	-2.07	-2.34	-8.89	2.68
Agriculture and livestock	5.86	4.62	3.69	7.82	5.00	-0.65	2.12	3.59	1.35	-0.93	6.92	-17.21	19.03
Crude oil and natural gas	36.48	34.91	-12.12	-21.49	5.74	-23.96	-4.20	-7.93	4.75	5.11	5.71	-4.01	-2.24
Metallic and non-metallic minerals	3.94	21.60	-6.02	0.83	-	2.39	-9.85	-7.83	-2.88	3.06	-7.78	-9.24	-18.74
Manufacturing industries	8.09	4.99	11.31	6.11	8.33	6.95	4.55	-1.60	-3.25	-7.75	-12.36	0.19	1.02
Construction and public works	4.01	3.30	7.46	12.23	5.01	10.94	2.78	-3.02	-30.22	-10.24	-8.87	0.43	-5.28
BASIC UTILITIES	6.95	7.13	14.13	11.99	11.34	13.10	12.36	12.62	-2.21	11.74	-3.88	0.71	8.02
Electricity, gas, and water	6.15	11.05	9.95	2.16	8.02	11.33	5.96	2.80	9.81	12.53	2.54	2.26	7.78
Transportation, storage, and telecommunications	7.09	6.44	14.90	13.73	11.87	13.37	13.33	13.67	-3.38	11.65	-4.59	0.53	8.05
OTHER SERVICES	4.29	4.18	5.15	7.82	6.18	4.04	3.76	2.16	1.63	2.23	-1.91	1.36	-7.05
Commerce	2.23	3.14	3.09	8.17	4.97	2.50	2.29	2.55	-2.65	8.72	-6.62	18.71	-17.14
Financial and real estate services	4.12	4.07	4.80	7.74	7.02	5.59	5.00	2.18	-2.52	-1.72	-2.53	-7.20	-0.52
Public administration	8.91	6.41	9.75	7.36	6.59	3.53	3.66	1.67	14.69	1.96	4.21	-3.18	-4.02
IMPORT DUTIES, VAT, IT AND OTHER INDIRECT TAXES	13.14	14.84	1.69	27.07	19.13	10.58	10.23	-9.78	1.54	14.14	-70.96	-47.52	83.22

Table 3c: GDP Growth, by Economic Activity (in %) continued

	1985	1986	1987	1988	1989	1990	1991	1992	1993	1994	1995	1996	1997
GDP AT MARKET PRICES	-0.97	-2.49	2.60	2.96	2.83	2.62	5.27	1.65	4.27	4.67	4.68	4.36	4.95
GOODS	-2.12	-6.03	2.57	7.75	4.46	2.84	6.01	-0.41	4.62	5.07	5.02	4.24	3.95
Agriculture and livestock	7.72	-3.52	3.51	2.42	-1.34	-1,98	9.86	-4.24	4.14	6.67	1.40	6.70	4.55
Crude oil and natural gas	-0.60	-1.81	1.50	3.44	4.37	3.69	0.74	0.93	2.38	8.58	3.32	2.24	14.13
Metallic and non-metallic minerals	-18.56	-26.51	1.54	41.03	25.31	10.63	3.33	1.61	8.28	0.03	10.15	-4.82	0.22
Manufacturing industries	-8.32	1.92	2.51	5.43	3.51	5.70	4.82	0.08	4.08	5.41	6.79	4.86	2.02
Construction and public works	-3.67	-21.45	-0.94	14.49	6.59	2.45	5.97	11.19	5.75	1.18	6.05	9.02	4.99
BASIC UTILITIES	3.82	5.54	4.00	0.91	2.38	3.10	6.62	4.63	6.04	6.82	6.38	6.25	8.49
Electricity, gas, and water	-3.80	7.40	-5.95	5.52	5.14	5.43	7.03	4.65	15.54	11.26	8.67	3.35	4.71
Transportation, storage, and telecommunications	4.75	5.33	5.13	0.44	2.09	2.85	6.55	4.63	4.40	5.97	5.92	6.85	9.25
OTHER SERVICES	-1.09	-1.35	1.74	-1.27	0.91	2.94	3.46	3.30	3.55	3.55	2.78	4.09	4.81
Commerce	0.55	10.90	8.17	-3.91	0.23	1.50	6.57	0.73	2.90	4.17	2.84	5.40	4.94
Financial and real estate services	0.97	-0.66	-3.77	1.22	1.31	3.22	3.38	4.29	4.23	3.72	2.92	4.88	4.81
Public administration	-5.76	-15.97	2.44	-1.50	1.23	4.58	0.82	4.07	3.01	2.71	2.48	1.54	4.69
IMPORT DUTIES, VAT, IT AND OTHER INDIRECT TAXES	24.62	51.68	14.89	-19.73	-0.88	-15,68	7.04	2.14	3.01	4.16	8.25	3.44	5.80

Table 3c: GDP Growth, by Economic Activity (in %) continued

	1998	1999	2000	2001	2002	2003	2004	2005	2006	2007	2008	2009	2010
GDP AT MARKET PRICES	5.03	0.43	2.51	1.68	2.49	2.71	4.17	4.42	4.80	4.56	6.15	3.36	4.13
GOODS	3.41	-0.87	2.80	1.24	1.96	3.35	4.37	6.16	6.19	4.71	8.46	2.99	2.24
Agriculture and livestock	-4.43	2.51	3.48	3.46	0.45	8.71	0.25	4.98	4.26	-0.51	2.62	3.68	-1.18
Crude oil and natural gas	12.88	-4.27	11.65	-0.05	4.72	8.87	24.20	14.59	4.60	5.24	2.04	-13.48	13.95
Metallic and non-metallic minerals	-0.47	-4.83	1.49	-3.07	0.09	0.58	-8.43	10.63	6.57	9.98	56.26	9.90	-4.07
Manufacturing industries	2.48	2.93	1.79	2.69	0.25	3.81	5.58	3.00	8.09	6.09	3.66	4.81	2.59
Construction and public works	35.74	-16.83	-4.17	-6.99	16.17	-23.67	2.18	6.35	8.25	14.35	9.20	10.82	7.46
BASIC UTILITIES	6.32	0.08	2.24	2.64	3.99	3.72	3.89	2.89	3.93	3.63	3.95	5.66	7.89
Electricity, gas, and water	2.52	4.73	1.80	0.67	2.23	2.93	3.09	2.72	4.03	4.31	3.58	6.11	7.34
Transportation, storage, and telecommunications	7.05	-0.78	2.33	3.02	4.33	3.87	4.03	2.93	3.92	3.50	4.02	5.58	7.99
OTHER SERVICES	5.24	5.18	2.04	1.66	1.18	1.49	2.55	1.64	2.91	4.22	3.54	4.66	4.01
Commerce	1.59	-0.15	3.91	0.59	2.15	2.46	3.91	3.07	3.85	5.59	4.77	4.90	3.96
Financial and real estate services	8.08	9.50	1.37	1.73	-0.29	-0.01	1.41	-0.21	1.99	3.59	2.71	3.43	4.27
Public administration	3.74	2.23	1.64	2.52	3.17	3.44	3.40	3.63	3.65	4.06	3.83	6.48	3.64
IMPORT DUTIES, VAT, IT AND OTHER INDIRECT TAXES	10.77	-10.44	3.41	2.68	8.48	2.88	9.98	8.57	5.95	6.25	6.90	-1.95	8.65

Notes: Values in table reflect author's own estimations based on data from the Central Bank of Bolivia (CBB), and the National Institute of Statistics (NIS).
Growth rates between years with different bases were estimated by converting values of first year with new base to values with old base.

Table 4c: Share of Each Economic Activity in GDP (in %)

	1958	1959	1960	1961	1962	1963	1964	1965	1966	1967	1968	1969	1970	1971
GDP AT MARKET PRICES	100.00	100.00	100.00	100.00	100.00	100.00	100.00	100.00	100.00	100.00	100.00	100.00	100.00	100.00
GOODS	58.84	60.90	58.93	58.70	57.89	58.63	50.09	51.66	51.24	51.07	50.28	48.70	47.00	47.03
Agriculture and livestock	31.73	32.36	31.02	31.88	29.90	29.67	21.70	21.84	21.13	19.28	18.41	16.02	18.11	18.29
Crude oil and natural gas	3.99	3.76	3.95	3.67	3.72	3.82	1.04	0.86	1.47	3.94	3.56	3.26	0.95	1.80
Metallic and non-metallic minerals	8.33	9.70	8.21	8.58	8.52	9.01	10.30	9.84	10.17	9.67	9.93	10.51	9.34	8.62
Manufacturing industries	11.16	11.31	11.71	11.38	11.84	11.85	13.38	13.93	14.60	14.30	13.91	14.33	14.47	14.29
Construction and public works	3.63	3.76	4.04	3.20	3.90	4.29	3.67	5.19	3.87	3.88	4.47	4.58	4.13	4.04
BASIC UTILITIES	10.03	9.79	9.87	9.81	9.85	9.91	10.25	9.99	10.09	9.90	10.01	10.30	8.88	9.09
Electricity, gas, and water	1.55	1.37	1.40	1.46	1.51	1.52	1.37	1.46	1.69	1.70	1.74	1.77	1.35	1.38
Transportation, storage, and telecommunications	8.48	8.42	8.47	8.35	8.34	8.38	8.87	8.53	8.40	8.20	8.26	8.53	7.53	7.71
OTHER SERVICES	31.13	29.31	31.20	31.48	32.26	31.46	39.66	38.35	38.67	39.03	39.71	41.00	45.18	44.94
Commerce	12.80	13.01	12.99	12.78	12.77	12.85	12.73	12.48	12.95	13.54	13.63	13.68	17.64	17.26
Financial and real estate services	10.63	8.33	10.36	10.20	10.28	9.66	19.49	17.53	17.21	17.19	18.03	19.12	19.57	19.28
Public administration	7.71	7.97	7.84	8.49	9.21	8.96	7.45	8.34	8.51	8.30	8.05	8.20	7.97	8.39
IMPORT DUTIES, VAT, IT AND OTHER INDIRECT TAXES	-	-	-	-	-	-	-	-	-	-	-	-	-1.06	-1.06

Table 4c: Share of Each Economic Activity in GDP (in %) continued

	1972	1973	1974	1975	1976	1977	1978	1979	1980	1981	1982	1983	1984
GDP AT MARKET PRICES	100.00	100.00	100.00	100.00	100.00	100.00	100.00	100.00	100.00	100.00	100.00	100.00	100.00
GOODS	47.64	48.73	47.90	47.13	46.74	45.97	54.78	53.59	52.43	50.88	51.95	49.54	51.18
Agriculture and livestock	18.30	17.94	17.69	17.90	17.71	16.89	17.26	17.86	18.35	18.02	20.14	17.45	20.90
Crude oil and natural gas	2.32	2.93	2.45	1.80	1.80	1.31	5.60	5.15	5.47	5.70	6.30	6.33	6.22
Metallic and non-metallic minerals	8.46	9.65	8.62	8.16	7.69	7.55	11.38	10.47	10.31	10.53	10.15	9.65	7.89
Manufacturing industries	14.60	14.37	15.21	15.14	15.46	15.86	15.17	14.90	14.62	13.36	12.24	12.84	13.05
Construction and public works	3.97	3.84	3.93	4.14	4.09	4.36	5.37	5.20	3.68	3.27	3.12	3.28	3.12
BASIC UTILITIES	9.19	9.23	10.02	10.53	11.05	11.99	5.93	6.67	6.61	7.32	7.36	7.75	8.43
Electricity, gas, and water	1.38	1.44	1.51	1.44	1.47	1.57	0.57	0.59	0.66	0.73	0.78	0.84	0.91
Transportation, storage, and telecommunications	7.81	7.79	8.51	9.08	9.58	10.42	5.35	6.08	5.95	6.59	6.57	6.91	7.52
OTHER SERVICES	44.29	43.25	43.25	43.75	43.78	43.71	36.41	37.15	38.28	38.78	39.77	42.20	39.46
Commerce	16.68	16.13	15.81	16.04	15.87	15.61	10.67	10.93	10.79	11.62	11.35	14.10	11.75
Financial and real estate services	18.97	18.51	18.45	18.65	18.81	19.06	16.83	17.17	16.97	16.53	16.84	16.36	16.37
Public administration	8.64	8.62	8.99	9.06	9.10	9.04	8.91	9.05	10.52	10.63	11.59	11.74	11.34
IMPORT DUTIES, VAT, IT AND OTHER INDIRECT TAXES	-1.13	-1.22	-1.18	-1.40	-1.57	-1.67	2.88	2.60	2.67	3.02	0.92	0.50	0.93

Table 4c: Share of Each Economic Activity in GDP (in %) continued

	1985	1986	1987	1988	1989	1990	1991	1992	1993	1994	1995	1996	1997
GDP AT MARKET PRICES	100.00	100.00	100.00	100.00	100.00	100.00	100.00	100.00	100.00	100.00	100.00	100.00	100.00
GOODS	50.58	48.74	48.73	51.00	51.80	45.63	45.95	45.03	45.18	45.35	45.50	45.45	45.01
Agriculture and livestock	22.73	22.49	22.69	22.57	21.66	15.35	16.02	15.10	15.08	15.37	14.89	15.22	15.16
Crude oil and natural gas	6.25	6.29	6.22	6.25	6.35	4.30	4.11	4.08	4.01	4.16	4.11	4.02	4.37
Metallic and non-metallic minerals	6.49	4.89	4.84	6.63	8.07	5.94	5.84	5.83	6.06	5.79	6.09	5.56	5.31
Manufacturing industries	12.08	12.63	12.62	12.92	13.00	16.96	16.89	16.63	16.60	16.72	17.06	17.14	16.66
Construction and public works	3.04	2.45	2.36	2.63	2.72	3.07	3.09	3.38	3.43	3.31	3.36	3.51	3.51
BASIC UTILITIES	8.83	9.56	9.69	9.50	9.46	10.93	11.07	11.39	11.59	11.82	12.02	12.24	12.65
Electricity, gas, and water	0.88	0.97	0.89	0.91	0.93	1.61	1.64	1.68	1.87	1.98	2.06	2.04	2.03
Transportation, storage, and telecommunications	7.95	8.59	8.80	8.58	8.52	9.32	9.43	9.71	9.72	9.84	9.96	10.20	10.61
OTHER SERVICES	39.41	39.87	39.54	37.92	37.21	35.16	34.55	35.12	34.87	34.50	33.88	33.79	33.74
Commerce	11.93	13.57	14.31	13.35	13.01	8.88	8.99	8.91	8.79	8.75	8.59	8.68	8.68
Financial and real estate services	16.69	17.01	15.95	15.68	15.45	16.23	15.94	16.35	16.34	16.20	15.93	16.00	15.98
Public administration	10.79	9.30	9.28	8.88	8.74	10.05	9.63	9.86	9.74	9.56	9.36	9.10	9.08
IMPORT DUTIES, VAT, IT AND OTHER INDIRECT TAXES	1.17	1.82	2.04	1.59	1.53	8.29	8.43	8.47	8.36	8.32	8.61	8.53	8.60

Table 4c: Share of Each Economic Activity in GDP (in %) continued

	1998	1999	2000	2001	2002	2003	2004	2005	2006	2007	2008	2009	2010
GDP AT MARKET PRICES	100.00	100.00	100.00	100.00	100.00	100.00	100.00	100.00	100.00	100.00	100.00	100.00	100.00
GOODS	44.32	43.75	43.87	43.68	43.45	43.72	43.81	44.54	45.13	45.19	46.18	46.01	45.18
Agriculture and livestock	13.80	14.08	14.22	14.46	14.18	15.00	14.44	14.52	14.44	13.74	13.28	13.33	12.65
Crude oil and natural gas	4.70	4.48	4.88	4.80	4.90	5.20	6.20	6.80	6.79	6.83	6.57	5.50	6.01
Metallic and non-metallic minerals	5.03	4.76	4.72	4.50	4.39	4.30	3.78	4.01	4.08	4.29	6.31	6.71	6.18
Manufacturing industries	16.26	16.66	16.54	16.71	16.34	16.52	16.74	16.51	17.03	17.28	16.88	17.11	16.86
Construction and public works	4.53	3.76	3.51	3.21	3.64	2.71	2.65	2.70	2.79	3.05	3.14	3.37	3.48
BASIC UTILITIES	12.80	12.76	12.72	12.84	13.03	13.16	13.13	12.93	12.83	12.71	12.45	12.73	13.19
Electricity, gas, and water	1.99	2.07	2.06	2.04	2.03	2.04	2.01	1.98	1.97	1.96	1.91	1.97	2.03
Transportation, storage, and telecommunications	10.82	10.69	10.67	10.81	11.00	11.13	11.11	10.95	10.86	10.75	10.53	10.76	11.16
OTHER SERVICES	33.81	35.41	35.25	35.24	34.79	34.38	33.84	32.94	32.35	32.24	31.45	31.85	31.81
Commerce	8.39	8.35	8.46	8.37	8.34	8.32	8.30	8.19	8.12	8.20	8.09	8.21	8.20
Financial and real estate services	16.45	17.93	17.73	17.74	17.26	16.80	16.36	15.63	15.21	15.07	14.58	14.59	14.61
Public administration	8.97	9.13	9.05	9.13	9.19	9.25	9.19	9.12	9.02	8.97	8.78	9.04	9.00
IMPORT DUTIES, VAT, IT AND OTHER INDIRECT TAXES	9.07	8.09	8.16	8.24	8.72	8.74	9.22	9.59	9.70	9.85	9.92	9.41	9.82

Note: Values in table reflect author's own estimations based on data from the Central Bank of Bolivia (CBB), and the National Institute of Statistics (NIS).

Table 5c: GDP by Type of Expenditure, 1964–2010

	US Dollars from 1968					
	1964	1965	1966	1967	1968	1969
CONSUMO	574,768,713.20	630,277,544.15	674,852,817.49	713,456,686.29	739,276,703.11	785,113,540.79
Final expenditures by institutions in government administration	63,835,155.59	78,132,884.78	80,824,222.04	83,431,455.00	90,664,423.89	94,196,804.04
Final expenditures by households and not-for-profit institutions	510,933,557.61	552,144,659.38	594,028,595.46	630,025,231.29	648,612,279.23	690,916,736.75
GROSS INVESTMENT	96,383,515.56	114,718,250.63	119,596,299.41	111,774,600.50	154,415,475.19	145,079,899.07
Gross fixed capital formation	91,505,466.78	98,822,539.95	88,057,190.92	100,252,312.87	148,864,592.09	131,118,587.05
Inventory provisions	4,878,048.78	15,895,710.68	31,539,108.49	11,522,287.64	5,550,883.10	13,961,312.03
BALANCE IN TRADE OF GOODS AND SERVICES	-10,428,931.88	-51,808,242.22	-51,555,929.35	-35,407,905.80	-36,501,261.56	-34,650,967.20
Exports of goods and services	115,979,814.97	120,353,238.02	136,248,948.70	168,713,204.37	169,554,247.27	174,095,878.89
Imports of goods and services	126,408,746.85	172,161,480.24	187,804,878.05	204,121,110.18	206,055,508.83	208,746,846.09
GDP AT MARKET PRICES	660,723,296.89	693,187,552.57	742,893,187.55	789,823,380.99	857,190,916.74	895,542,472.67

Table 5c: GDP by Type of Expenditure, 1964–2010 continued

	US Dollars from 1970							
	1970	1971	1972	1973	1974	1975	1976	1977
CONSUMO	864,507,989.91	901,345,668.63	922,371,740.96	1,003,448,275.86	1,044,154,751.89	1,098,402,018.50	1,181,076,534.90	1,238,015,138.77
Final expenditures by institutions in government administration	111,354,079.06	121,278,385.20	134,566,862.91	150,462,573.59	164,087,468.46	182,169,890.66	193,187,552.57	199,158,957.11
Final expenditures by households and not-for-profit institutions	753,153,910.85	780,067,283.43	787,804,878.05	852,985,702.27	880,067,283.43	916,232,127.84	987,888,982.34	1,038,856,181.67
GROSS INVESTMENT	177,544,154.75	197,056,349.87	241,211,101.77	213,624,894.87	211,942,809.08	303,448,275.86	274,348,191.76	282,590,412.11
Gross fixed capital formation	150,714,886.46	165,853,658.54	185,281,749.37	180,824,222.04	196,972,245.58	236,669,470.14	247,687,132.04	261,816,652.65
Inventory provisions	26,829,268.29	31,202,691.34	55,929,352.40	32,800,672.83	14,970,563.50	66,778,805.72	26,661,059.71	20,773,759.46
BALANCE IN TRADE OF GOODS AND SERVICES	-1,682,085.79	-7,064,760.30	-8,915,054.67	14,718,250.63	39,108,494.53	-21,110,176.62	9,503,784.69	5,971,404.54
Exports of goods and services	209,756,097.56	233,978,132.88	258,368,376.79	287,384,356.60	284,524,810.77	271,993,271.66	301,261,564.34	295,206,055.51
Imports of goods and services	211,438,183.35	241,042,893.19	267,283,431.46	272,666,105.97	245,416,316.23	293,103,448.28	291,757,779.65	289,234,650.97
GDP AT MARKET PRICES	1,040,370,058.87	1,091,337,258.20	1,154,667,788.06	1,231,791,421.36	1,295,206,055.51	1,380,740,117.75	1,464,928,511.35	1,526,576,955.42

Table 5c: GDP by Type of Expenditure, 1964–2010 continued

	US Dollars from 1980					
	1978	1979	1980	1981	1982	1983
CONSUMO	3,862,250,305.75	3,985,161,027.31	4,001,712,189.16	4,067,549,938.85	3,906,604,158.17	3,574,887,892.38
Final expenditures by institutions in government administration	597,676,314.72	692,662,046.47	648,348,960.46	702,649,816.55	682,185,079.49	602,038,320.42
Final expenditures by households and not-for-profit institutions	3,264,573,991.03	3,292,498,980.84	3,353,363,228.70	3,364,900,122.30	3,224,419,078.68	2,972,849,571.95
GROSS INVESTMENT	1,176,559,315.12	1,024,500,611.50	736,159,804.32	846,392,172.85	495,801,059.93	471,667,346.11
Gross fixed capital formation	1,010,354,667.75	939,788,014.68	713,982,878.11	696,494,088.87	495,271,096.62	422,339,991.85
Inventory provisions	166,204,647.37	84,712,596.82	22,176,926.21	149,898,083.98	529,963.31	49,327,354.26
BALANCE IN TRADE OF GOODS AND SERVICES	36,200,570.73	72,115,776.60	274,194,863.43	144,476,151.65	435,507,541.79	575,458,622.10
Exports of goods and services	1,328,903,383.61	1,349,612,719.12	1,284,997,961.68	1,326,294,333.47	1,285,038,728.09	1,314,227,476.56
Imports of goods and services	1,292,702,812.88	1,277,496,942.52	1,010,803,098.25	1,181,818,181.82	849,531,186.30	738,768,854.46
GDP AT MARKET PRICES	5,075,010,191.60	5,081,777,415.41	5,012,066,856.91	5,058,418,263.35	4,837,912,759.89	4,622,013,860.58

Table 5c: GDP by Type of Expenditure, 1964–2010 continued						
	US Dollars from 1980					
	1984	1985	1986	1987	1988	1989
CONSUMO	3,654,871,585.81	3,726,416,632.69	3,819,608,642.48	4,029,637,178.96	4,076,763,147.17	4,184,019,567.88
Final expenditures by institutions in government administration	624,989,808.40	578,719,934.77	497,024,052.18	557,521,402.36	535,222,176.93	553,933,958.42
Final expenditures by households and not-for-profit institutions	3,029,881,777.42	3,147,696,697.92	3,322,584,590.30	3,472,115,776.60	3,541,540,970.24	3,630,085,609.46
GROSS INVESTMENT	643,538,524.26	854,382,388.91	743,538,524.26	826,579,698.33	625,601,304.53	563,147,166.73
Gross fixed capital formation	467,672,238.08	562,739,502.65	593,151,243.38	621,850,794.94	637,505,095.80	658,092,132.08
Inventory provisions	175,866,286.18	291,642,886.26	150,387,280.88	204,728,903.38	-11,903,791.28	-94,944,965.35
BALANCE IN TRADE OF GOODS AND SERVICES	295,801,059.93	-30,941,704.04	-126,620,464.74	-304,280,472.89	-15,735,833.67	72,278,842.23
Exports of goods and services	1,224,785,976.36	1,086,832,450.06	1,210,680,799.02	1,138,809,620.87	1 210,803,098.25	1,358,010,599.27
Imports of goods and services	928,984,916.43	1,117,774,154.10	1,337,301,263.76	1,443,090,093.76	1,226,538,931.92	1,285,731,757.03
GDP AT MARKET PRICES	4,594,211,170.00	4,549,857,317.57	4,436,526,702.00	4,551,936,404.40	4,686,628,618.02	4,819,445,576.84

Table 5c: GDP by Type of Expenditure, 1964-2010 continued

	Thousands of US Dollars from 1990						
	1990	1991	1992	1993	1994	1995	1996
CONSUMO	4,326,683.84	4,470,576.35	4,630,340.82	4,779,423.96	4,920,887.76	5,089,863.10	5,251,512.49
Final expenditures by institutions in government administration	573,953.53	593,128.36	615,028.45	630,605.75	650,358.52	693,479.92	711,548.53
Final expenditures by households and not-for-profit institutions	3,752,730.32	3,877,447.99	4,015,312.36	4,148,818.21	4,270,529.24	4,396,383.18	4,539,963.96
GROSS INVESTMENT	611,863.42	791,060.07	833,165.98	832,590.26	744,316.16	835,932.34	992,984.51
Gross fixed capital formation	613,159.97	730,075.25	818,169.46	839,675.94	772,349.35	878,938.98	982,023.71
Inventory provisions	-1,296.55	60,984.82	14,996.52	-7,085.68	-28,033.20	-43,006.64	10,960.80
BALANCE IN TRADE OF GOODS AND SERVICES	-56,114.45	-122,068.61	-239,316.47	-164,787.54	36,259.25	42,398.04	-16,010.12
Exports of goods and services	1,112,070.82	1,193,183.05	1,206,460.95	1,270,458.74	1,462,253.56	1,595,586.15	1,660,505.22
Imports of goods and services	1,168,185.27	1,315,251.66	1,445,777.43	1,435,246.29	1,425,994.31	1,553,188.11	1,676,515.33
GDP AT MARKET PRICES	4,882,432.82	5,139,567.82	5,224,190.33	5,447,226.68	5,701,463.17	5,968,193.49	6,228,486.88

Table 5c: GDP by Type of Expenditure, 1964–2010 continued

	Thousands of US Dollars from 1990						
	1997	1998	1999	2000	2001	2002	2003
CONSUMO	5,521,895.98	5,801,291.50	5,964,965.22	6,100,577.62	6,190,824.85	6,329,091.69	6,462,781.85
Final expenditures by institutions in government administration	735,457.48	763,410.69	787,917.80	804,294.97	827,319.63	855,920.96	886,501.11
Final expenditures by households and not-for-profit institutions	4,786,438.51	5,037,880.81	5,177,047.42	5,296,282.64	5,363,505.22	5,473,170.72	5,576,280.75
GROSS INVESTMENT	1,293,198.86	1,661,890.61	1,350,084.73	1,250,484.03	1,032,035.41	1,216,369.59	1,060,336.07
Gross fixed capital formation	1,244,843.19	1,608,545.68	1,362,821.06	1,241,544.74	975,245.34	1,155,742.02	1,030,394.56
Inventory provisions	48,355.67	53,344.93	-12,736.33	8,939.30	56,790.07	60,627.57	29,941.51
BALANCE IN TRADE OF GOODS AND SERVICES	-278,035.41	-597,351.25	-419,909.90	-283,004.43	-35,791.02	-179,752.77	42,299.72
Exports of goods and services	1,625,465.06	1,730,834.65	1,509,204.87	1,736,198.23	1,881,643.69	1,988,770.15	2,230,665.19
Imports of goods and services	1,903,500.47	2,328,185.90	1,929,114.76	2,019,202.66	1,917,434.71	2,168,522.92	2,188,365.48
GDP AT MARKET PRICES	6,537,059.44	6,865,830.86	6,895,140.06	7,068,057.22	7,187,069.24	7,365,708.50	7,565,417.64

Table 5c: GDP by Type of Expenditure, 1964–2010 continued

	Thousands of US Dollars from 1990						
	2004	2005	2006	2007	2008	2009	2010[p]
CONSUMO	6,652,961.11	6,874,705.34	7,147,049.64	7,441,139.42	7,833,210.24	8,122,481.19	8,435,630.73
Final expenditures by institutions in government administration	914,410.69	945,097.69	976,034.46	1,012,812.84	1,052,423.96	1,092,626.94	1,126,156.50
Final expenditures by households and not-for-profit institutions	5,738,550.43	5,929,607.65	6,171,015.18	6,428,326.59	6,780,786.28	7,029,854.25	7,309,474.23
GROSS INVESTMENT	934,739.80	1,185,863.42	1,125,501.74	1,249,942.46	1,616,342.71	1,679,036.67	1,799,037.62
Gross fixed capital formation	1,018,877.65	1,086,803.35	1,187,822.32	1,338,006.32	1,587,848.56	1,633,721.47	1,755,658.87
Inventory provisions	-84,137.84	99,060.07	-62,320.58	-88,063.86	28,494.15	45,315.21	43,378.75
BALANCE IN TRADE OF GOODS AND SERVICES	293,443.88	169,036.04	351,828.33	326,947.20	122,950.05	92,333.86	67,474.87
Exports of goods and services	2,601,413.85	2,818,276.00	3,137,779.32	3,234,710.72	3,305,050.58	2,949,570.66	3,240,180.84
Imports of goods and services	2,307,969.97	2,649,239.96	2,785,951.00	2,907,763.52	3,182,100.54	2,857,236.80	3,172,705.98
GDP AT MARKET PRICES	7,881,144.80	8,229,604.81	8,624,379.70	9,018,029.09	9,572,503.00	9,893,851.72	10,302,143.22

Notes: Values in table reflect author's own estimations based on data from the Central Bank of Bolivia (CBB), and the National Institute of Statistics (NIS).
(p) Preliminary.

Table 6c: Gross Domestic Product Growth, by Expenditure (in %)

	1965	1966	1967	1968	1969	1970	1971	1972	1973	1974	1975	1976	1977	1978	1979
CONSUMO	9.66	7.07	5.72	3.62	6.20	6.42	4.26	2.33	8.79	4.06	5.20	7.53	4.82	5.56	3.18
Final expenditures by institutions in government administration	22.40	3.44	3.23	8.67	3.90	5.36	8.91	10.96	11.81	9.06	11.02	6.05	3.09	2.87	15.89
Final expenditures by households and not-for-profit institutions	8.07	7.59	6.06	2.95	6.52	6.56	3.57	0.99	8.27	3.17	4.11	7.82	5.16	6.08	0.86
GROSS INVESTMENT	19.02	4.25	- 6.54	38.15	- 6.05	2.26	10.99	22.41	- 11.44	- 0.79	43.17	- 9.59	3.00	0.95	- 12.92
Gross fixed capital formation	8.00	- 10.89	13.85	48.49	- 11.92	0.32	10.04	11.71	- 2.41	8.93	20.15	4.66	5.70	9.57	- 6.98
Inventory provisions	225.86	98.41	- 63.47	- 51.82	151.52	20.48	16.30	79.25	- 41.35	- 54.36	346.07	- 60.08	- 22.08	- 107.69	- 49.03
BALANCE IN TRADE OF GOODS AND SERVICES	-	-	-	-	-	-	-	-	-	-	-	-	-	-	-
Exports of goods and services	3.77	13.21	23.83	0.50	2.68	- 9.71	11.55	10.42	11.23	- 1.00	- 4.40	10.76	- 2.01	- 2.99	1.56
Imports of goods and services	36.19	9.09	8.69	0.95	1.31	- 4.83	14.00	10.89	2.01	- 9.99	19.43	- 0.46	- 0.86	3.98	- 1.18
GDP AT MARKET PRICES	4.91	7.17	6.32	8.53	4.47	5.23	4.90	5.80	6.68	5.15	6.60	6.10	4.21	3.36	0.13

Table 6c: Gross Domestic Product Growth, by Expenditure (in %) continued

	1980	1981	1982	1983	1984	1985	1986	1987	1988	1989	1990	1991	1992	1993	1994
CONSUMO	0.42	1.65	- 3.96	- 8.49	2.24	1.96	2.50	5.50	1.17	2.63	1.92	3.33	3.57	3.22	2.96
Final expenditures by institutions in government administration	- 6.40	8.38	- 2.91	- 11.75	3.81	- 7.40	- 14.12	12.17	- 4.00	3.50	4.00	3.34	3.69	2.53	3.13
Final expenditures by households and not-for-profit institutions	1.85	0.34	- 4.17	- 7.80	1.92	3.89	5.56	4.50	2.00	2.50	1.60	3.32	3.56	3.32	2.93
GROSS INVESTMENT	- 28.14	14.97	- 41.42	- 4.87	36.44	32.76	- 12.97	11.17	- 24.31	- 9.98	-6,44	29.29	5.32	- 0.07	- 10.60
Gross fixed capital formation	- 24.03	- 2.45	- 28.89	- 14.73	10.73	20.33	5.40	4.84	2.52	3.23	-4,26	19.07	12.07	2.63	- 8.02
Inventory provisions	- 73.82	575.92	- 99.65	9,207.69	256.53	65.83	- 48.43	36.13	- 105.81	697.60	8.67	- 4,803.61	- 75.41	- 147.25	295.63
BALANCE IN TRADE OF GOODS AND SERVICES	-	-	-	-	-	-	-	-	-	-	-	-	-	-	-
Exports of goods and services	- 4.79	3.21	- 3.11	2.27	- 6.81	- 11.26	11.40	- 5.94	6.32	12.16	14.95	7.29	1.11	5.30	15.10
Imports of goods and services	- 20.88	16.92	- 28.12	- 13.04	25.75	20.32	19.64	7.91	- 15.01	4.83	9.40	12.59	9.92	- 0.73	- 0.64
GDP AT MARKET PRICES	- 1.37	0.92	- 4.36	- 4.46	- 0.60	- 0.97	- 2.49	2.60	2.96	2.83	2.62	5.27	1.65	4.27	4.67

Table 6c: Gross Domestic Product Growth, by Expenditure (in %) continued

	1995	1996	1997	1998	1999	2000	2001	2002	2003	2004	2005	2006	2007	2008	2009	2010
CONSUMO	3.43	3.18	5.15	5.06	2.82	2.27	1.48	2.23	2.11	2.94	3.33	3.96	4.11	5.27	3.69	3.86
Final expenditures by institutions in government administration	6.63	2.61	3.36	3.80	3.21	2.08	2.86	3.46	3.57	3.15	3.36	3.27	3.77	3.91	3.82	3.07
Final expenditures by households and not-for-profit institutions	2.95	3.27	5.43	5.25	2.76	2.30	1.27	2.04	1.88	2.91	3.33	4.07	4.17	5.48	3.67	3.98
GROSS INVESTMENT	12.31	18.79	30.23	28.51	- 18.76	- 7.38	- 17.47	17.86	- 12.83	- 11.84	26.87	- 5.09	11.06	29.31	3.88	7.15
Gross fixed capital formation	13.80	11.73	26.76	29.22	- 15.28	- 8.90	- 21.45	18.51	- 10.85	- 1.12	6.67	9.30	12.64	18.67	2.89	7.46
Inventory provisions	53.41	- 125.49	341.17	10.32	- 123.88	- 170.19	535.29	6.76	- 50.61	- 381.01	- 217.74	- 162.91	41.31	- 132.36	59.03	- 4.27
BALANCE IN TRADE OF GOODS AND SERVICES	-	-	-	-	-	-	-	-	-	-	-	-	-	-	-	-
Exports of goods and services	9.12	4.07	- 2.11	6.48	- 12.80	15.04	8.38	5.69	12.16	16.62	8.34	11.34	3.09	2.17	- 10.76	9.85
Imports of goods and services	8.92	7.94	13.54	22.31	- 17.14	4.67	- 5.04	13.10	0.92	5.47	14.79	5.16	4.37	9.43	- 10.21	11.04
GDP AT MARKET PRICES	4.68	4.36	4.95	5.03	0.43	2.51	1.68	2.49	2.71	4.17	4.42	4.80	4.56	6.15	3.36	4.13

Notes: Values in table reflect author's own estimations based on data from the Central Bank of Bolivia (CBB), and the National Institute of Statistics (NIS).
Growth rates between years with different bases were estimated by converting values of first year with new base to values with old base.

Table 7c: Share of Each Type of Expenditure in GDP (in %)

	1964	1965	1966	1967	1968	1969	1970	1971	1972	1973	1974	1975	1976	1977	1978
CONSUMO	86.99	90.92	90.84	90.33	86.24	87.67	83.10	82.59	79.88	81.46	80.62	79.55	80.62	81.10	76.10
Final expenditures by institutions in government administration	9.66	11.27	10.88	10.56	10.58	10.52	10.70	11.11	11.65	12.21	12.67	13.19	13.19	13.05	11.78
Final expenditures by households and not-for-profit institutions	77.33	79.65	79.96	79.77	75.67	77.15	72.39	71.48	68.23	69.25	67.95	66.36	67.44	68.05	64.33
GROSS INVESTMENT	14.59	16.55	16.10	14.15	18.01	16.20	17.07	18.06	20.89	17.34	16.36	21.98	18.73	18.51	23.18
Gross fixed capital formation	13.85	14.26	11.85	12.69	17.37	14.64	14.49	15.20	16.05	14.68	15.21	17.14	16.91	17.15	19.91
Inventory provisions	0.74	2.29	4.25	1.46	0.65	1.56	2.58	2.86	4.84	2.66	1.16	4.84	1.82	1.36	3.27
TOTAL SHARE OF TRADE ON GDP	36.69	42.20	43.62	47.20	43.82	42.75	40.49	43.53	45.52	45.47	40.92	40.93	40.48	38.28	51.66
Exports of goods and services	17.55	17.36	18.34	21.36	19.78	19.44	20.16	21.44	22.38	23.33	21.97	19.70	20.56	19.34	26.19
Imports of goods and services	19.13	24.84	25.28	25.84	24.04	23.31	20.32	22.09	23.15	22.14	18.95	21.23	19.92	18.95	25.47
GDP AT MARKET PRICES	100.00	100.00	100.00	100.00	100.00	100.00	100.00	100.00	100.00	100.00	100.00	100.00	100.00	100.00	100.00

Table 7c: Share of Each Type of Expenditure in GDP (in %) continued															
	1979	1980	1981	1982	1983	1984	1985	1986	1987	1988	1989	1990	1991	1992	1993
CONSUMO	78.42	79.84	80.41	80.75	77.34	79.55	81.90	86.09	88.53	86.99	86.82	88.62	86.98	88.63	87.74
Final expenditures by institutions in government administration	13.63	12.94	13.89	14.10	13.03	13.60	12.72	11.20	12.25	11.42	11.49	11.76	11.54	11.77	11.58
Final expenditures by households and not-for-profit institutions	64.79	66.91	66.52	66.65	64.32	65.95	69.18	74.89	76.28	75.57	75.32	76.86	75.44	76.86	76.16
GROSS INVESTMENT	20.16	14.69	16.73	10.25	10.20	14.01	18.78	16.76	18.16	13.35	11.68	12.53	15.39	15.95	15.28
Gross fixed capital formation	18.49	14.25	13.77	10.24	9.14	10.18	12.37	13.37	13.66	13.60	13.65	12.56	14.20	15.66	15.41
Inventory provisions	1.67	0.44	2.96	0.01	1.07	3.83	6.41	3.39	4.50	-0.25	-1.97	-0.03	1.19	0.29	-0.13
TOTAL SHARE OF TRADE ON GDP	51.70	45.81	49.58	44.12	44.42	46.88	48.45	57.43	56.72	52.01	54.86	46.70	48.81	50.77	49.67
Exports of goods and services	26.56	25.64	26.22	26.56	28.43	26.66	23.89	27.29	25.02	25.84	28.18	22.78	23.22	23.09	23.32
Imports of goods and services	25.14	20.17	23.36	17.56	15.98	20.22	24.57	30.14	31.70	26.17	26.68	23.93	25.59	27.67	26.35
GDP AT MARKET PRICES	100.00	100.00	100.00	100.00	100.00	100.00	100.00	100.00	100.00	100.00	100.00	100.00	100.00	100.00	100.00

Table 7c: Share of Each Type of Expenditure in GDP (in %) continued

	1994	1995	1996	1997	1998	1999	2000	2001	2002	2003	2004	2005	2006	2007	2008	2009	2010
CONSUMO	86.31	85.28	84.31	84.47	84.50	86.51	86.31	86.14	85.93	85.43	84.42	83.54	82.87	82.51	81.83	82.10	81.88
Final expenditures by institutions in government administration	11.41	11.62	11.42	11.25	11.12	11.43	11.38	11.51	11.62	11.72	11.60	11.48	11.32	11.23	10.99	11.04	10.93
Final expenditures by households and not-for-profit institutions	74.90	73.66	72.89	73.22	73.38	75.08	74.93	74.63	74.31	73.71	72.81	72.05	71.55	71.28	70.84	71.05	70.95
GROSS INVESTMENT	13.05	14.01	15.94	19.78	24.21	19.58	17.69	14.36	16.51	14.02	11.86	14.41	13.05	13.86	16.89	16.97	17.46
Gross fixed capital formation	13.55	14.73	15.77	19.04	23.43	19.76	17.57	13.57	15.69	13.62	12.93	13.21	13.77	14.84	16.59	16.51	17.04
Inventory provisions	-0.49	-0.72	0.18	0.74	0.78	-0.18	0.13	0.79	0.82	0.40	-1.07	1.20	-0.72	-0.98	0.30	0.46	0.42
TOTAL SHARE OF TRADE ON GDP	50.66	52.76	53.58	53.98	59.12	49.87	53.13	52.86	56.44	58.41	62.29	66.44	68.69	68.11	67.77	58.69	62.25
Exports of goods and services	25.65	26.73	26.66	24.87	25.21	21.89	24.56	26.18	27.00	29.49	33.01	34.25	36.38	35.87	34.53	29.81	31.45
Imports of goods and services	25.01	26.02	26.92	29.12	33.91	27.98	28.57	26.68	29.44	28.93	29.28	32.19	32.30	32.24	33.24	28.88	30.80
GDP AT MARKET PRICES	100.00	100.00	100.00	100.00	100.00	100.00	100.00	100.00	100.00	100.00	100.00	100.00	100.00	100.00	100.00	100.00	100.00

Note: Values in table reflect author's own estimations based on data from the Central Bank of Bolivia (CBB), and the National Institute of Statistics (NIS).

Table 8c: GDP by Department (current US dollars)

	La Paz	Santa Cruz	Cochabamba	Oruro	Potosí	Chuquisaca	Tarija	Beni	Pando	Bolivia
1988	1,278,666,335.20	1,173,466,524.31	851,347,492.55	264,367,503.09	282,987,437.58	303,568,451.67	219,318,558.18	190,417,669.40	33,475,642.06	4,597,615,614.04
1989	1,301,737,419.84	1,223,298,441.93	848,361,040.97	284,876,164.66	301,022,269.61	306,805,597.77	227,390,349.95	188,358,042.97	34,129,378.24	4,715,978,705.93
1990	1,315,547,117.34	1,308,783,830.35	859,274,110.53	265,749,190.35	292,303,459.64	331,296,698.89	253,555,680.36	204,630,206.28	36,442,471.74	4,867,582,765.48
1991	1,464,682,513.27	1,463,605,895.04	966,423,470.07	273,285,244.63	290,862,720.47	348,215,635.54	273,851,204.29	224,321,298.93	38,011,506.46	5,343,259,488.69
1992	1,588,036,422.61	1,535,770,696.06	1,025,804,390.47	291,193,329.29	311,112,745.75	350,723,229.52	276,397,561.34	226,221,702.61	38,604,435.84	5,643,864,513.50
1993	1,644,728,753.27	1,582,048,694.13	1,055,710,375.76	289,447,044.24	278,113,434.46	341,785,098.54	274,437,527.79	228,029,513.62	40,403,074.34	5,734,703,516.15
1994	1,736,613,882.05	1,655,018,532.06	1,098,796,830.77	333,071,050.94	285,906,176.86	322,562,208.72	273,032,452.70	232,452,161.52	43,765,667.78	5,981,218,963.40
1995	1,983,275,692.26	1,848,831,016.69	1,215,932,364.79	388,328,548.89	325,996,625.39	350,202,397.59	292,175,247.64	260,220,203.41	50,202,353.27	6,715,164,449.93
1996	2,178,720,439.36	2,083,011,786.03	1,321,053,364.80	424,377,073.00	364,926,729.95	365,530,925.70	320,771,957.16	283,386,604.82	55,173,136.99	7,396,952,017.82
1997	2,205,601,370.43	2,307,693,741.46	1,418,520,835.34	470,237,547.38	375,823,704.03	400,126,552.46	389,649,244.20	298,078,194.40	60,002,609.68	7,925,733,799.38
1998	2,172,685,620.76	2,630,000,430.01	1,531,221,269.77	518,161,264.04	373,302,303.23	443,183,528.57	441,705,815.29	317,139,093.76	70,099,950.35	8,497,499,275.78
1999	2,153,678,899.30	2,434,067,711.00	1,540,321,906.95	487,854,421.85	389,945,928.72	460,999,548.76	425,001,409.61	321,307,967.39	71,883,797.01	8,285,061,590.60
2000	2,159,167,910.54	2,522,881,936.32	1,568,023,136.71	475,171,901.67	399,199,943.52	444,924,657.12	440,729,048.66	312,616,184.79	75,143,486.51	8,397,858,205.83
2001	2,050,977,844.12	2,502,446,052.05	1,492,133,930.59	455,638,454.79	375,383,361.90	430,079,076.72	453,648,954.94	303,995,046.95	77,210,505.07	8,141,513,227.14
2002	2,030,777,994.25	2,399,206,219.34	1,422,656,029.14	428,368,824.31	360,239,807.51	411,326,163.78	495,715,892.30	284,651,692.77	72,542,526.67	7,905,485,150.07
2003	2,082,793,522.83	2,455,822,029.01	1,404,897,750.36	417,867,299.32	381,591,627.95	401,709,875.00	588,677,524.89	278,995,792.22	70,041,052.65	8,082,396,474.24
2004	2,181,852,977.73	2,639,106,685.81	1,525,138,491.24	441,953,380.13	425,252,125.92	434,082,685.90	763,186,407.77	287,791,725.73	75,087,273.21	8,773,451,753.44
2005	2,344,643,875.41	2,827,086,595.02	1,610,694,078.16	468,133,314.92	431,699,750.23	418,152,097.42	1,073,743,683.86	288,790,080.35	86,252,826.33	9,549,196,301.70
2006	2,766,764,008.46	3,348,282,328.73	1,843,670,118.71	549,455,539.04	624,741,895.17	518,067,497.41	1,350,313,438.33	360,794,992.23	89,207,647.87	11,451,297,465.95
2007	3,240,721,975.83	3,723,972,580.51	2,090,961,481.32	644,692,136.50	703,127,018.64	574,318,994.90	1,675,957,757.30	352,473,616.27	114,291,881.88	13,120,517,443.16
2008	4,111,297,940.14	4,641,248,973.87	2,558,146,102.86	908,043,148.14	1,059,921,025.43	761,141,415.49	2,045,415,291.78	448,706,494.59	141,095,378.83	16,675,015,771.13
2009	4,372,163,392.69	4,727,887,177.56	2,644,566,332.73	969,382,508.67	1,184,135,765.45	774,308,221.16	2,012,788,437.37	506,721,314.06	148,039,041.54	17,339,992,191.23
2010	4,933,861,283.11	5,355,370,674.12	2,929,485,642.82	1,158,580,691.19	1,407,420,474.92	880,595,346.86	2,223,838,090.17	573,093,497.11	187,478,955.28	19,649,724,655.58

Notes: All values in current US Dollars, converted from Bolivianos at yearly average market buying exchange rate (Bs/$).
Values in table reflect author's own estimations based on data from the Central Bank of Bolivia (CBB), and the National Institute of Statistics (NIS).

Table 9c: GDP Growth, by Department (%)

	La Paz	Santa Cruz	Cochabamba	Oruro	Potosí	Chuquisaca	Tarija	Beni	Pando	Bolivia
1989	1.80	4.25	-0.35	7.76	6.37	1.07	3.68	-1.08	1.95	2.57
1990	1.06	6.99	1.29	-6.71	-2.90	7.98	11.51	8.64	6.78	3.21
1991	11.34	11.83	12.47	2.84	-0.49	5.11	8.00	9.62	4.31	9.77
1992	8.42	4.93	6.14	6.55	6.96	0.72	0.93	0.85	1.56	5.63
1993	3.57	3.01	2.92	-0.60	-10.61	-2.55	-0.71	0.80	4.66	1.61
1994	5.59	4.61	4.08	15.07	2.80	-5.62	-0.51	1.94	8.32	4.30
1995	14.20	11.71	10.66	16.59	14.02	8.57	7.01	11.95	14.71	12.27
1996	9.85	12.67	8.65	9.28	11.94	4.38	9.79	8.90	9.90	10.15
1997	1.23	10.79	7.38	10.81	2.99	9.46	21.47	5.18	8.75	7.15
1998	-1.49	13.97	7.94	10.19	-0.67	10.76	13.36	6.39	16.83	7.21
1999	-0.87	-7.45	0.59	-5.85	4.46	4.02	-3.78	1.31	2.54	-2.50
2000	0.25	3.65	1.80	-2.60	2.37	-3.49	3.70	-2.71	4.53	1.36
2001	-5.01	-0.81	-4.84	-4.11	-5.97	-3.34	2.93	-2.76	2.75	-3.05
2002	-0.98	-4.13	-4.66	-5.98	-4.03	-4.36	9.27	-6.36	-6.05	-2.90
2003	2.56	2.36	-1.25	-2.45	5.93	-2.34	18.75	-1.99	-3.45	2.24
2004	4.76	7.46	8.56	5.76	11.44	8.06	29.64	3.15	7.20	8.55
2005	7.46	7.12	5.61	5.92	1.52	-3.67	40.69	0.35	14.87	8.84
2006	18.00	18.44	14.46	17.37	44.72	23.89	25.76	24.93	3.43	19.92
2007	17.13	11.22	13.41	17.33	12.55	10.86	24.12	-2.31	28.12	14.58
2008	26.86	24.63	22.34	40.85	50.74	32.53	22.04	27.30	23.45	27.09
2009	6.35	1.87	3.38	6.76	11.72	1.73	-1.60	12.93	4.92	3.99
2010	12.85	13.27	10.77	19.52	18.86	13.73	10.49	13.10	26.64	13.32

Notes: Values in table reflect author's own estimations based on data from the Central Bank of Bolivia (CBB), and the National Institute of Statistics (NIS). Growth rates were estimated utilizing yearly GDP valued at current Dollars (Table 8c).

Table 10c: GDP per Capita by Department (current US dollars)

	La Paz	Santa Cruz	Cochabamba	Oruro	Potosí	Chuquisaca	Tarija	Beni	Pando	Bolivia
1988	744.40	1,034.00	866.20	829.09	456.11	719.43	850.14	778.82	1,022.39	722.50
1989	738.88	1,029.40	837.26	879.12	480.32	714.01	854.98	747.28	1,003.79	724.60
1990	728.05	1,051.78	822.59	806.97	461.75	757.13	924.76	787.49	1,032.17	731.04
1991	790.32	1,123.27	897.41	816.58	454.88	781.47	968.82	837.37	1,036.77	784.18
1992	835.46	1,125.61	923.98	856.16	481.68	772.93	948.49	819.13	1,013.98	809.25
1993	844.18	1,109.60	923.22	837.63	426.33	739.92	914.34	801.62	1,023.36	803.38
1994	869.61	1,110.79	932.91	948.69	433.93	685.95	883.16	793.37	1,068.98	818.87
1995	968.90	1,187.44	1,002.29	1,088.66	489.88	731.57	917.55	862.28	1,182.45	898.84
1996	1,038.42	1,280.23	1,057.23	1,170.99	542.95	750.09	978.02	911.69	1,253.16	968.49
1997	1,025.59	1,357.25	1,102.16	1,277.10	553.63	806.56	1,153.42	931.02	1,314.23	1,015.56
1998	985.64	1,480.20	1,155.08	1,385.09	544.47	877.56	1,269.43	961.71	1,480.61	1,066.02
1999	953.19	1,310.93	1,128.10	1,283.54	563.11	896.69	1,185.85	945.97	1,464.11	1,017.97
2000	932.31	1,300.25	1,114.94	1,230.49	570.77	850.12	1,193.92	893.57	1,475.90	1,010.91
2001	872.58	1,233.05	1,025.02	1,162.73	529.44	807.23	1,193.12	843.62	1,469.98	960.46
2002	838.82	1,142.21	944.24	1,066.48	498.61	749.54	1,245.23	766.94	1,302.93	914.28
2003	835.25	1,129.62	900.93	1,014.96	518.32	710.70	1,412.37	729.80	1,186.79	916.80
2004	849.49	1,172.88	944.96	1,047.28	566.85	745.60	1,748.86	730.88	1,200.28	976.68
2005	891.37	1,183.48	963.42	1,079.94	561.96	694.81	2,339.31	709.59	1,293.36	1,044.01
2006	1,035.16	1,356.99	1,078.29	1,256.96	808.65	846.99	2,863.48	869.89	1,282.81	1,230.44
2007	1,193.63	1,462.17	1,196.27	1,463.02	905.43	924.26	3,460.94	834.39	1,578.03	1,386.43
2008	1,491.23	1,766.95	1,432.30	2,044.71	1,358.19	1,206.13	4,115.62	1,043.38	1,872.91	1,733.65
2009	1,562.24	1,746.89	1,449.81	2,166.37	1,509.87	1,208.41	3,948.90	1,157.86	1,891.87	1,774.20
2010	1,737.31	1,922.41	1,573.37	2,569.97	1,785.15	1,353.58	4,257.46	1,287.17	2,309.99	1,979.02

Notes: All values in current US Dollars.
Values in table reflect author's own estimations based on data from the Central Bank of Bolivia (CBB), and the National Institute of Statistics (NIS).
GDP per capita values were estimated utilizing yearly GDP valued at current Dollars (Table 8c).

Table 11c: GDP per Capita Growth, by Department (%)

	La Paz	Santa Cruz	Cochabamba	Oruro	Potosí	Chuquisaca	Tarija	Beni	Pando	Bolivia
1989	-0.74	-0.44	- 3.34	6.03	5.31	-0.75	0.57	-4.05	-1.82	0.29
1990	-1.47	2.17	- 1.75	-8.21	-3.87	6.04	8.16	5.38	2.83	0.89
1991	8.55	6.80	9.10	1.19	-1.49	3.21	4.76	6.33	0.45	7.27
1992	5.71	0.21	2.96	4.85	5.89	-1.09	-2.10	-2.18	-2.20	3.20
1993	1.04	-1.42	- 0.08	-2.17	-11.49	-4.27	-3.60	-2.14	0.92	-0.73
1994	3.01	0.11	1.05	13.26	1.78	-7.29	-3.41	-1.03	4.46	1.93
1995	11.42	6.90	7.44	14.75	12.89	6.65	3.89	8.69	10.61	9.77
1996	7.18	7.81	5.48	7.56	10.83	2.53	6.59	5.73	5.98	7.75
1997	-1.24	6.02	4.25	9.06	1.97	7.53	17.93	2.12	4.87	4.86
1998	-3.89	9.06	4.80	8.46	-1.65	8.80	10.06	3.30	12.66	4.97
1999	-3.29	-11.44	- 2.34	-7.33	3.42	2.18	-6.58	-1.64	-1.11	-4.51
2000	-2.19	-0.81	- 1.17	-4.13	1.36	-5.19	0.68	-5.54	0.80	-0.69
2001	-6.41	-5.17	- 8.06	-5.51	-7.24	-5.05	-0.07	-5.59	-0.40	-4.99
2002	-3.87	-7.37	- 7.88	-8.28	-5.82	-7.15	4.37	-9.09	-11.36	-4.81
2003	-0.43	-1.10	- 4.59	-4.83	3.95	-5.18	13.42	-4.84	-8.91	0.28
2004	1.70	3.83	4.89	3.18	9.36	4.91	23.82	0.15	1.14	6.53
2005	4.93	0.90	1.95	3.12	-0.86	-6.81	33.76	-2.91	7.75	6.89
2006	16.13	14.66	11.92	16.39	43.90	21.90	22.41	22.59	-0.82	17.86
2007	15.31	7.75	10.94	16.39	11.97	9.12	20.86	-4.08	23.01	12.68
2008	24.93	20.84	19.73	39.76	50.01	30.50	18.92	25.05	18.69	25.04
2009	4.76	-1.14	1.22	5.95	11.17	0.19	-4.05	10.97	1.01	2.34
2010	11.21	10.05	8.52	18.63	18.23	12.01	7.81	11.17	22.10	11.54

Note: Values in table reflect author's own estimations based on data from the Central Bank of Bolivia (CBB), and the National Institute of Statistics (NIS).

Table 12c: Share of Each Department in National GDP (%)

	La Paz	Santa Cruz	Cochabamba	Oruro	Potosí	Chuquisaca	Tarija	Beni	Pando
1988	27.81	25.52	18.52	5.75	6.16	6.60	4.77	4.14	0.73
1989	27.60	25.94	17.99	6.04	6.38	6.51	4.82	3.99	0.72
1990	27.03	26.89	17.65	5.46	6.01	6.81	5.21	4.20	0.75
1991	27.41	27.39	18.09	5.11	5.44	6.52	5.13	4.20	0.71
1992	28.14	27.21	18.18	5.16	5.51	6.21	4.90	4.01	0.68
1993	28.68	27.59	18.41	5.05	4.85	5.96	4.79	3.98	0.70
1994	29.03	27.67	18.37	5.57	4.78	5.39	4.56	3.89	0.73
1995	29.53	27.53	18.11	5.78	4.85	5.22	4.35	3.88	0.75
1996	29.45	28.16	17.86	5.74	4.93	4.94	4.34	3.83	0.75
1997	27.83	29.12	17.90	5.93	4.74	5.05	4.92	3.76	0.76
1998	25.57	30.95	18.02	6.10	4.39	5.22	5.20	3.73	0.82
1999	25.99	29.38	18.59	5.89	4.71	5.56	5.13	3.88	0.87
2000	25.71	30.04	18.67	5.66	4.75	5.30	5.25	3.72	0.89
2001	25.19	30.74	18.33	5.60	4.61	5.28	5.57	3.73	0.95
2002	25.69	30.35	18.00	5.42	4.56	5.20	6.27	3.60	0.92
2003	25.77	30.38	17.38	5.17	4.72	4.97	7.28	3.45	0.87
2004	24.87	30.08	17.38	5.04	4.85	4.95	8.70	3.28	0.86
2005	24.55	29.61	16.87	4.90	4.52	4.38	11.24	3.02	0.90
2006	24.16	29.24	16.10	4.80	5.46	4.52	11.79	3.15	0.78
2007	24.70	28.38	15.94	4.91	5.36	4.38	12.77	2.69	0.87
2008	24.66	27.83	15.34	5.45	6.36	4.56	12.27	2.69	0.85
2009	25.21	27.27	15.25	5.59	6.83	4.47	11.61	2.92	0.85
2010	25.11	27.25	14.91	5.90	7.16	4.48	11.32	2.92	0.95

Notes: Values in table reflect author's own estimations based on data from the Central Bank of Bolivia (CBB), and the National Institute of Statistics (NIS).
Shares of each Department on GDP were estimated utilizing yearly national and departamental GDPs valued at current Dollars.

Table 13c: Quarterly GDP by Economic Activity, 1990–2011 (thousands of current US dollars)

Year	Agriculture, forestry, livestock, and fisheries	Crude oil and natural gas	Metallic and non-metallic minerals	Manufacturing industry	Electricity, gas, and water	Construction industry	Commerce industry	Transport and communications	Finance, insurance, real estate, and other business services	Public administration services	Other services	Imputed banking services	GDP at basic prices	Import duties, VAT, IT, and other indirect taxes	GDP at market prices
1990	**751,223.31**	**208,640.53**	**290,556.12**	**828,622.24**	**78,520.99**	**148,872.99**	**433,115.27**	**454,921.32**	**495,939.89**	**488,248.10**	**376,266.47**	**-79,516.11**	**4,475,411.11**	**403,698.23**	**4,879,109.35**
I Quarter	193,260.54	45,717.74	74,934.46	203,445.00	19,137.01	26,059.59	106,354.09	113,601.01	121,464.68	96,877.46	96,178.50	-15,162.99	1,081,867.11	94,107.90	1,175,975.01
II Quarter	196,293.23	37,085.00	73,375.90	215,951.24	20,508.38	36,847.93	101,747.73	111,662.12	126,577.70	121,751.44	94,928.79	-21,310.08	1,115,419.37	89,783.50	1,205,202.87
III Quarter	201,555.08	60,417.52	73,715.12	211,979.75	18,908.57	38,837.16	115,395.51	115,947.44	119,983.83	114,836.64	93,893.11	-16,279.46	1,149,190.27	112,395.57	1,261,585.84
IV Quarter	160,114.46	65,420.27	68,530.63	197,246.26	19,967.03	47,128.29	109,617.94	113,710.75	127,913.68	154,782.56	91,266.07	-26,763.59	1,128,934.36	107,411.27	1,236,345.63
1991	**832,999.33**	**179,228.18**	**238,931.85**	**948,051.24**	**106,007.10**	**164,069.19**	**472,346.87**	**529,068.35**	**549,837.78**	**543,120.67**	**395,739.04**	**-96,450.06**	**4,862,949.54**	**483,782.15**	**5,346,731.69**
I Quarter	225,029.96	45,888.85	59,440.58	226,907.92	24,963.56	35,658.62	109,820.45	116,458.85	130,185.96	96,278.21	96,337.93	-19,488.98	1,147,481.91	113,242.68	1,260,724.59
II Quarter	208,903.93	43,343.01	59,518.31	236,089.99	25,143.05	33,570.91	110,167.95	132,306.67	141,187.53	144,479.39	98,306.07	-27,663.35	1,205,353.47	118,820.99	1,324,174.46
III Quarter	215,809.43	44,650.39	61,024.39	231,978.41	28,383.81	39,279.13	127,783.27	139,005.53	133,841.77	137,854.85	99,617.61	-15,807.82	1,243,420.78	121,069.01	1,364,489.79
IV Quarter	183,256.01	45,345.94	58,948.56	253,074.93	27,516.68	55,560.53	124,575.21	141,297.30	144,622.52	164,508.22	101,477.43	-33,489.92	1,266,693.39	130,649.47	1,397,342.85
1992	**814,918.63**	**164,254.56**	**246,835.50**	**968,463.72**	**148,456.06**	**174,278.09**	**470,426.78**	**593,798.99**	**583,642.25**	**616,656.87**	**417,558.52**	**-124,471.78**	**5,074,818.20**	**571,108.04**	**5,645,926.24**
I Quarter	218,037.28	41,669.95	53,902.29	235,829.43	31,025.99	29,989.55	115,507.77	138,124.64	140,066.53	117,882.40	102,391.47	-28,701.71	1,195,725.58	130,830.09	1,326,555.67
II Quarter	197,751.68	42,995.96	63,841.30	256,827.88	33,492.79	38,561.26	115,165.90	150,498.03	154,855.88	155,845.43	106,748.22	-28,443.55	1,288,140.77	137,916.98	1,426,057.75
III Quarter	213,945.45	41,217.97	65,992.20	222,712.84	43,468.05	42,417.83	126,349.73	151,805.02	142,818.62	152,335.55	102,651.11	-29,323.73	1,276,390.63	146,195.74	1,422,586.37
IV Quarter	185,184.22	38,370.69	63,099.72	253,093.58	40,469.22	63,309.45	113,403.38	153,371.31	145,901.23	190,593.49	105,767.72	-38,002.79	1,314,561.22	156,165.22	1,470,726.45
1993	**842,152.60**	**115,562.17**	**181,527.50**	**968,193.68**	**184,147.89**	**192,498.17**	**471,496.81**	**635,921.68**	**604,983.68**	**656,868.33**	**437,635.57**	**-143,605.69**	**5,147,382.41**	**590,138.02**	**5,737,520.43**
I Quarter	236,607.54	28,801.65	35,722.58	225,336.97	38,141.31	50,530.13	113,947.51	148,644.28	138,439.44	140,016.45	108,575.58	-28,800.03	1,235,963.41	133,136.04	1,369,099.46
II Quarter	190,933.33	30,910.09	42,014.20	255,442.08	45,345.39	43,333.85	109,388.22	157,569.70	164,971.32	172,792.29	110,484.31	-37,217.25	1,285,967.55	146,356.83	1,432,324.38
III Quarter	224,615.52	28,537.27	49,449.11	240,753.86	51,852.95	42,022.76	127,522.35	167,080.16	153,473.23	149,227.05	108,934.57	-37,664.38	1,305,804.45	149,056.69	1,454,861.14
IV Quarter	189,996.21	27,313.16	54,341.61	246,660.77	48,808.24	56,611.42	120,638.73	162,627.54	148,099.69	194,832.54	109,641.11	-39,924.03	1,319,647.00	161,588.46	1,481,235.47
1994	**913,793.68**	**54,924.14**	**238,186.30**	**996,405.71**	**205,959.93**	**186,994.19**	**508,398.85**	**647,838.64**	**615,540.08**	**685,362.95**	**434,098.55**	**-157,117.11**	**5,330,385.91**	**653,627.62**	**5,984,013.53**
I Quarter	272,683.22	11,229.93	59,226.77	219,463.68	40,574.13	35,922.62	122,574.17	150,031.83	141,032.82	148,847.02	107,839.14	-31,821.39	1,277,603.93	143,524.38	1,421,128.32
II Quarter	186,098.06	13,160.27	55,994.63	249,450.28	49,181.81	34,567.78	112,490.74	160,019.38	163,989.24	152,137.45	104,335.70	-35,981.30	1,245,444.05	152,316.56	1,397,760.61
III Quarter	240,564.59	15,980.53	57,539.66	253,468.20	60,642.09	55,144.64	136,427.53	174,372.93	148,807.16	193,834.71	105,646.29	-37,594.88	1,404,833.46	169,558.82	1,574,392.28
IV Quarter	214,447.81	14,553.41	65,425.22	274,023.56	55,561.90	61,359.15	136,906.39	163,414.50	161,710.87	190,543.77	116,277.43	-51,719.54	1,402,504.47	188,227.86	1,590,732.33
1995	**999,377.39**	**80,618.64**	**324,700.36**	**1,123,774.96**	**229,297.13**	**198,668.47**	**565,630.47**	**677,533.25**	**662,202.72**	**746,051.03**	**487,166.51**	**-182,830.99**	**5,912,189.95**	**805,182.78**	**6,717,372.73**
I Quarter	304,052.91	19,401.45	72,712.38	250,107.73	45,040.57	40,673.93	142,177.04	156,665.70	158,307.44	154,239.08	120,926.77	-42,020.19	1,422,284.81	184,840.97	1,607,125.78
II Quarter	194,383.24	22,433.16	83,190.64	289,753.52	52,076.65	39,529.40	129,214.26	170,520.03	168,395.88	163,945.10	119,397.28	-47,268.58	1,385,570.58	196,940.68	1,582,511.25
III Quarter	269,550.76	19,623.10	82,549.28	295,589.51	68,764.48	56,048.69	151,167.02	184,746.44	161,494.59	188,872.27	121,495.73	-39,411.39	1,560,490.51	200,014.86	1,760,505.37
IV Quarter	231,390.47	19,160.93	86,248.05	288,324.20	63,415.43	62,416.45	143,072.14	165,601.08	174,004.81	238,994.58	125,346.74	-54,130.83	1,543,844.05	223,386.27	1,767,230.32
1996	**1,051,024.62**	**93,447.88**	**343,722.09**	**1,215,382.03**	**220,824.23**	**194,568.59**	**603,296.59**	**768,276.67**	**781,992.76**	**807,752.54**	**551,484.53**	**-224,213.67**	**6,407,558.85**	**989,431.59**	**7,396,990.44**
I Quarter	333,253.29	22,064.32	86,257.14	282,229.04	47,521.09	42,893.60	155,245.49	171,705.48	181,949.44	166,090.87	134,223.49	-46,921.04	1,576,512.21	221,317.28	1,797,829.49
II Quarter	196,118.86	23,983.64	90,694.41	327,670.40	57,723.74	42,042.97	139,509.71	188,589.35	186,864.98	199,698.33	132,293.35	-43,481.92	1,541,707.82	233,501.27	1,775,209.09

Table 13c: Quarterly GDP by Economic Activity, 1990–2011 (thousands of current US dollars) continued

Year	Agriculture, forestry, livestock, and fisheries	Crude oil and natural gas	Metallic and non-metallic minerals	Manufacturing industry	Electricity, gas, and water	Construction industry	Commerce industry	Transport and communications	Finance, insurance, real estate, and other business services	Public administration services	Other services	Imputed banking services	GDP at basic prices	Import duties, VAT, IT, and other indirect taxes	GDP at market prices
III Quarter	285,801.45	21,526.40	81,944.69	315,602.54	51,257.95	50,061.90	159,152.34	205,348.63	202,111.55	208,515.77	140,349.08	-55,857.00	1,665,815.29	246,322.83	1,912,138.12
IV Quarter	235,851.02	25,873.52	84,825.85	289,880.05	64,321.45	59,570.12	149,389.05	202,633.21	211,066.79	233,447.57	144,618.60	-77,953.72	1,623,523.52	288,290.22	1,911,813.74
1997	**1,184,188.80**	**163,367.92**	**336,812.59**	**1,152,174.51**	**217,102.10**	**227,347.55**	**627,434.87**	**860,989.25**	**921,090.48**	**888,626.58**	**605,118.40**	**-320,495.04**	**6,863,758.01**	**1,068,049.26**	**7,931,807.27**
I Quarter	373,917.94	30,925.85	78,769.87	267,675.30	46,518.69	42,655.29	162,895.00	191,479.35	214,274.57	182,325.53	147,931.61	-69,475.37	1,669,893.64	240,570.83	1,910,464.47
II Quarter	219,881.52	42,768.81	88,177.08	318,080.00	55,701.11	54,249.42	140,198.92	202,005.28	233,979.14	220,604.65	148,218.21	-65,490.11	1,658,374.02	254,706.87	1,913,080.90
III Quarter	318,521.41	41,518.66	85,372.09	287,583.93	49,138.03	61,029.57	167,760.00	223,966.74	229,463.13	224,663.98	154,153.74	-90,784.54	1,752,386.73	274,438.52	2,026,825.25
IV Quarter	271,867.93	48,154.60	84,493.55	278,835.29	65,744.28	69,413.27	156,580.94	243,537.88	243,373.63	261,032.42	154,814.64	-94,745.01	1,783,103.62	298,333.04	2,081,436.65
1998	**1,075,663.40**	**162,617.76**	**308,807.74**	**1,190,396.40**	**237,275.34**	**324,030.50**	**653,689.20**	**1,016,717.69**	**1,045,272.80**	**1,002,564.35**	**678,786.54**	**-375,505.13**	**7,320,316.58**	**1,184,328.24**	**8,504,644.82**
I Quarter	346,093.36	41,638.27	94,002.99	282,828.88	53,405.01	72,454.56	171,831.86	258,369.20	241,995.98	220,726.73	173,665.27	-91,973.07	1,865,039.03	271,717.33	2,136,756.36
II Quarter	216,286.35	38,726.46	78,836.77	336,444.30	60,399.81	74,728.40	148,398.73	248,557.70	258,336.06	235,992.48	171,267.53	-89,213.03	1,778,761.52	286,933.10	2,065,694.62
III Quarter	279,036.42	43,592.67	76,114.19	301,692.34	55,783.11	90,927.07	174,100.77	269,603.68	273,760.25	247,724.49	175,663.94	-123,332.25	1,864,666.67	304,431.41	2,169,098.08
IV Quarter	234,247.27	38,660.37	59,853.79	269,430.87	67,687.42	85,920.48	159,357.84	240,187.11	271,180.51	298,120.64	158,189.79	-70,986.72	1,811,849.37	321,246.39	2,133,095.76
1999	**1,102,352.53**	**168,404.08**	**281,287.09**	**1,129,076.18**	**236,562.44**	**270,477.25**	**611,026.82**	**981,433.09**	**1,212,371.44**	**994,169.59**	**699,119.29**	**-403,969.25**	**7,282,310.54**	**1,013,857.83**	**8,296,168.37**
I Quarter	360,970.19	33,296.81	69,640.63	279,788.65	54,577.05	55,285.87	159,470.74	249,455.36	309,804.68	234,982.44	173,050.69	-119,796.33	1,860,526.72	243,881.19	2,104,407.91
II Quarter	219,697.83	38,919.57	67,005.91	316,306.56	62,119.44	62,066.97	130,662.09	237,219.92	315,103.29	234,278.41	174,800.54	-90,676.53	1,767,503.98	233,093.23	2,000,597.22
III Quarter	277,852.87	46,930.18	69,260.93	288,760.25	54,100.81	67,825.91	161,607.19	255,978.82	316,865.89	224,012.28	182,313.07	-135,888.81	1,809,619.38	252,390.89	2,062,010.27
IV Quarter	243,831.64	49,257.52	75,379.63	244,220.72	65,765.15	85,298.51	159,286.81	238,778.99	270,597.58	300,896.46	168,955.00	-57,607.54	1,844,660.46	284,492.52	2,129,152.97
2000	**1,093,285.39**	**267,437.26**	**283,611.32**	**1,113,920.63**	**244,481.30**	**254,540.58**	**604,666.50**	**954,008.60**	**1,143,052.33**	**984,240.57**	**700,404.37**	**-376,385.79**	**7,267,263.07**	**1,143,169.65**	**8,410,432.72**
I Quarter	368,780.37	53,775.88	75,519.29	264,426.34	57,407.69	55,037.33	149,647.91	247,453.72	289,074.04	211,461.01	176,936.51	-97,451.25	1,852,068.84	262,274.89	2,114,343.73
II Quarter	217,293.42	60,484.09	70,326.46	298,482.27	64,910.20	59,100.18	132,185.33	244,171.13	295,582.59	228,012.78	177,878.76	-94,164.87	1,754,262.33	276,438.42	2,030,700.75
III Quarter	266,865.93	71,631.36	72,905.71	287,838.71	55,801.66	61,859.65	164,056.77	243,857.51	281,720.75	251,231.12	172,836.75	-97,601.60	1,833,004.32	293,407.81	2,126,412.13
IV Quarter	240,345.67	81,545.93	64,859.86	263,173.31	66,361.76	78,543.42	158,776.48	218,526.25	276,674.95	293,535.66	172,752.34	-87,168.07	1,827,927.58	311,048.53	2,138,976.12
2001	**1,084,114.12**	**266,836.79**	**249,604.80**	**1,087,767.67**	**242,193.68**	**226,253.44**	**586,077.27**	**941,363.66**	**1,060,953.63**	**1,008,169.00**	**695,527.08**	**-343,501.81**	**7,105,359.31**	**1,049,353.62**	**8,154,712.93**
I Quarter	366,024.08	69,996.15	63,232.61	249,028.30	54,894.63	54,197.79	142,815.03	241,912.13	267,310.00	237,517.58	174,504.92	-88,731.69	1,832,701.51	245,315.94	2,078,017.45
II Quarter	222,584.52	77,378.05	66,080.54	293,940.05	60,661.51	56,733.17	140,618.30	233,157.64	271,350.61	230,449.94	174,742.72	-86,469.30	1,741,227.75	263,433.54	2,004,661.29
III Quarter	272,998.13	63,363.40	62,646.31	273,677.52	56,040.32	57,412.76	147,015.54	248,215.56	261,050.56	252,411.26	172,178.72	-88,838.24	1,778,171.83	263,778.02	2,041,949.85
IV Quarter	222,507.40	56,099.18	57,645.34	271,121.80	70,597.22	57,909.72	155,628.39	218,078.33	261,242.46	287,790.22	174,100.73	-79,462.58	1,753,258.21	276,826.12	2,030,084.34
2002	**1,029,367.40**	**265,117.56**	**241,184.34**	**1,032,117.53**	**230,388.30**	**245,971.88**	**564,670.22**	**944,828.32**	**956,094.09**	**986,202.28**	**688,842.49**	**-299,296.94**	**6,885,487.47**	**1,031,224.11**	**7,916,711.58**
I Quarter	350,166.57	49,647.24	59,177.78	239,668.98	52,406.40	45,207.32	135,808.79	247,345.50	254,370.85	214,468.44	176,737.20	-78,645.95	1,746,359.11	232,054.64	1,978,413.75
II Quarter	208,203.08	64,964.47	63,596.52	285,327.44	60,746.94	65,216.75	127,623.29	243,282.50	248,555.00	251,917.52	170,905.76	-80,308.05	1,710,031.21	260,169.63	1,970,200.83
III Quarter	249,037.73	68,434.99	60,202.94	263,086.48	53,401.13	73,344.48	143,772.98	248,491.73	235,326.38	255,966.79	169,644.56	-75,075.22	1,745,635.01	260,930.52	2,006,565.53
IV Quarter	221,960.02	82,070.87	58,207.09	244,034.63	63,833.82	62,203.33	157,465.15	205,708.59	217,841.86	263,849.53	171,554.97	-65,267.72	1,683,462.14	278,069.33	1,961,531.47

Table 13c: Quarterly GDP by Economic Activity, 1990–2011 (thousands of current US dollars) continued

Year	Agriculture, forestry, livestock, and fisheries	Crude oil and natural gas	Metallic and non-metallic minerals	Manufacturing industry	Electricity, gas, and water	Construction industry	Commerce industry	Transport and communications	Finance, insurance, real estate, and other business services	Public administration services	Other services	Imputed banking services	GDP at basic prices	Import duties, VAT, IT, and other indirect taxes	GDP at market prices
2003	**1,088,413.18**	**349,626.20**	**261,552.89**	**1,034,387.01**	**238,669.41**	**186,333.07**	**553,176.12**	**998,639.28**	**886,463.39**	**1,020,890.11**	**690,845.78**	**-261,084.46**	**7,047,911.97**	**1,044,450.92**	**8,092,362.89**
I Quarter	375,899.22	70,138.68	63,250.72	223,396.79	52,420.85	37,555.45	131,383.34	250,798.75	229,902.93	224,302.99	173,835.46	-70,764.22	1,762,120.97	244,323.13	2,006,444.10
II Quarter	213,906.85	95,579.47	68,900.42	293,558.71	63,815.01	50,632.32	118,630.30	254,385.81	229,068.49	257,854.05	170,219.34	-66,777.40	1,749,773.38	256,371.94	2,006,145.32
III Quarter	264,027.43	78,858.78	66,389.76	263,905.24	56,006.57	51,208.11	146,095.87	270,690.28	216,709.99	257,737.52	171,681.59	-65,027.56	1,778,283.57	269,695.63	2,047,979.20
IV Quarter	234,579.68	105,049.27	63,011.98	253,526.27	66,426.98	46,937.19	157,066.61	222,764.43	210,781.99	280,995.55	175,109.38	-58,515.28	1,757,734.05	274,060.22	2,031,794.27
2004	**1,171,696.14**	**530,906.99**	**299,094.60**	**1,098,582.74**	**242,510.69**	**185,769.53**	**612,760.26**	**1,041,739.27**	**863,164.49**	**1,090,023.96**	**721,198.85**	**-245,628.46**	**7,611,819.06**	**1,172,113.13**	**8,783,932.19**
I Quarter	411,020.79	104,998.53	72,800.54	237,349.09	53,192.25	35,775.53	149,086.01	264,402.39	221,008.41	249,284.52	179,203.54	-63,915.18	1,914,206.40	273,778.03	2,187,984.43
II Quarter	228,656.09	143,801.66	76,534.19	319,534.13	64,863.43	49,713.58	131,383.53	257,872.86	220,868.84	275,777.46	176,379.44	-61,020.90	1,884,364.30	283,357.13	2,167,721.43
III Quarter	284,613.79	134,476.19	70,661.79	275,114.30	57,541.22	52,094.75	158,121.55	284,664.53	213,935.41	275,083.05	183,405.42	-64,489.36	1,925,222.64	305,274.98	2,230,497.62
IV Quarter	247,405.47	147,630.62	79,098.08	266,585.21	66,913.80	48,185.68	174,169.18	234,799.49	207,351.83	289,878.93	182,210.45	-56,203.03	1,888,025.71	309,702.99	2,197,728.70
2005	**1,129,779.34**	**611,609.28**	**332,095.22**	**1,113,751.48**	**248,537.63**	**211,003.33**	**633,655.53**	**1,079,149.98**	**892,616.36**	**1,153,849.63**	**726,891.44**	**-274,293.98**	**7,858,645.23**	**1,724,003.43**	**9,582,648.66**
I Quarter	379,756.65	129,381.85	69,819.89	248,713.12	53,137.08	38,636.19	150,862.16	266,758.62	217,771.64	262,353.19	178,619.35	-61,593.10	1,934,216.64	338,816.22	2,273,032.86
II Quarter	218,864.28	167,583.98	77,811.20	318,595.34	65,608.36	48,546.79	135,146.49	266,180.81	230,340.80	289,987.80	174,126.33	-72,042.88	1,920,749.32	362,256.74	2,283,006.06
III Quarter	272,845.71	146,574.85	81,800.40	277,804.41	59,899.06	62,336.63	164,805.84	295,797.24	225,294.05	296,716.63	185,680.43	-73,257.09	1,996,298.16	479,450.54	2,475,748.69
IV Quarter	258,312.71	168,068.60	102,663.72	268,638.61	69,893.12	61,483.71	182,841.04	250,413.31	219,209.88	304,792.00	188,465.33	-67,400.91	2,007,381.12	543,479.92	2,550,861.05
2006	**1,262,251.58**	**740,619.65**	**600,522.73**	**1,308,298.49**	**267,710.28**	**275,593.67**	**740,500.43**	**1,174,599.30**	**987,213.89**	**1,266,336.84**	**810,807.64**	**-334,609.53**	**9,099,844.96**	**2,444,994.29**	**11,544,839.25**
I Quarter	409,366.77	147,949.71	123,092.07	276,765.99	57,829.88	53,365.17	173,569.13	272,721.94	244,292.75	289,293.61	199,453.93	-83,299.82	2,164,401.13	555,119.31	2,719,520.45
II Quarter	259,729.73	178,090.57	168,516.66	362,421.16	71,359.17	65,855.01	145,168.92	292,502.60	259,216.02	309,999.38	195,542.95	-88,416.02	2,219,986.15	585,070.97	2,805,057.12
III Quarter	306,284.37	216,573.90	155,122.31	333,448.45	63,587.53	78,082.43	199,982.09	325,808.69	254,402.44	336,878.08	208,791.47	-90,902.91	2,388,058.84	644,502.81	3,032,561.64
IV Quarter	286,870.71	198,005.48	153,791.70	335,662.89	74,933.70	78,291.05	221,780.29	283,566.06	229,302.67	330,165.77	207,019.29	-71,990.78	2,327,398.83	660,301.21	2,987,700.04
2007	**1,325,293.26**	**859,899.52**	**770,675.14**	**1,512,935.32**	**290,438.73**	**319,127.20**	**900,730.52**	**1,242,112.81**	**1,143,204.61**	**1,461,129.38**	**887,226.05**	**-406,478.28**	**10,306,294.26**	**2,951,564.65**	**13,257,858.91**
I Quarter	428,531.15	162,575.71	161,135.94	302,601.97	60,473.47	41,580.92	202,712.21	305,574.66	278,853.95	321,967.21	213,661.31	-97,635.69	2,382,032.80	671,419.35	3,053,452.15
II Quarter	247,075.95	211,754.21	184,764.69	428,025.02	76,301.56	64,661.26	181,414.71	295,334.33	290,455.62	375,189.51	211,719.78	-102,335.49	2,464,361.15	695,697.87	3,160,059.02
III Quarter	340,638.43	242,172.64	180,704.51	396,239.75	69,204.54	98,335.76	244,630.80	347,108.01	297,633.30	384,478.71	230,750.52	-109,546.11	2,722,350.86	766,853.50	3,489,204.35
IV Quarter	309,047.73	243,396.97	244,070.01	386,068.58	84,459.15	114,549.25	271,972.80	294,095.82	276,261.74	379,493.94	231,094.43	-96,960.99	2,737,549.44	817,593.93	3,555,143.38
2008	**1,752,843.63**	**955,231.15**	**1,443,738.87**	**1,884,128.15**	**340,804.18**	**393,571.00**	**1,185,020.19**	**1,417,241.82**	**1,404,915.72**	**1,764,481.51**	**1,061,689.70**	**-530,178.29**	**13,073,487.63**	**3,786,383.58**	**16,859,871.20**
I Quarter	560,873.23	211,145.93	281,570.06	374,434.73	70,475.87	48,664.92	260,067.32	333,876.79	328,268.00	355,394.99	244,874.86	-128,219.34	2,941,427.35	854,045.57	3,795,472.93
II Quarter	345,660.37	334,398.83	402,597.74	555,278.98	89,636.07	81,301.98	258,689.09	341,707.09	361,518.15	422,234.25	253,653.74	-137,065.47	3,309,610.82	1,046,936.92	4,356,547.74
III Quarter	451,181.95	260,003.80	471,934.10	504,334.18	82,480.54	125,594.06	358,001.19	400,520.11	369,921.46	466,976.60	281,014.87	-142,732.70	3,629,230.15	1,049,846.06	4,679,076.21
IV Quarter	395,128.08	149,682.60	287,636.97	450,080.26	98,211.70	138,010.04	308,262.59	341,137.83	345,208.11	519,875.68	282,146.23	-122,160.79	3,193,219.30	835,555.02	4,028,774.33
2009p	**1,941,528.82**	**874,542.29**	**1,381,714.48**	**2,021,688.38**	**376,209.60**	**432,850.49**	**1,255,352.50**	**1,533,088.36**	**1,521,780.13**	**2,074,167.93**	**1,187,956.47**	**-565,132.91**	**14,035,746.54**	**3,369,463.07**	**17,405,209.62**
I Quarter	626,872.88	210,211.73	313,869.49	439,112.90	80,773.31	81,849.21	243,226.21	300,645.50	324,159.71	434,371.29	280,669.98	-148,789.74	3,186,972.47	980,653.69	4,167,626.16

Table 13c: Quarterly GDP by Economic Activity, 1990–2011 (thousands of current US dollars) continued

Year	Agriculture, forestry, livestock, and fisheries	Crude oil and natural gas	Metallic and non-metallic minerals	Manufacturing industry	Electricity, gas, and water	Construction industry	Commerce industry	Transport and communications	Finance, insurance, real estate, and other business services	Public administration services	Other services	Imputed banking services	GDP at basic prices	Import duties, VAT, IT, and other indirect taxes	GDP at market prices
II Quarter	458,482.55	282,673.63	283,538.82	477,514.23	93,180.88	116,249.99	407,239.74	370,013.67	438,460.40	505,884.28	286,011.04	-143,902.83	3,575,346.39	799,395.53	4,374,741.92
III Quarter	456,752.46	219,800.96	414,847.06	519,593.78	86,252.42	89,293.06	291,208.20	421,249.85	359,378.46	533,175.36	318,524.54	-150,280.95	3,559,795.21	762,815.06	4,322,610.27
IV Quarter	399,420.92	161,855.97	369,459.11	585,467.48	116,002.98	145,458.23	313,678.35	441,179.33	399,781.55	600,737.00	302,750.92	-122,159.39	3,713,632.47	826,598.80	4,540,231.27
2010p	**2,040,149.55**	**1,012,785.54**	**1,740,701.39**	**2,213,595.41**	**428,968.46**	**524,289.78**	**1,452,148.48**	**1,763,119.21**	**1,709,076.58**	**2,339,685.28**	**1,289,950.56**	**-638,296.97**	**15,876,174.13**	**3,764,307.79**	**19,640,481.92**
I Quarter	635,668.01	217,900.00	443,183.61	487,147.18	90,939.14	98,973.94	281,322.93	333,314.75	362,085.24	507,854.69	302,012.51	-162,913.83	3,597,488.03	785,790.71	4,383,278.74
II Quarter	472,431.19	309,122.54	379,592.99	525,033.78	106,307.58	143,158.77	469,517.60	428,618.86	483,059.53	542,131.81	309,280.01	-161,448.95	4,006,806.86	880,135.18	4,886,942.04
III Quarter	487,990.55	273,851.04	457,187.81	569,027.64	96,849.86	107,312.88	334,264.77	465,882.43	399,176.60	604,669.70	346,456.69	-170,803.35	3,971,866.61	989,640.15	4,961,506.76
IV Quarter	444,059.80	211,911.96	460,736.98	632,386.81	134,871.89	174,844.20	367,043.17	535,303.17	464,755.21	685,029.07	332,201.36	-143,130.84	4,300,012.63	1,108,741.75	5,408,754.38
2011p	**1,933,216.04**	**1,151,928.52**	**1,944,203.54**	**1,797,303.19**	**330,056.20**	**418,610.69**	**1,335,863.28**	**1,454,169.80**	**1,432,547.12**	**1,897,863.61**	**1,095,693.08**	**-594,533.34**	**14,196,921.59**	**3,723,228.71**	**17,920,150.29**
I Quarter	722,496.33	371,341.51	657,601.90	540,360.30	100,716.57	117,515.17	332,752.06	385,547.28	417,366.88	576,441.76	338,887.75	-189,926.50	4,371,101.03	1,133,053.25	5,504,154.27
II Quarter	625,635.10	392,620.62	543,792.94	608,879.09	117,721.45	171,959.28	596,144.44	515,199.64	555,323.08	623,383.37	356,946.43	-195,256.41	4,912,348.89	1,188,964.27	6,101,313.16
III Quarter	585,084.60	387,966.39	742,808.70	648,063.81	111,618.18	129,136.23	406,966.77	553,422.88	459,857.16	698,038.47	399,858.90	-209,350.43	4,913,471.66	1,401,211.19	6,314,682.86
IV Quarter															-

Notes: All values in current Dollars.

Values in table reflect author's own estimations based on data from the Central Bank of Bolivia (CBB), and the National Institute of Statistics (NIS).

GDP values reported on this table may differ from those on previous tables due to (i) difference in yearly and quarterly conversion exchange rates; and (ii) most estimations of GDP reported in this work utilize prices of different base years (constant, as opposed to current values).

The conversion from Bs to Dollars was carried out utilizing the quarterly average buying Bs/$ rate in the parallel markets.

(p) preliminary.

Table 14c: GDP Quarterly Growth, by Economic Activity, 1990–2011 (%)

Year, Quarter	Agriculture, forestry, livestock, and fisheries	Crude oil and natural gas	Metallic and non-metallic minerals	Manufacturing industry	Electricity, gas, and water	Construction industry	Commerce industry	Transport and communications	Finance, insurance, real estate, and other business services	Public administration services	Other services	Imputed banking services	GDP at basic prices	Import duties, VAT, IT, and other indirect taxes	GDP at market prices
1990, I	-	-	-	-	-	-	-	-	-	-	-	-	-	-	-
II	1.57	-18.88	-2.08	6.15	7.17	41.40	-4.33	-1.71	4.21	25.68	-1.30	40.54	3.10	-4.60	2.49
III	2.68	62.92	0.46	-1.84	-7.80	5.40	13.41	3.84	-5.21	-5.68	-1.09	-23.61	3.03	25.19	4.68
IV	-20.56	8.28	-7.03	-6.95	5.60	21.35	-5.01	-1.93	6.61	34.78	-2.80	64.40	-1.76	-4.43	-2.00
1991, I	40.54	-29.86	-13.26	15.04	25.02	-24.34	0.18	2.42	1.78	-37.80	5.56	-27.18	1.64	5.43	1.97
II	-7.17	-5.55	0.13	4.05	0.72	-5.85	0.32	13.61	8.45	50.06	2.04	41.94	5.04	4.93	5.03
III	3.31	3.02	2.53	-1.74	12.89	17.00	15.99	5.06	-5.20	-4.59	1.33	-42.86	3.16	1.89	3.04
IV	-15.08	1.56	-3.40	9.09	-3.06	41.45	-2.51	1.65	8.05	19.33	1.87	111.86	1.87	7.91	2.41
1992, I	18.98	-8.11	-8.56	-6.81	12.75	-46.02	-7.28	-2.25	-3.15	-28.34	0.90	-14.30	-5.60	0.14	-5.07
II	-9.30	3.18	18.44	8.90	7.95	28.58	-0.30	8.96	10.56	32.20	4.25	-0.90	7.73	5.42	7.50
III	8.19	-4.14	3.37	-13.28	29.78	10.00	9.71	0.87	-7.77	-2.25	-3.84	3.09	-0.91	6.00	-0.24
IV	-13.44	-6.91	-4.38	13.64	-6.90	49.25	-10.25	1.03	2.16	25.11	3.04	29.60	2.99	6.82	3.38
1993, I	27.77	-24.94	-43.39	-10.97	-5.75	-20.19	0.48	-3.08	-5.11	-26.54	2.65	-24.22	-5.98	-14.75	-6.91
II	-19.30	7.32	17.61	13.36	18.89	-14.24	-4.00	6.00	19.16	23.41	1.76	29.23	4.05	9.93	4.62
III	17.64	-7.68	17.70	-5.75	14.35	-3.03	16.58	6.04	-6.97	-13.64	-1.40	1.20	1.54	1.84	1.57
IV	-15.41	-4.29	9.89	2.45	-5.87	34.72	-5.40	-2.66	-3.50	30.56	0.65	6.00	1.06	8.41	1.81
1994, I	43.52	-58.88	8.99	-11.03	-16.87	-36.55	1.60	-7.75	-4.77	-23.60	-1.64	-20.30	-3.19	-11.18	-4.06
II	-31.75	17.19	-5.46	13.66	21.21	-3.77	-8.23	6.66	16.28	2.21	-3.25	13.07	-2.52	6.13	-1.64
III	29.27	21.43	2.76	1.61	23.30	59.53	21.28	8.97	-9.26	27.41	1.26	4.48	12.80	11.32	12.64
IV	-10.86	-8.93	13.70	8.11	-8.38	11.27	0.35	-6.28	8.67	-1.70	10.06	37.57	-0.17	11.01	1.04
1995, I	41.78	33.31	11.14	-8.73	-18.94	-33.71	3.85	-4.13	-2.10	-19.05	4.00	-18.75	1.41	-1.80	1.03
II	-36.07	15.63	14.41	15.85	15.62	-2.81	-9.12	8.84	6.37	6.29	-1.26	12.49	-2.58	6.55	-1.53
III	38.67	-12.53	-0.77	2.01	32.04	41.79	16.99	8.34	-4.10	15.20	1.76	-16.62	12.62	1.56	11.25
IV	-14.16	-2.36	4.48	-2.46	-7.78	11.36	-5.35	-10.36	7.75	26.54	3.17	37.35	-1.07	11.68	0.38
1996, I	44.02	15.15	0.01	-2.11	-25.06	-31.28	8.51	3.69	4.57	-30.50	7.08	-13.32	2.12	-0.93	1.73
II	-41.15	8.70	5.14	16.10	21.47	-1.98	-10.14	9.83	2.70	20.23	-1.44	-7.33	-2.21	5.51	-1.26
III	45.73	-10.25	-9.65	-3.68	-11.20	19.07	14.08	8.89	8.16	4.42	6.09	28.46	8.05	5.49	7.71
IV	-17.48	20.19	3.52	-8.15	25.49	18.99	-6.13	-1.32	4.43	11.96	3.04	39.56	-2.54	17.04	-0.02
1997, I	58.54	19.53	-7.14	-7.66	-27.68	-28.39	9.04	-5.50	1.52	-21.90	2.29	-10.88	2.86	-16.55	-0.07
II	-41.20	38.29	11.94	18.83	19.74	27.18	-13.93	5.50	9.20	20.99	0.19	-5.74	-0.69	5.88	0.14

Table 14c: GDP Quarterly Growth, by Economic Activity, 1990–2011 (%) continued

Year, Quarter	Agriculture, forestry, livestock, and fisheries	Crude oil and natural gas	Metallic and non-metallic minerals	Manufacturing industry	Electricity, gas, and water	Construction industry	Commerce industry	Transport and communications	Finance, insurance, real estate, and other business services	Public administration services	Other services	Imputed banking services	GDP at basic prices	Import duties, VAT, IT, and other indirect taxes	GDP at market prices
III	44.86	-2.92	-3.18	-9.59	-11.78	12.50	19.66	10.87	-1.93	1.84	4.00	38.62	5.67	7.75	5.95
IV	-14.65	15.98	-1.03	-3.04	33.80	13.74	-6.66	8.74	6.06	16.19	0.43	4.36	1.75	8.71	2.69
1998, I	27.30	-13.53	11.25	1.43	-18.77	4.38	9.74	6.09	-0.57	-15.44	12.18	-2.93	4.60	-8.92	2.66
II	-37.51	-6.99	-16.13	18.96	13.10	3.14	-13.64	-3.80	6.75	6.92	-1.38	-3.00	-4.63	5.60	-3.33
III	29.01	12.57	-3.45	-10.33	-7.64	21.68	17.32	8.47	5.97	4.97	2.57	38.24	4.83	6.10	5.01
IV	-16.05	-11.31	-21.36	-10.69	21.34	-5.51	-8.47	-10.91	-0.94	20.34	-9.95	-42.44	-2.83	5.52	-1.66
1999, I	54.10	-13.87	16.35	3.84	-19.37	-35.65	0.07	3.86	14.24	-21.18	9.39	68.76	2.69	-24.08	-1.34
II	-39.14	16.89	-3.78	13.05	13.82	12.27	-18.07	-4.90	1.71	-0.30	1.01	-24.31	-5.00	-4.42	-4.93
III	26.47	20.58	3.37	-8.71	-12.91	9.28	23.68	7.91	0.56	-4.38	4.30	49.86	2.38	8.28	3.07
IV	-12.24	4.96	8.83	-15.42	21.56	25.76	-1.44	-6.72	-14.60	34.32	-7.33	-57.61	1.94	12.72	3.26
2000, I	51.24	9.17	0.19	8.27	-12.71	-35.48	-6.05	3.63	6.83	-29.72	4.72	69.16	0.40	-7.81	-0.70
II	-41.08	12.47	-6.88	12.88	13.07	7.38	-11.67	-1.33	2.25	7.83	0.53	-3.37	-5.28	5.40	-3.96
III	22.81	18.43	3.67	-3.57	-14.03	4.67	24.11	-0.13	-4.69	10.18	-2.83	3.65	4.49	6.14	4.71
IV	-9.94	13.84	-11.04	-8.57	18.92	26.97	-3.22	-10.39	-1.79	16.84	-0.05	-10.69	-0.28	6.01	0.59
2001, I	52.29	-14.16	-2.51	-5.37	-17.28	-31.00	-10.05	10.70	-3.38	-19.08	1.01	1.79	0.26	-21.13	-2.85
II	-39.19	10.55	4.50	18.03	10.51	4.68	-1.54	-3.62	1.51	-2.98	0.14	-2.55	-4.99	7.39	-3.53
III	22.65	-18.11	-5.20	-6.89	-7.62	1.20	4.55	6.46	-3.80	9.53	-1.47	2.74	2.12	0.13	1.86
IV	-18.49	-11.46	-7.98	-0.93	25.98	0.87	5.86	-12.14	0.07	14.02	1.12	-10.55	-1.40	4.95	-0.58
2002, I	57.37	-11.50	2.66	-11.60	-25.77	-21.93	-12.74	13.42	-2.63	-25.48	1.51	-1.03	-0.39	-16.17	-2.55
II	-40.54	30.85	7.47	19.05	15.92	44.26	-6.03	-1.64	-2.29	17.46	-3.30	2.11	-2.08	12.12	-0.42
III	19.61	5.34	-5.34	-7.79	-12.09	12.46	12.65	2.14	-5.32	1.61	-0.74	-6.52	2.08	0.29	1.85
IV	-10.87	19.93	-3.32	-7.24	19.54	-15.19	9.52	-17.22	-7.43	3.08	1.13	-13.06	-3.56	6.57	-2.24
2003, I	69.35	-14.54	8.66	-8.46	-17.88	-39.62	-16.56	21.92	5.54	-14.99	1.33	8.42	4.67	-12.14	2.29
II	-43.09	36.27	8.93	31.41	21.74	34.82	-9.71	1.43	-0.36	14.96	-2.08	-5.63	-0.70	4.93	-0.01
III	23.43	-17.49	-3.64	-10.10	-12.24	1.14	23.15	6.41	-5.40	-0.05	0.86	-2.62	1.63	5.20	2.09
IV	-11.15	33.21	-5.09	-3.93	18.61	-8.34	7.51	-17.71	-2.74	9.02	2.00	-10.01	-1.16	1.62	-0.79
2004, I	75.22	-0.05	15.53	-6.38	-19.92	-23.78	-5.08	18.69	4.85	-11.29	2.34	9.23	8.90	-0.10	7.69
II	-44.37	36.96	5.13	34.63	21.94	38.96	-11.87	-2.47	-0.06	10.63	-1.58	-4.53	-1.56	3.50	-0.93
III	24.47	-6.48	-7.67	-13.90	-11.29	4.79	20.35	10.39	-3.14	-0.25	3.98	5.68	2.17	7.74	2.90
IV	-13.07	9.78	11.94	-3.10	16.29	-7.50	10.15	-17.52	-3.08	5.38	-0.65	-12.85	-1.93	1.45	-1.47

Table 14c: GDP Quarterly Growth, by Economic Activity, 1990–2011 (%) continued

Year, Quarter	Agriculture, forestry, livestock, and fisheries	Crude oil and natural gas	Metallic and non-metallic minerals	Manufacturing industry	Electricity, gas, and water	Construction industry	Commerce industry	Transport and communications	Finance, insurance, real estate, and other business services	Public administration services	Other services	Imputed banking services	GDP at basic prices	Import duties, VAT, IT, and other indirect taxes	GDP at market prices
2005, I	53.50	-12.36	-11.73	-6.70	-20.59	-19.82	-13.38	13.61	5.03	-9.50	-1.97	9.59	2.45	9.40	3.43
II	-42.37	29.53	11.45	28.10	23.47	25.65	-10.42	-0.22	5.77	10.53	-2.52	16.97	-0.70	6.92	0.44
III	24.66	-12.54	5.13	-12.80	-8.70	28.41	21.95	11.13	-2.19	2.32	6.64	1.69	3.93	32.35	8.44
IV	-5.33	14.66	25.51	-3.30	16.68	-1.37	10.94	-15.34	-2.70	2.72	1.50	-7.99	0.56	13.35	3.03
2006, I	58.48	-11.97	19.90	3.03	-17.26	-13.20	-5.07	8.91	11.44	-5.08	5.83	23.59	7.82	2.14	6.61
II	-36.55	20.37	36.90	30.95	23.39	23.40	-16.36	7.25	6.11	7.16	-1.96	6.14	2.57	5.40	3.15
III	17.92	21.61	-7.95	-7.99	-10.89	18.57	37.76	11.39	-1.86	8.67	6.78	2.81	7.57	10.16	8.11
IV	-6.34	-8.57	-0.86	0.66	17.84	0.27	10.90	-12.97	-9.87	-1.99	-0.85	-20.80	-2.54	2.45	-1.48
2007, I	49.38	-17.89	4.78	-9.85	-19.30	-46.89	-8.60	7.76	21.61	-2.48	3.21	35.62	2.35	1.68	2.20
II	-42.34	30.25	14.66	41.45	26.17	55.51	-10.51	-3.35	4.16	16.53	-0.91	4.81	3.46	3.62	3.49
III	37.87	14.36	-2.20	-7.43	-9.30	52.08	34.85	17.53	2.47	2.48	8.99	7.05	10.47	10.23	10.42
IV	-9.27	0.51	35.07	-2.57	22.04	16.49	11.18	-15.27	-7.18	-1.30	0.15	-11.49	0.56	6.62	1.89
2008, I	81.48	-13.25	15.36	-3.01	-16.56	-57.52	-4.38	13.53	18.82	-6.35	5.96	32.24	7.45	4.46	6.76
II	-38.37	58.37	42.98	48.30	27.19	67.06	-0.53	2.35	10.13	18.81	3.59	6.90	12.52	22.59	14.78
III	30.53	-22.25	17.22	-9.17	-7.98	54.48	38.39	17.21	2.32	10.60	10.79	4.13	9.66	0.28	7.40
IV	-12.42	-42.43	-39.05	-10.76	19.07	9.89	-13.89	-14.83	-6.68	11.33	0.40	-14.41	-12.01	-20.41	-13.90
2009, I	58.65	40.44	9.12	-2.44	-17.76	-40.69	-21.10	-11.87	-6.10	-16.45	-0.52	21.80	-0.20	17.37	3.45
II	-26.86	34.47	-9.66	8.75	15.36	42.03	67.43	23.07	35.26	16.46	1.90	-3.28	12.19	-18.48	4.97
III	-0.38	-22.24	46.31	8.81	-7.44	-23.19	-28.49	13.85	-18.04	5.39	11.37	4.43	-0.43	-4.58	-1.19
IV	-12.55	-26.36	-10.94	12.68	34.49	62.90	7.72	4.73	11.24	12.67	-4.95	-18.71	4.32	8.36	5.03
2010, I	59.15	34.63	19.95	-16.79	-21.61	-31.96	-10.31	-24.45	-9.43	-15.46	-0.24	33.36	-3.13	-4.94	-3.46
II	-25.68	41.86	-14.35	7.78	16.90	44.64	66.90	28.59	33.41	6.75	2.41	-0.90	11.38	12.01	11.49
III	3.29	-11.41	20.44	8.38	-8.90	-25.04	-28.81	8.69	-17.36	11.54	12.02	5.79	-0.87	12.44	1.53
IV	-9.00	-22.62	0.78	11.13	39.26	62.93	9.81	14.90	16.43	13.29	-4.11	-16.20	8.26	12.03	9.01
2011, I	62.70	75.23	42.73	-14.55	-25.32	-32.79	-9.34	-27.98	-10.20	-15.85	2.01	32.69	1.65	2.19	1.76
II	-13.41	5.73	-17.31	12.68	16.88	46.33	79.16	33.63	33.05	8.14	5.33	2.81	12.38	4.93	10.85
III	-6.48	-1.19	36.60	6.44	-5.18	-24.90	-31.73	7.42	-17.19	11.98	12.02	7.22	0.02	17.85	3.50

Note: Values in table reflect author's own estimations based on data from the Central Bank of Bolivia (CBB), and the National Institute of Statistics (NIS).

Table 15c: Share of Economic Activity in GDP, 1990–2011 (%)

Year, Quarter	Agriculture, forestry, livestock, and fisheries	Crude oil and natural gas	Metallic and non-metallic minerals	Manufacturing industry	Electricity, gas, and water	Construction industry	Commerce industry	Transport and communications	Finance, insurance, real estate, and other business services	Public administration services	Other services	Imputed banking services	GDP at basic prices	Import duties, VAT, IT, and other indirect taxes
1990, I	16.43	3.89	6.37	17.30	1.63	2.22	9.04	9.66	10.33	8.24	8.18	-1.29	92.00	8.00
II	16.29	3.08	6.09	17.92	1.70	3.06	8.44	9.27	10.50	10.10	7.88	-1.77	92.55	7.45
III	15.98	4.79	5.84	16.80	1.50	3.08	9.15	9.19	9.51	9.10	7.44	-1.29	91.09	8.91
IV	12.95	5.29	5.54	15.95	1.62	3.81	8.87	9.20	10.35	12.52	7.38	-2.16	91.31	8.69
1991, I	17.85	3.64	4.71	18.00	1.98	2.83	8.71	9.24	10.33	7.64	7.64	-1.55	91.02	8.98
II	15.78	3.27	4.49	17.83	1.90	2.54	8.32	9.99	10.66	10.91	7.42	-2.09	91.03	8.97
III	15.82	3.27	4.47	17.00	2.08	2.88	9.36	10.19	9.81	10.10	7.30	-1.16	91.13	8.87
IV	13.11	3.25	4.22	18.11	1.97	3.98	8.92	10.11	10.35	11.77	7.26	-2.40	90.65	9.35
1992, I	16.44	3.14	4.06	17.78	2.34	2.26	8.71	10.41	10.56	8.89	7.72	-2.16	90.14	9.86
II	13.87	3.02	4.48	18.01	2.35	2.70	8.08	10.55	10.86	10.93	7.49	-1.99	90.33	9.67
III	15.04	2.90	4.64	15.66	3.06	2.98	8.88	10.67	10.04	10.71	7.22	-2.06	89.72	10.28
IV	12.59	2.61	4.29	17.21	2.75	4.30	7.71	10.43	9.92	12.96	7.19	-2.58	89.38	10.62
1993, I	17.28	2.10	2.61	16.46	2.79	3.69	8.32	10.86	10.11	10.23	7.93	-2.10	90.28	9.72
II	13.33	2.16	2.93	17.83	3.17	3.03	7.64	11.00	11.52	12.06	7.71	-2.60	89.78	10.22
III	15.44	1.96	3.40	16.55	3.56	2.89	8.77	11.48	10.55	10.26	7.43	-2.59	89.75	10.25
IV	12.83	1.84	3.67	16.65	3.30	3.82	8.14	10.98	10.00	13.15	7.40	-2.70	89.09	10.91
1994, I	19.19	0.79	4.17	15.44	2.86	2.53	8.63	10.56	9.92	10.47	7.59	-2.24	89.90	10.10
II	13.31	0.94	4.01	17.85	3.52	2.47	8.05	11.45	11.73	10.88	7.46	-2.57	89.10	10.90
III	15.28	1.02	3.65	16.10	3.85	3.50	8.67	11.08	9.45	12.31	6.71	-2.39	89.23	10.77
IV	13.48	0.91	4.11	17.23	3.49	3.86	8.61	10.27	10.17	11.98	7.31	-3.25	88.17	11.83
1995, I	18.92	1.21	4.52	15.56	2.80	2.53	8.85	9.75	9.85	9.60	7.52	-2.61	88.50	11.50
II	12.28	1.42	5.26	18.31	3.29	2.50	8.17	10.78	10.64	10.36	7.54	-2.99	87.56	12.44
III	15.31	1.11	4.69	16.79	3.91	3.18	8.59	10.49	9.17	10.73	6.90	-2.24	88.64	11.36
IV	13.09	1.08	4.88	16.32	3.59	3.53	8.10	9.37	9.85	13.52	7.09	-3.06	87.36	12.64
1996, I	18.54	1.23	4.80	15.70	2.64	2.39	8.64	9.55	10.12	9.24	7.47	-2.61	87.69	12.31
II	11.05	1.35	5.11	18.46	3.25	2.37	7.86	10.62	10.53	11.25	7.45	-2.45	86.85	13.15
III	14.95	1.13	4.29	16.51	2.68	2.62	8.32	10.74	10.57	10.90	7.34	-2.92	87.12	12.88
IV	12.34	1.35	4.44	15.16	3.36	3.12	7.81	10.60	11.04	12.21	7.56	-4.08	84.92	15.08
1997, I	19.57	1.62	4.12	14.01	2.43	2.23	8.53	10.02	11.22	9.54	7.74	-3.64	87.41	12.59

Table 15c: Share of Economic Activity in GDP, 1990-2011 (%) continued

Year, Quarter	Agriculture, forestry, livestock, and fisheries	Crude oil and natural gas	Metallic and non-metallic minerals	Manufacturing industry	Electricity, gas, and water	Construction industry	Commerce industry	Transport and communications	Finance, insurance, real estate, and other business services	Public administration services	Other services	Imputed banking services	GDP at basic prices	Import duties, VAT, IT, and other indirect taxes
II	11.49	2.24	4.61	16.63	2.91	2.84	7.33	10.56	12.23	11.53	7.75	-3.42	86.69	13.31
III	15.72	2.05	4.21	14.19	2.42	3.01	8.28	11.05	11.32	11.08	7.61	-4.48	86.46	13.54
IV	13.06	2.31	4.06	13.40	3.16	3.33	7.52	11.70	11.69	12.54	7.44	-4.55	85.67	14.33
1998, I	16.20	1.95	4.40	13.24	2.50	3.39	8.04	12.09	11.33	10.33	8.13	-4.30	87.28	12.72
II	10.47	1.87	3.82	16.29	2.92	3.62	7.18	12.03	12.51	11.42	8.29	-4.32	86.11	13.89
III	12.86	2.01	3.51	13.91	2.57	4.19	8.03	12.43	12.62	11.42	8.10	-5.69	85.97	14.03
IV	10.98	1.81	2.81	12.63	3.17	4.03	7.47	11.26	12.71	13.98	7.42	-3.33	84.94	15.06
1999, I	17.15	1.58	3.31	13.30	2.59	2.63	7.58	11.85	14.72	11.17	8.22	-5.69	88.41	11.59
II	10.98	1.95	3.35	15.81	3.11	3.10	6.53	11.86	15.75	11.71	8.74	-4.53	88.35	11.65
III	13.47	2.28	3.36	14.00	2.62	3.29	7.84	12.41	15.37	10.86	8.84	-6.59	87.76	12.24
IV	11.45	2.31	3.54	11.47	3.09	4.01	7.48	11.21	12.71	14.13	7.94	-2.71	86.64	13.36
2000, I	17.44	2.54	3.57	12.51	2.72	2.60	7.08	11.70	13.67	10.00	8.37	-4.61	87.60	12.40
II	10.70	2.98	3.46	14.70	3.20	2.91	6.51	12.02	14.56	11.23	8.76	-4.64	86.39	13.61
III	12.55	3.37	3.43	13.54	2.62	2.91	7.72	11.47	13.25	11.81	8.13	-4.59	86.20	13.80
IV	11.24	3.81	3.03	12.30	3.10	3.67	7.42	10.22	12.93	13.72	8.08	-4.08	85.46	14.54
2001, I	17.61	3.37	3.04	11.98	2.64	2.61	6.87	11.64	12.86	11.43	8.40	-4.27	88.19	11.81
II	11.10	3.86	3.30	14.66	3.03	2.83	7.01	11.63	13.54	11.50	8.72	-4.31	86.86	13.14
III	13.37	3.10	3.07	13.40	2.74	2.81	7.20	12.16	12.78	12.36	8.43	-4.35	87.08	12.92
IV	10.96	2.76	2.84	13.36	3.48	2.85	7.67	10.74	12.87	14.18	8.58	-3.91	86.36	13.64
2002, I	17.70	2.51	2.99	12.11	2.65	2.29	6.86	12.50	12.86	10.84	8.93	-3.98	88.27	11.73
II	10.57	3.30	3.23	14.48	3.08	3.31	6.48	12.35	12.62	12.79	8.67	-4.08	86.79	13.21
III	12.41	3.41	3.00	13.11	2.66	3.66	7.17	12.38	11.73	12.76	8.45	-3.74	87.00	13.00
IV	11.32	4.18	2.97	12.44	3.25	3.17	8.03	10.49	11.11	13.45	8.75	-3.33	85.82	14.18
2003, I	18.73	3.50	3.15	11.13	2.61	1.87	6.55	12.50	11.46	11.18	8.66	-3.53	87.82	12.18
II	10.66	4.76	3.43	14.63	3.18	2.52	5.91	12.68	11.42	12.85	8.48	-3.33	87.22	12.78
III	12.89	3.85	3.24	12.89	2.73	2.50	7.13	13.22	10.58	12.58	8.38	-3.18	86.83	13.17
IV	11.55	5.17	3.10	12.48	3.27	2.31	7.73	10.96	10.37	13.83	8.62	-2.88	86.51	13.49
2004, I	18.79	4.80	3.33	10.85	2.43	1.64	6.81	12.08	10.10	11.39	8.19	-2.92	87.49	12.51
II	10.55	6.63	3.53	14.74	2.99	2.29	6.06	11.90	10.19	12.72	8.14	-2.81	86.93	13.07
III	12.76	6.03	3.17	12.33	2.58	2.34	7.09	12.76	9.59	12.33	8.22	-2.89	86.31	13.69

Table 15c: Share of Economic Activity in GDP, 1990–2011 (%) continued

Year, Quarter	Agriculture, forestry, livestock, and fisheries	Crude oil and natural gas	Metallic and non-metallic minerals	Manufacturing industry	Electricity, gas, and water	Construction industry	Commerce industry	Transport and communications	Finance, insurance, real estate, and other business services	Public administration services	Other services	Imputed banking services	GDP at basic prices	Import duties, VAT, IT, and other indirect taxes
IV	11.26	6.72	3.60	12.13	3.04	2.19	7.92	10.68	9.43	13.19	8.29	-2.56	85.91	14.09
2005, I	16.71	5.69	3.07	10.94	2.34	1.70	6.64	11.74	9.58	11.54	7.86	-2.71	85.09	14.91
II	9.59	7.34	3.41	13.96	2.87	2.13	5.92	11.66	10.09	12.70	7.63	-3.16	84.13	15.87
III	11.02	5.92	3.30	11.22	2.42	2.52	6.66	11.95	9.10	11.98	7.50	-2.96	80.63	19.37
IV	10.13	6.59	4.02	10.53	2.74	2.41	7.17	9.82	8.59	11.95	7.39	-2.64	78.69	21.31
2006, I	15.05	5.44	4.53	10.18	2.13	1.96	6.38	10.03	8.98	10.64	7.33	-3.06	79.59	20.41
II	9.26	6.35	6.01	12.92	2.54	2.35	5.18	10.43	9.24	11.05	6.97	-3.15	79.14	20.86
III	10.10	7.14	5.12	11.00	2.10	2.57	6.59	10.74	8.39	11.11	6.88	-3.00	78.75	21.25
IV	9.60	6.63	5.15	11.23	2.51	2.62	7.42	9.49	7.67	11.05	6.93	-2.41	77.90	22.10
2007, I	14.03	5.32	5.28	9.91	1.98	1.36	6.64	10.01	9.13	10.54	7.00	-3.20	78.01	21.99
II	7.82	6.70	5.85	13.54	2.41	2.05	5.74	9.35	9.19	11.87	6.70	-3.24	77.98	22.02
III	9.76	6.94	5.18	11.36	1.98	2.82	7.01	9.95	8.53	11.02	6.61	-3.14	78.02	21.98
IV	8.69	6.85	6.87	10.86	2.38	3.22	7.65	8.27	7.77	10.67	6.50	-2.73	77.00	23.00
2008, I	14.78	5.56	7.42	9.87	1.86	1.28	6.85	8.80	8.65	9.36	6.45	-3.38	77.50	22.50
II	7.93	7.68	9.24	12.75	2.06	1.87	5.94	7.84	8.30	9.69	5.82	-3.15	75.97	24.03
III	9.64	5.56	10.09	10.78	1.76	2.68	7.65	8.56	7.91	9.98	6.01	-3.05	77.56	22.44
IV	9.81	3.72	7.14	11.17	2.44	3.43	7.65	8.47	8.57	12.90	7.00	-3.03	79.26	20.74
2009, I	15.04	5.04	7.53	10.54	1.94	1.96	5.84	7.21	7.78	10.42	6.73	-3.57	76.47	23.53
II	10.48	6.46	6.48	10.92	2.13	2.66	9.31	8.46	10.02	11.56	6.54	-3.29	81.73	18.27
III	10.57	5.08	9.60	12.02	2.00	2.07	6.74	9.75	8.31	12.33	7.37	-3.48	82.35	17.65
IV	8.80	3.56	8.14	12.90	2.56	3.20	6.91	9.72	8.81	13.23	6.67	-2.69	81.79	18.21
2010, I	14.50	4.97	10.11	11.11	2.07	2.26	6.42	7.60	8.26	11.59	6.89	-3.72	82.07	17.93
II	9.67	6.33	7.77	10.74	2.18	2.93	9.61	8.77	9.88	11.09	6.33	-3.30	81.99	18.01
III	9.84	5.52	9.21	11.47	1.95	2.16	6.74	9.39	8.05	12.19	6.98	-3.44	80.05	19.95
IV	8.21	3.92	8.52	11.69	2.49	3.23	6.79	9.90	8.59	12.67	6.14	-2.65	79.50	20.50
2011, I	13.13	6.75	11.95	9.82	1.83	2.14	6.05	7.00	7.58	10.47	6.16	-3.45	79.41	20.59
II	10.25	6.44	8.91	9.98	1.93	2.82	9.77	8.44	9.10	10.22	5.85	-3.20	80.51	19.49
III	9.27	6.14	11.76	10.26	1.77	2.05	6.44	8.76	7.28	11.05	6.33	-3.32	77.81	22.19

Note: Values in table reflect author's own estimations based on data from the Central Bank of Bolivia (CBB), and the National Institute of Statistics (NIS).

Table 1d: Money Supply (*M1*), in old Bolivianos			
Balances at the end of:	Bills and Coins with the Public (A)	Checking Deposits (B)	M1 (A + B)
1911	1,200,000.00	2,400,000.00	3,600,000.00
1912	2,500,000.00	6,200,000.00	8,700,000.00
1913	6,500,000.00	12,700,000.00	19,200,000.00
1914	13,300,000.00	11,600,000.00	24,900,000.00
1915	15,800,000.00	12,700,000.00	28,500,000.00
1916	16,800,000.00	14,300,000.00	31,100,000.00
1917	20,300,000.00	21,900,000.00	42,200,000.00
1918	23,200,000.00	21,100,000.00	44,300,000.00
1919	26,900,000.00	21,900,000.00	48,800,000.00
1920	33,800,000.00	15,200,000.00	49,000,000.00
1921	27,400,000.00	19,700,000.00	47,100,000.00
1922	24,400,000.00	28,000,000.00	52,400,000.00
1923	26,400,000.00	21,500,000.00	47,900,000.00
1924	31,600,000.00	20,800,000.00	52,400,000.00
1925	37,200,000.00	24,900,000.00	62,100,000.00
1926	36,600,000.00	21,300,000.00	57,900,000.00
1927	38,700,000.00	20,100,000.00	58,800,000.00
1928	43,700,000.00	22,100,000.00	65,800,000.00
1929	42,526,000.00	17,887,000.00	60,413,000.00
1930	31,795,000.00	14,659,000.00	46,454,000.00
1931	26,626,000.00	11,229,000.00	37,855,000.00
1932	37,614,000.00	42,341,000.00	79,955,000.00
1933	53,774,000.00	53,965,000.00	107,739,000.00
1934	83,597,000.00	138,965,000.00	222,562,000.00
1935	145,946,000.00	231,759,000.00	377,705,000.00
1936	210,296,000.00	232,672,000.00	442,968,000.00
1937	252,459,000.00	277,504,000.00	529,963,000.00
1938	288,090,000.00	218,128,000.00	506,218,000.00
1939	368,760,000.00	310,773,000.00	679,533,000.00
1940	475,856,000.00	387,239,000.00	863,095,000.00
1941	641,573,000.00	597,290,000.00	1,238,863,000.00
1942	818,299,000.00	797,779,000.00	1,616,078,000.00
1943	1,075,190,000.00	803,649,000.00	1,878,839,000.00
1944	1,252,522,000.00	681,621,000.00	1,934,143,000.00
1945	1,540,861,000.00	1,017,549,000.00	2,558,410,000.00
1946	1,608,353,000.00	1,225,585,000.00	2,833,938,000.00
1947	1,747,455,000.00	1,058,758,000.00	2,806,213,000.00
1948	2,100,353,000.00	1,476,539,000.00	3,576,892,000.00
1949	2,434,084,000.00	1,619,605,000.00	4,053,689,000.00
1950	3,327,072,000.00	2,197,582,000.00	5,524,654,000.00

Table 1d: Money Supply (*M1*), in old Bolivianos continued			
Balances at the end of:	Bills and Coins with the Public (A)	Checking Deposits (B)	M1 (A + B)
1951	3,967,078,000.00	2,925,820,000.00	6,892,898,000.00
1952	6,213,544,000.00	4,383,098,000.00	10,596,642,000.00
1953	11,599,742,000.00	8,957,600,000.00	20,557,342,000.00
1954	20,048,593,000.00	14,961,970,000.00	35,010,563,000.00
1955	39,197,939,000.00	33,914,692,000.00	73,112,631,000.00
1956	148,815,141,000.00	98,776,552,000.00	247,591,693,000.00
1957	210,731,000,000.00	82,520,000,000.00	293,251,000,000.00
1958	236,404,000,000.00	57,158,000,000.00	293,562,000,000.00
1959	318,422,000,000.00	65,200,000,000.00	383,622,000,000.00
1960	352,523,000,000.00	66,613,000,000.00	419,136,000,000.00
1961	413,151,000,000.00	80,908,000,000.00	494,059,000,000.00
1962	457,103,000,000.00	98,314,000,000.00	555,417,000,000.00
1963	537,048,000,000.00	125,410,000,000.00	662,458,000,000.00
1964	656,231,000,000.00	141,970,000,000.00	798,201,000,000.00
1965	805,100,000,000.00	185,144,000,000.00	990,244,000,000.00
1966	880,372,000,000.00	230,196,000,000.00	1,110,568,000,000.00
1967	904,500,000,000.00	241,800,000,000.00	1,146,300,000,000.00
1968	948,600,000,000.00	282,900,000,000.00	1,231,500,000,000.00
1969	1,041,300,000,000.00	299,100,000,000.00	1,340,400,000,000.00
1970	1,152,600,000,000.00	357,700,000,000.00	1,510,300,000,000.00
1971	1,281,400,000,000.00	417,800,000,000.00	1,699,200,000,000.00
1972	1,597,600,000,000.00	555,000,000,000.00	2,152,600,000,000.00
1973	2,069,600,000,000.00	848,700,000,000.00	2,918,300,000,000.00
1974	2,736,800,000,000.00	1,458,700,000,000.00	4,195,500,000,000.00
1975	3,048,400,000,000.00	1,605,200,000,000.00	4,653,600,000,000.00
1976	3,966,700,000,000.00	2,425,200,000,000.00	6,391,900,000,000.00
1977	4,858,500,000,000.00	2,872,800,000,000.00	7,731,300,000,000.00
1978	5,803,800,000,000.00	2,828,700,000,000.00	8,632,500,000,000.00
1979	7,171,600,000,000.00	2,915,500,000,000.00	10,087,100,000,000.00
1980	9,460,600,000,000.00	4,777,400,000,000.00	14,238,000,000,000.00
1981	10,851,700,000,000.00	6,300,800,000,000.00	17,152,500,000,000.00
1982	38,898,200,000,000.00	17,659,400,000,000.00	56,557,600,000,000.00
1983	124,755,000,000,000.00	50,368,000,000,000.00	175,123,000,000,000.00
1984	2,870,909,000,000,000.00	424,607,000,000,000.00	3,295,516,000,000,000.00

Table 1d: Money Supply (*M1*), in old Bolivianos continued			
Balances at the end of:	Bills and Coins with the Public (A)	Checking Deposits (B)	M1 (A + B)
1985	173,819,231,000,000,000.00	24,859,114,000,000,000.00	198,678,345,000,000,000.00
1986	294,372,647,000,000,000.00	68,931,046,000,000,000.00	363,303,693,000,000,000.00
1987	396,874,215,000,000,000.00	105,636,317,000,000,000.00	502,510,532,000,000,000.00
1988	526,078,440,000,000,000.00	158,179,377,000,000,000.00	684,257,817,000,000,000.00
1989	500,299,000,000,000,000.00	206,004,000,000,000,000.00	706,303,000,000,000,000.00
1990	638,838,000,000,000,000.00	349,538,000,000,000,000.00	988,376,000,000,000,000.00
1991	753,713,000,000,000,000.00	693,070,000,000,000,000.00	1,446,783,000,000,000,000.00
1992	886,991,000,000,000,000.00	1,036,974,000,000,000,000.00	1,923,965,000,000,000,000.00
1993	1,033,600,000,000,000,000.00	1,465,861,000,000,000,000.00	2,499,461,000,000,000,000.00
1994	1,405,990,000,000,000,000.00	1,825,985,000,000,000,000.00	3,231,975,000,000,000,000.00
1995	1,693,986,000,000,000,000.00	2,219,026,000,000,000,000.00	3,913,012,000,000,000,000.00
1996	1,795,704,000,000,000,000.00	2,972,487,000,000,000,000.00	4,768,191,000,000,000,000.00
1997	2,050,244,000,000,000,000.00	3,687,668,000,000,000,000.00	5,737,912,000,000,000,000.00
1998	2,183,162,000,000,000,000.00	4,158,496,000,000,000,000.00	6,341,658,000,000,000,000.00
1999	2,157,814,000,000,000,000.00	3,735,163,000,000,000,000.00	5,892,977,000,000,000,000.00
2000	2,175,276,000,000,000,000.00	4,230,588,000,000,000,000.00	6,405,864,000,000,000,000.00
2001	2,396,358,000,000,000,000.00	5,136,461,000,000,000,000.00	7,532,819,000,000,000,000.00
2002	2,677,868,000,000,000,000.00	5,437,441,000,000,000,000.00	8,115,309,000,000,000,000.00
2003	3,193,035,000,000,000,000.00	6,013,062,000,000,000,000.00	9,206,097,000,000,000,000.00
2004	3,865,381,000,000,000,000.00	5,506,121,000,000,000,000.00	9,371,502,000,000,000,000.00
2005	5,594,201,000,000,000,000.00	5,889,132,000,000,000,000.00	11,483,333,000,000,000,000.00
2006	8,012,031,000,000,000,000.00	6,879,013,000,000,000,000.00	14,891,044,000,000,000,000.00
2007	13,117,459,000,000,000,000.00	8,208,072,000,000,000,000.00	21,325,531,000,000,000,000.00
2008	15,807,424,000,000,000,000.00	9,838,148,000,000,000,000.00	25,645,572,000,000,000,000.00
2009	17,079,537,000,000,000,000.00	13,215,945,000,000,000,000.00	30,295,482,000,000,000,000.00
2010	22,484,784,000,000,000,000.00	14,759,466,000,000,000,000.00	37,244,250,000,000,000,000.00
2011	25,813,629,000,000,000,000.00	17,007,790,000,000,000,000.00	42,821,419,000,000,000,000.00

Notes: Values in table reflect author's own estimations based on data from the Central Bank of Bolivia (CBB).
Numbers in table are end-of-period values.
Unit of account changed twice during the 1911–2011 period: the first in 1962, when a new currency, the Peso Boliviano, was introduced: the exchange rate between new and old currencies was set at 1 Peso Boliviano = 1,000 Bolivianos.
In 1987 the unit of account was changed again. The exchange rate between new and old currencies was set at 1 Boliviano = 1,000,000 Pesos Bolivianos.
Checking deposits include those in Bolivian and foreign currency.
All values in old, unadjusted Bolivianos.
M1=Bills and Coins + Checking Deposits; Official M1 calculated by the CBB differs from the one reported here.

Table 2d: Foreign Reserves of Central Bank of Bolivia (millions of current US dollars), 1929-2011							
Year	Net Reserves	Gold	Foreign Exchange	Silver Coins	Other	Total Reserves	Total Liabilities
1929	20.50	3.33	16.68	0.01	0.48	20.50	-
1930	14.36	0.99	12.88	0.01	0.48	14.36	-
1931	9.14	1.09	7.58	0.04	0.44	9.14	-
1932	6.52	1.32	4.93	0.04	0.23	6.52	-
1933	2.95	1.57	1.33	0.04	0.02	2.95	-
1934	3.33	2.27	1.01	0.04	0.01	3.33	-
1935	6.93	4.64	2.13	0.04	0.11	6.93	-
1936	12.22	7.39	4.77	0.02	0.04	12.22	-
1937	8.58	2.97	5.54	0.01	0.06	8.58	-
1938	3.29	1.99	1.27	0.01	0.02	3.29	-
1939	4.87	2.89	1.98	0.01	0.00	4.87	-
1940	7.52	2.61	4.91	-	-	7.52	-
1941	17.41	8.70	8.70	-	0.01	17.41	-
1942	20.16	10.71	9.44	-	0.01	20.16	-
1943	22.30	12.96	9.33	-	0.01	22.30	-
1944	23.77	14.14	9.56	0.05	0.02	23.77	-
1945	35.15	21.53	13.56	0.05	0.01	35.15	-
1946	33.47	21.68	11.73	0.05	0.01	33.47	-
1947	30.31	22.41	7.85	0.05	-	30.31	-
1948	31.17	22.50	8.62	0.05	-	31.17	-
1949	27.65	22.53	5.07	0.05	-	27.65	-
1950	42.57	24.45	18.08	0.04	-	42.57	-
1951	51.00	22.61	28.35	0.04	-	51.00	-
1952	70.66	23.04	11.87	0.04	35.71	70.66	-
1953	95.56	29.83	-0,03	0.01	65.75	95.56	-
1954	18.75	5.91	11.37	0.01	1.46	18.75	-
1955	6.97	0.06	0.15	-	6.76	6.97	-
1956	27.40	0.08	2.78	-	24.54	27.40	-
1957	56.60	3.47	6.49	0.11	46.53	56.60	-
1958	63.22	4.35	1.69	0.09	57.09	63.22	-
1959	53.05	5.00	1.00	0.05	47.00	53.05	-
1960	41.48	5.25	1.20	0.03	35.00	41.48	-
1961	29.80	6.00	0.80	-	23.00	29.80	-
1962	19.45	6.25	3.20	-	10.00	19.45	
1963	5.70	7.60	8.40	-	-	16.00	10.30
1964	22.40	10.30	17.60	-	-	27.90	5.50
1965	36.10	6.70	28.50	-	5.60	40.80	4.70
1966	40.90	7.30	25.90	-	8.30	41.50	0.60
1967	32.70	9.30	19.90	-	9.10	38.30	5.60
1968	32.40	10.80	25.80	-	10.10	46.70	14.30
1969	32.80	11.70	27.20	-	10.30	49.20	16.40
1970	36.30	12.70	26.60	-	15.60	54.90	18.60
1971	33.80	13.50	20.40	-	23.30	57.20	23.40

Table 2d: Foreign Reserves of Central Bank of Bolivia (millions of current US dollars), 1929–2011 continued							
Year	Net Reserves	Gold	Foreign Exchange	Silver coins	Other	Total Reserves	Total Liabilities
1972	48.60	15.50	37.00	-	17.30	69.80	21.20
1973	40.20	17.20	47.40	-	17.40	82.00	41.80
1974	163.10	17.20	157.40	-	26.70	201.30	38.20
1975	115.40	17.30	120.70	-	22.00	160.00	44.60
1976	171.50	17.60	107.40	-	48.30	173.30	1.80
1977	216.40	25.40	189.50	-	23.50	238.40	22.00
1978	169.10	27.20	123.50	-	41.10	191.80	22.70
1979	3.10	28.80	157.50	-	27.30	213.60	210.50
1980	-101.90	31.20	84.90	-	19.40	135.50	237.40
1981	-264.10	34.20	89.30	-	12.90	136.40	400.50
1982	-326.60	36.10	147.10	-	32.60	215.80	542.40
1983	-44.70	37.00	150.80	-	55.00	242.80	287.50
1984	104.00	37.90	243.50	-	43.20	324.60	220.60
1985	136.20	37.80	167.10	-	64.00	268.90	132.70
1986	246.60	37.80	265.30	-	202.20	505.30	258.70
1987	168.40	37.90	162.60	-	213.00	413.50	245.10
1988	160.90	38.00	230.60	-	135.80	404.40	243.50
1989	18.60	38.00	228.40	-	106.90	373.30	354.70
1990	132.30	37.90	269.30	-	68.50	375.70	243.40
1991	200.40	39.50	247.40	-	106.10	393.00	192.60
1992	258.00	39.50	293.70	-	109.70	442.90	184.90
1993	370.90	39.70	377.80	-	76.80	494.30	123.40
1994	502.30	39.60	557.50	-	61.80	658.90	156.60
1995	650.30	39.60	694.80	-	55.30	789.70	139.40
1996	950.80	39.60	1,017.90	-	49.60	1,107.10	156.30
1997	1,066.00	39.60	1,103.70	-	46.20	1,189.50	123.50
1998	1,063.70	256.90	888.50	-	47.70	1,193.10	129.40
1999	1,113.60	260.00	915.30	-	47.40	1,222.70	109.10
2000	1,084.80	244.80	869.30	-	45.60	1,159.70	74.90
2001	1,076.10	252.70	830.90	-	55.60	1,139.20	63.10
2002	853.90	316.40	521.20	-	59.30	896.90	43.00
2003	975.80	379.40	663.30	-	53.40	1,096.10	120.30
2004	1,123.30	399.40	817.30	-	55.00	1,271.70	148.40
2005	1,714.10	470.60	1,276.70	-	51.10	1,798.40	84.30
2006	3,177.30	577.60	2,561.20	-	53.50	3,192.30	15.00
2007	5,319.20	764.30	4,497.70	-	56.50	5,318.50	-0,7
2008	7,722.00	794.50	6,871.40	-	56.30	7,722.20	0.20
2009	8,580.10	997.60	7,311.30	-	271.60	8,580.50	0.40
2010	9,729.70	1,596.20	7,866.20	-	267.80	9,730.20	0.50
2011	12,018.60	2,109.10	9,643.90	-	266.10	12,019.10	0.50

Notes: Values in table reflect author's own estimations based on data from the Central Bank of Bolivia (CBB).
Numbers in table are end-of-period values.
Before 1962 no information on liabilities is available.
Figures in Bolivian currency were converted to Dollars at current, official selling (spot) rate between Bolivian currency and Dollars.

Table 1e: Central Government Operations (current US dollars)			
Year	Total Revenues	Total Expenditures	Balance
1940	13,236,466.10	14,443,440.46	-1,206,974.36
1941	20,139,235.47	23,485,480.81	-3,346,245.34
1942	19,849,803.55	25,017,464.58	-5,167,661.02
1943	25,152,848.89	25,481,806.60	-328,957.71
1944	25,034,598.21	27,500,239.85	-2,465,641.64
1945	26,295,486.19	26,575,941.97	-280,455.78
1946	24,023,010.25	28,459,830.51	-4,436,820.25
1947	23,851,412.40	29,961,203.94	-6,109,791.54
1948	31,378,087.32	29,746,698.77	1,631,388.54
1949	31,702,064.80	21,105,499.76	10,596,565.05
1950	27,847,443.86	25,384,685.53	2,462,758.34
1951	44,567,495.18	46,783,434.13	-2,215,938.95
1952	48,185,130.56	56,185,806.20	-8,000,675.64
1953	42,688,850.89	39,201,976.50	3,486,874.39
1954	39,154,070.42	42,240,242.37	-3,086,171.95
1955	66,561,919.71	72,337,908.52	-5,775,988.81
1956	49,921,439.78	53,916,863.58	-3,995,423.79
1957	35,619,289.96	35,495,818.63	123,471.33
1958	31,737,704.45	32,044,117.12	-306,412.67
1959	31,037,090.53	31,037,090.53	-
1960	34,885,206.38	35,797,905.40	-912,699.03
1961	36,180,058.90	36,180,058.90	-
1962	39,040,807.74	42,751,283.13	-3,710,475.39
1963	36,028,607.49	44,341,607.07	-8,312,999.58
1964	43,020,614.22	53,538,073.20	- 10,517,458.98
1965	51,577,618.85	72,149,768.62	- 20,572,149.77
1966	60,849,810.69	74,118,636.94	- 13,268,826.25
1967	64,938,998.74	79,537,231.80	- 14,598,233.07
1968	70,416,491.38	85,788,809.42	- 15,372,318.05
1969	73,319,310.05	81,018,090.03	-7,698,779.97
1970	90,063,104.75	105,082,036.18	- 15,018,931.43
1971	91,973,075.31	116,836,348.34	- 24,863,273.03
1972	95,561,742.25	148,598,114.05	- 53,036,371.80
1973	123,351,648.35	143,956,043.96	- 20,604,395.60
1974	253,231,768.23	275,959,040.96	- 22,727,272.73
1975	284,155,844.16	319,450,549.45	- 35,294,705.29
1976	341,703,296.70	411,578,421.58	- 69,875,124.88
1977	381,678,321.68	547,157,842.16	-165,479,520.48

Table 1e: Central Government Operations (current US dollars) continued			
Year	Total Revenues	Total Expenditures	Balance
1978	426,578,421.58	576,523,476.52	-149,945,054.95
1979	403,626,670.36	723,832,026.99	-320,205,356.62
1980	473,033,020.79	810,415,817.37	-337,382,796.58
1981	573,550,754.18	936,661,231.15	-363,110,476.97
1982	287,908,779.25	841,077,791.75	-553,169,012.50
1983	157,523,411.85	610,471,452.33	-452,948,040.48
1984	206,018,447.38	1,315,076,132.42	-1,109,057,685.04
1985	460,872,726.75	1,751,848,686.14	-1,290,975,959.39
1986	438,799,515.79	856,936,179.41	-418,136,663.61
1987	498,484,400.50	982,609,596.09	-484,125,195.59
1988	530,780,256.29	1,011,230,865.89	-480,450,609.59
1989	577,392,077.19	1,076,368,933.24	-498,976,856.06
1990	585,940,783.37	1,118,544,355.97	-532,603,572.60
1991	779,644,165.53	1,304,136,764.22	-524,492,598.69
1992	1,282,187,422.34	1,423,392,115.88	-141,204,693.54
1993	1,784,730,679.16	2,132,271,662.76	-347,540,983.61
1994	1,997,537,796.98	2,175,809,935.21	-178,272,138.23
1995	2,175,264,033.26	2,296,428,274.43	-121,164,241.16
1996	2,249,744,094.49	2,392,834,645.67	-143,090,551.18
1997	2,411,577,946.77	2,685,114,068.44	-273,536,121.67
1998	2,654,692,028.99	3,049,311,594.20	-394,619,565.22
1999	2,698,161,512.03	2,985,549,828.18	-287,388,316.15
2000	2,826,090,468.50	3,139,644,588.05	-313,554,119.55
2001	2,478,323,262.84	3,032,447,129.91	-554,123,867.07
2002	2,187,785,515.32	2,885,250,696.38	-697,465,181.06
2003	1,932,881,355.93	2,555,971,316.82	-623,089,960.89
2004	2,304,075,471.70	2,800,616,352.20	-496,540,880.50
2005	2,893,807,169.34	3,111,755,253.40	-217,948,084.05
2006	3,721,464,019.85	3,326,302,729.53	395,161,290.32
2007	4,270,797,468.35	3,975,493,670.89	295,303,797.47
2008	5,421,362,420.25	5,422,967,688.82	-1,605,268.57
2009	5,653,437,057.99	5,997,920,792.08	-344,483,734.09
2010	6,001,542,161.86	6,020,614,035.09	- 19,071,873.23
2011	7,789,742,489.27	8,062,703,862.66	-272,961,373.39

Notes: Values in table reflect author's own estimations based on data from the Central Bank of Bolivia (CBB), and Ministry of Economy and Public Finances.

Exchange rate used to convert values in Bolivian currency to US Dollar is the yearly average, official selling (spot) exchange rate between Bolivian currency and the US Dollar.

Table 2e: Tax Collection Revenues by Department (thousands of current US dollars)										
	Chuquisaca	La Paz	Cochabamba	Oruro	Potosí	Tarija	Santa Cruz	Beni	Pando	Total
1987	4,068.49	119,613.99	27,734.93	6,388.10	2,430.78	3,214.37	42,228.85	994.75	92.26	206,766.53
1988	5,468.43	168,015.16	35,459.17	6,298.33	2,285.06	4,271.64	44,338.38	1,245.38	153.11	267,534.65
1989	5,339.76	174,771.55	41,163.41	7,173.83	2,489.59	4,483.88	56,394.93	1,499.21	187.02	293,503.17
1990	6,053.64	200,897.59	49,187.93	8,308.84	2,169.09	7,062.62	63,132.26	2,174.02	161.59	339,147.56
1991	6,466.66	190,989.74	57,846.64	8,807.84	2,647.19	5,879.82	71,103.58	2,622.02	245.87	346,609.36
1992	8,477.28	236,520.27	71,525.38	12,446.26	3,316.47	9,055.61	109,896.06	2,273.27	286.47	453,797.06
1993	12,474.89	266,833.58	75,825.75	13,968.46	3,453.63	11,114.60	133,857.47	2,177.59	299.18	520,005.16
1994	11,106.88	272,515.32	88,765.79	20,923.33	4,849.94	12,131.25	156,431.89	2,656.69	333.44	569,714.55
1995	14,089.09	364,888.88	102,878.92	25,458.12	4,982.08	12,455.51	181,871.38	2,811.61	606.94	710,042.52
1996	15,821.47	382,698.62	119,370.34	30,285.06	5,888.70	16,419.78	201,025.90	3,198.75	468.00	775,176.64
1997	17,805.78	404,697.26	136,284.87	32,676.99	5,764.37	16,195.70	255,235.86	3,282.27	393.42	872,336.53
1998	21,276.18	413,455.48	144,210.49	38,960.14	9,290.82	33,368.53	384,372.34	3,807.30	471.55	1,049,212.84
1999	18,985.66	371,992.14	124,810.64	27,647.23	9,102.66	27,607.43	371,183.71	4,501.53	479.86	956,310.87
2000	17,401.11	412,702.25	128,462.68	30,101.53	7,449.29	37,782.94	364,592.33	3,604.53	453.08	1,002,549.73
2001	16,094.94	370,368.18	123,715.52	33,532.94	6,801.51	94,201.89	349,161.60	4,206.21	263.76	998,346.55
2002	13,111.25	295,504.37	70,065.63	6,754.09	4,013.43	9,574.50	230,639.05	3,204.77	152.93	633,020.02
2003	12,933.57	313,996.17	68,053.56	5,772.00	4,118.49	11,312.87	253,069.27	3,391.87	199.76	672,847.54
2004	14,759.79	317,374.76	77,197.63	10,548.22	5,316.75	13,747.20	309,954.37	4,988.10	329.54	754,216.36
2005	16,219.12	359,878.10	89,661.04	13,948.43	8,152.35	11,426.47	387,379.41	5,889.87	530.64	893,085.43
2006	20,775.17	433,065.84	112,740.67	14,366.53	17,649.62	20,223.06	264,355.20	8,393.61	642.45	892,212.16
2007	20,321.91	523,950.48	134,641.16	17,815.63	26,700.30	25,877.01	300,697.33	10,358.80	914.47	1,061,277.10
2008	27,908.12	680,450.46	184,944.48	22,072.07	30,071.29	31,351.11	452,036.22	12,408.14	909.57	1,442,151.45
2009	33,982.07	789,679.97	192,986.80	17,555.02	37,764.80	36,902.52	452,206.17	13,164.98	1,259.67	1,575,501.99
2010	40,267.50	839,072.28	214,712.58	18,212.86	138,873.08	38,844.62	833,380.76	14,655.66	2,276.61	2,140,295.96

Notes: Values in table reflect author's own estimations based on data from the National Tax Revenue Authority (NTRA) and the National Institute of Statistics (NIS).

Starting in 2005, the National Tax Revenue Authority (NTRA) does not include the special tax on hydrocarbons and derivatives (known for its Spanish acronym IEHD), the direct tax on hydrocarbons (Spanish acronym IDH), the financial transactions tax (Spanish acronym ITF), and the import tax in its revenue reports by Department.

Exchange rate utilized to convert values from Bolivianos to US Dollars was the average yearly buying exchange rate between Bolivianos and Dollars in the parallel market.

Table 3e: Central Government Expenditures, by Sector (current US dollars)						
Year	Total Government Expenditures	Infrastructure	Education	Health	National Defense	Other
1940	14,443,440.46	1,860,715.11	2,354,687.62	742,238.49	4,479,025.36	5,006,773.87
1941	23,485,480.81	2,276,730.78	2,527,107.05	1,081,084.81	4,734,131.71	12,866,426.47
1942	25,017,464.58	2,692,746.45	2,699,526.47	1,419,931.12	4,989,238.05	13,216,022.47
1943	25,481,806.60	3,052,630.16	3,915,171.29	1,213,658.98	5,732,929.39	11,567,416.79
1944	27,500,239.85	2,980,056.11	3,987,478.10	1,225,836.87	6,452,984.39	12,853,884.38
1945	26,575,941.97	2,997,289.01	4,562,024.35	1,652,865.39	6,258,840.17	11,104,923.04
1946	28,459,830.51	2,418,433.36	5,049,844.27	1,611,504.01	6,494,578.03	12,885,470.84
1947	29,961,203.94	1,827,679.57	5,817,856.34	1,611,098.68	5,370,328.93	15,334,240.41
1948	29,746,698.77	2,207,509.92	6,903,714.52	1,559,941.96	6,988,229.67	12,087,302.70
1949	21,105,499.76	1,630,523.83	6,441,891.10	1,616,063.72	8,464,876.78	2,952,144.33
1950	25,384,685.53	1,346,000.07	5,611,869.74	1,206,008.34	6,142,611.41	11,078,195.97
1951	46,783,434.13	2,111,580.85	7,443,172.45	1,308,399.20	9,083,549.18	26,836,732.45
1952	56,185,806.20	2,277,414.78	9,364,958.27	1,831,490.82	10,580,149.02	32,131,793.32
1953	39,201,976.50	2,458,697.20	9,671,206.80	1,973,626.77	7,158,976.19	17,939,469.54
1954	42,240,242.37	436,934.67	1,754,479.20	374,717.48	1,184,595.95	38,489,515.08
1955	72,337,908.52	376,720.69	1,391,759.25	375,433.46	1,118,332.09	69,075,663.03
1956	53,916,863.58	436,164.03	2,212,021.44	310,236.87	876,951.91	50,081,489.32
1957	35,495,818.63	809,633.75	2,682,411.88	833,780.10	2,080,090.79	29,089,902.11
1958	32,044,117.12	1,078,280.88	3,852,923.61	882,154.02	2,916,683.60	23,314,075.01
1959	31,037,090.53	1,239,882.20	3,939,082.88	1,068,489.69	3,190,912.92	21,598,722.84
1960	35,797,905.40	1,476,987.80	4,227,261.25	1,087,841.82	3,264,619.27	25,741,195.27
1961	36,180,058.90	1,735,044.17	4,607,236.01	1,218,510.73	4,271,350.44	24,347,917.54
1962	42,751,283.13	1,763,483.38	5,603,618.01	1,216,996.21	4,825,494.32	29,341,691.21
1963	44,341,607.07	2,025,073.62	6,627,513.67	1,405,973.92	5,489,356.33	28,793,689.52
1964	53,538,073.20	2,159,528.82	7,879,848.55	1,460,075.73	5,969,289.02	36,069,331.09
1965	72,149,768.62	4,594,026.08	13,504,417.33	2,002,524.19	11,762,726.13	40,286,074.88
1966	74,118,636.94	5,090,450.15	16,238,956.67	2,271,771.14	10,323,937.74	40,193,521.25

Table 3e: Central Government Expenditures, by Sector (current US dollars) continued						
Year	Total Government Expenditures	Infrastructure	Education	Health	National Defense	Other
1967	79,537,231.80	5,839,293.23	17,198,148.93	2,414,808.58	11,998,317.21	42,086,663.86
1968	85,788,809.42	7,395,877.16	18,754,732.86	3,466,554.48	12,461,085.40	43,710,559.53
1969	81,018,090.03	6,916,281.03	17,517,879.68	3,129,995.79	12,099,284.81	41,354,648.72
1970	105,082,036.18	8,498,106.86	29,314,261.67	7,143,458.14	16,575,515.36	43,550,694.15
1971	116,836,348.34	9,894,825.41	35,885,570.05	10,307,109.80	15,692,048.80	45,056,794.28
1972	148,598,114.05	10,173,327.35	35,491,692.86	9,634,485.86	19,541,984.73	73,756,623.26
1973	143,956,043.96	11,813,186.81	35,354,645.35	10,964,035.96	24,595,404.60	61,228,771.23
1974	275,959,040.96	25,064,935.06	65,909,090.91	21,443,556.44	41,898,101.90	121,643,356.64
1975	319,450,549.45	35,344,655.34	73,446,553.45	25,839,160.84	57,812,187.81	127,007,992.01
1976	411,578,421.58	47,532,467.53	92,312,687.31	28,626,373.63	66,198,801.20	176,908,091.91
1977	547,157,842.16	68,071,928.07	106,108,891.11	34,020,979.02	68,656,343.66	270,299,700.30
1978	576,523,476.52	61,148,851.15	130,934,065.93	44,150,849.15	81,748,251.75	258,541,458.54
1979	723,832,026.99	138,982,566.16	226,606,719.63	128,347,889.22	169,509,721.65	60,385,130.32
1980	810,415,817.37	47,452,099.47	153,298,002.45	52,706,889.52	79,094,985.73	477,863,840.20
1981	936,661,231.15	105,715,450.47	211,663,269.47	70,081,532.82	204,883,815.74	344,317,162.66
1982	841,077,791.75	75,454,959.38	129,003,235.96	42,985,158.79	130,565,063.34	463,069,374.29
1983	610,471,452.33	60,324,713.84	87,673,219.20	29,436,971.77	93,405,687.14	339,630,860.38
1984	1,315,076,132.42	52,759,591.06	67,008,210.82	22,662,878.27	74,825,999.04	1,097,819,453.23
1985	1,751,848,686.14	45,194,468.29	46,343,202.44	15,888,784.76	56,246,310.94	1,588,175,919.70
1986	856,936,179.41	135,212,556.10	138,649,332.47	47,535,976.89	168,277,396.78	367,260,917.16
1987	982,609,596.09	162,272,028.99	4,800,000.00	5,500,000.00	201,953,985.61	608,083,581.49
1988	1,011,230,865.89	162,800,000.00	2,500,000.00	2,900,000.00	204,605,873.83	638,424,992.05
1989	1,076,368,933.24	150,100,000.00	1,300,000.00	4,500,000.00	218,443,944.69	702,024,988.55
1990	1,118,544,355.97	113,500,000.00	100,000.00	15,300,000.00	221,977,727.53	767,666,628.44
1991	1,304,136,764.22	174,900,000.00	1,900,000.00	10,900,000.00	256,407,118.70	860,029,645.52
1992	1,423,392,115.88	255,200,000.00	7,800,000.00	22,600,000.00	279,975,732.04	857,816,383.84
1993	2,132,271,662.76	239,900,000.00	7,700,000.00	22,800,000.00	295,293,674.31	1,566,577,988.46

Table 3e: Central Government Expenditures, by Sector (current US dollars) continued

Year	Total Government Expenditures	Infrastructure	Education	Health	National Defense	Other
1994	2,175,809,935.21	233,500,000.00	14,600,000.00	23,800,000.00	302,747,205.51	1,601,162,729.70
1995	2,296,428,274.43	219,600,000.00	36,800,000.00	25,900,000.00	319,523,975.49	1,694,604,298.94
1996	2,392,834,645.67	231,600,000.00	63,500,000.00	31,300,000.00	332,283,811.71	1,734,150,833.95
1997	2,685,114,068.44	197,570,000.00	76,300,000.00	32,700,000.00	372,896,609.45	2,005,647,458.99
1998	3,049,311,594.20	176,650,000.00	64,180,000.00	34,880,000.00	181,557,971.01	2,592,043,623.19
1999	2,985,549,828.18	177,480,000.00	76,300,000.00	41,260,000.00	145,282,534.25	2,545,227,293.93
2000	3,139,644,588.05	203,130,000.00	83,710,000.00	60,970,000.00	139,964,573.27	2,651,870,014.78
2001	3,032,447,129.91	229,830,000.00	107,220,000.00	49,370,000.00	166,313,253.01	2,479,713,876.90
2002	2,885,250,696.38	222,060,000.00	95,930,000.00	53,200,000.00	147,599,167.82	2,366,461,528.56
2003	2,555,971,316.82	227,650,000.00	65,740,000.00	37,010,000.00	151,220,052.08	2,074,351,264.74
2004	2,800,616,352.20	296,720,000.00	54,210,000.00	45,030,000.00	147,172,110.55	2,257,484,241.65
2005	3,111,755,253.40	326,030,000.00	42,490,000.00	40,370,000.00	145,594,561.19	2,557,270,692.21
2006	3,326,302,729.53	481,460,000.00	75,190,000.00	61,150,000.00	92,672,456.58	2,615,830,272.95
2007	3,975,493,670.89	550,930,000.00	77,730,000.00	63,030,000.00	169,680,203.05	3,114,123,467.84
2008	5,422,967,688.82	590,600,000.00	108,630,000.00	60,180,000.00	246,061,728.40	4,417,495,960.43
2009	5,997,920,792.08	611,384,016.97	112,216,053.75	62,686,209.34	254,614,356.44	4,957,020,155.59
2010	6,020,614,035.09	607,227,298.44	111,453,111.74	62,260,014.14	252,883,267.33	4,986,790,343.43

Notes: Values in table reflect author's own estimations based on data from the National Institute of Statistics (NIS).
Estimates for each sector are aggregate values and were calculated by adding what the central government apportioned to each sector in its consolidated end-of-the-year statements.
Values above may not include expenditures made by Departments and by decentralized government agencies.

Index

Note: Page numbers followed by "n" refer to foot notes.

L

M

N

O

P

Q

R

S

T